For Mary Ellen,
who can do the s[...] [...]
38' sailboat (w[...]
me)— her loving husband
Christmas '98

SONNET

One Woman's Voyage
from Maryland to Greece

SONNET

One Woman's Voyage
from Maryland to Greece

LYDIA BIRD

North Point Press
Farrar, Straus and Giroux
New York

North Point Press
A division of Farrar, Straus and Giroux
19 Union Square West, New York 10003

Published simultaneously in Canada by HarperCollinsCanadaLtd
Printed in the United States of America
Designed by Jonathan D. Lippincott
First edition, 1997

LIBRARY OF CONGRESS CATALOGING-IN-PUBLICATION DATA
Bird, Lydia, 1954-
    Sonnet : one woman's voyage from Maryland to Greece / Lydia Bird.
    p.   cm.
    ISBN 0-86547-507-5 (pbk. : alk. paper)
    1. Bird, Lydia, 1954-   —Journeys.   2. Sonnet (Sailboat)
3. North Atlantic Ocean.   I. Title.
G470.B57   1997
910.4'5—dc21   96-50352

Excerpts from "If I Had a Boat" by Lyle Lovett, with permission of Criterion
Music Corp. Copyright © 1987 by Michael H. Goldsen, Inc./Lyle Lovett
(ASCAP). "Twelfth Morning, or What You Will" by Elizabeth Bishop, from
The Complete Poems 1927-1979, with permission of Farrar, Straus and Giroux.
Copyright © 1983 by Mary Alice Methfessel. Excerpts from "The Lost Son" by
Theodore Roethke, from The Collected Poem of Theodore Roethke with permission
of Bantam Doubleday Dell Publishing, Inc. Copyright © 1947 by Theodore
Roethke.

Grateful acknowledgment is made to Sail Magazine, in which a portion of this
book first appeared.

for Lydia M., Rachie, and Lydia G.

I

Self-Reliance

1

Black hull.
I'd imagined white,
though black looked right
when the fax came in. Dull
ache, I don't believe a full-
keeled boat will reconstruct my soul. Night
is black. Sea is black, down deep. Fight-
ing back. The lull
like ice-
cubes clack-
ing softly in a glass.
I'll listen again. Once, twice,
in case the resilience comes back.
Letting the shatter part pass.

Nearly midnight at Yacht Maintenance Co. on Maryland's Eastern Shore. The sensible thing, at this point, would be to crawl in my bunk, get a decent night's sleep, and leave in the morning, but I wasn't going to do it. For weeks now, months really, preparing this boat for departure had felt like that classic word-problem in math: If you keep moving halfway to your goal, when do you get there?

I was leaving *today*, tonight; one more night's sleep wasn't going to make a difference.

The wind was blowing hard. An hour ago, barely able to handle the dock lines alone, I'd inched *Sonnet* back as far as I could, out of the protection of the big looming shed, out to where her stern was as close as I could get it to the channel. If I had someone to help me, and if that end section of dock were a little better suited to a boat, I could move her ninety degrees around and take off in forward gear with the wind behind me, a whole lot easier than backing out stern first.

If.

I started the engine. The bow and stern lines were looped around pilings and back to the boat so I could release them from on deck; at blast-off I would release the bow line first, then move quickly aft and handle the stern line from the helm. I was trying hard to control my jumpiness, a product of this eerie nighttime departure, no send-off, no one to cast off my dock lines, aware of how long it would be before I spoke face-to-face with another human being, how long it would be before I set foot again on land.

I was ready, or ready enough.

I moved to the foredeck and released the bow line. In a heartbeat, the bow blew away from the dock. No way to stop the swing. No way to get to the stern and maneuver *Sonnet* out of there. Within seconds the boat was streaming perpendicular to the dock, held by her stern line, her bow within inches of a piling between this dock and the next.

Angry, panicky despair. What the hell now? No way to release the stern and get under way without the wind blowing the boat into the piling. I could tie together a couple of lines and drag her bow back to where it was before, but what the hell then? *Why hadn't I thought this through more?*

Think, Lydia. Slow *down* a little. What do you know. What knowledge do you have to get yourself out of this.

I could hear Steve say to me: *Deep breath.*

For the moment, the boat was going nowhere, smashing into nothing. I took a deep breath. Or reasonably deep, considering.

What I knew how to do was to back a boat down on a stern line, springing out the bow; the maneuver, in my present quandary, would allow me to clear the piling. To pull it off, I'd have to move *Sonnet* backward until eight or ten feet of her starboard side were alongside that dubious end section of dock.

I thought it through a minute, then headed up to the bow, looping the long bow line through a cleat on the piling and back to the foredeck, giving myself control from both bow and stern in case the wind shifted.

With a couple of people to help, I could have moved the boat in minutes. Instead, it took an hour, shifting the inflated rubber fenders which protected the hull from jutting wood, shifting dock lines, grinding hard on winches against the wind.

For the first forty minutes I heard voices. Mentors, telling me what to do. Critics, judging me for screwing this up, for taking so long to straighten it out again. And then I settled into something very calm, very clear: it was only me here.

This was the very point of it. To use my own brain, no one else's. To use my own muscles. If my muscles weren't as big as a linebacker's I might have to use my brain more, might have to think about mechanical advantage, might have to take more time.

I kept inching her back. Ease the bow line, shift the fenders, grind in one of the two stern lines, scramble down onto the dock to shift the other line for a clearer lead. An inch at a time, until finally *Sonnet* was where she needed to be.

The wind blew hard in the darkness. I stood quietly at the stern, visualizing how the maneuver would work. One line from the stern led backward to a piling on the dock, keeping the boat from blowing forward. A second line led forward to a big wooden cleat. With the engine in reverse, this forward-led spring line would suck the stern in toward the dock, forcing the bow out into the channel.

I positioned the fenders carefully—five of them—so nothing would be damaged in the pivot. I clambered down onto the dock, bad knee protesting, and cleared some old rope away from the spring line's cleat to be absolutely certain the line would come free cleanly when I shifted into forward and *Sonnet* pulled away. I climbed back onto the boat for the final time.

Up to the bow to remove the bow line. Committed now. Back to the stern. Engine in reverse, remove the stern line, shaking a little, heart pounding. Three turns around a winch with the spring line, hand-hold it, punch up the revs. The engine roared in the darkness. The spring line went taut, the fenders shifted and moaned, and *Sonnet's* bow sprang out, slowly slowly. Throttle back, wheel hard to port and gearshift in forward, give her the gas, ease off the spring line as we go.

Into the dark of the channel, into the Choptank River, out toward Chesapeake Bay.

1800 How many lifetimes have I lived this one day in the
Chesapeake? Seems to have gone on forever, three-minute naps,
and then seven, and then sixteen, which wasn't so hot an idea,
one freighter bearing down on me from astern, another I had to
tack to avoid. The last line of squalls was terrifying, lightning
streaking straight down, no sleeping at all, not knowing whether
or not to reduce sail further. These squalls aren't pods like in the
Pacific—squalls you can track around—but a dark unbroken
wall.

A couple of months back, I'd called Sparkman & Stephens—*Sonnet*'s
designers—to ask advice on an aluminum problem. The naval architect
I'd talked to had said, "Prudence would dictate some coastal cruising
before taking off on a voyage of this kind."

Prudence also dictated taking off before the hurricane season.

By the time I finally left the dock—six weeks into the hurricane
season—I'd sailed *Sonnet* only once, for only four hours, but I'd worked
on virtually all of her systems, and knew her well. I knew she was exceptionally seaworthy. I knew my way around boats; this would be my
seventh ocean crossing, my second long-distance singlehanded passage.
Still, the prudence lecture echoed in my head. I told myself the hundred
miles to the mouth of the Chesapeake qualified as coastal cruising. If
something drastic went wrong I could pull into Norfolk for a remedy;
otherwise, it was east through the gap in the bridge and into the Atlantic.

I soon got the hang of reefing *Sonnet* alone—reducing mainsail area
and increasing it again at the threat and retreat of the squalls—and
tacking her alone, swinging her bow through the eye of the wind, scrambling to shift the sails from one side to the other.

I reawakened my navigational skills to keep from going aground on
the Chesapeake shoals, using a hand-held Global Positioning System
which pinpointed my position within feet.

I'd finished installing the Monitor self-steering wind vane only a couple of days back, and spent long periods watching it work, standing in
the companionway trying to stay awake, pleased and impressed and a
little hypnotized, watching the vane react to the wind and activate the

paddle which activated lines linked to the wheel to bring the boat back on course. It seemed like a cognizant creature, a second crew member.

Just past the Davidson Wreck, in a lull between squalls, I talked to Steve on the VHF radio through the Point Lookout marine operator. I'd talked to him from the pay phone at Yacht Maintenance the day before, swearing this was *for sure* the day I'd be leaving. Phone calls from that pay phone had made up the greater part of our relationship for weeks.

If things had gone as I'd originally envisioned—if I'd bought a boat a few months earlier than April—I would have left five weeks ago, and in a few days I'd be meeting Steve in Vienna, the boat tucked snugly in southern Spain. If things had gone as I'd subsequently envisioned he at least would have cast off my dock lines. I'd set target date after target date, the tenth of June (I was dreaming), the tenth of July (try again), the fourteenth (Bastille day, and Steve could see me off), the fifteenth the sixteenth the seventeenth. I told him on the VHF that I didn't even make the seventeenth, missed it by an hour. Immediately he said, "It's good luck, you left on my birthday."

It was his thirty-eighth birthday, and the day of his twentieth high-school reunion, and his third day in California, visiting friends and family before heading overseas. If I'd never launched this project I would have been there with him. After California I would have flown to Europe with him and Butch, our African cat, to pick up our car in Austria, and drive through Italy and Greece and into Bulgaria. Instead, I'd thrown us deeply in debt by buying a 42-foot sailboat, and taken off alone, uninsured, on the first leg of a five-thousand-mile voyage.

I made my way south through the thundersqualls. Names on the chart—Rappahannock, Occohannock, Piankatank—jumped out at me, stirring the few drops in my veins of East Coast Native American blood. Dusk roiled briefly, and I continued on in darkness, following the lights of the buoys that marked the Chesapeake Channel, opting against Norfolk, heading on out.

Just after 10 p.m. I passed through the gap of the bridge-tunnel at the entrance of the Bay, a profusion of bright-on-black lights, steering sleep-deprived toward that four-second flashing green to starboard, four-second flashing red to port, toward and between them, leaving civilization behind. An hour later I crossed the imaginary line between

Cape Charles and Cape Henry—Chuck and Hank—and was officially in the Atlantic.

By dawn the loom of the big cape lighthouses was behind me, as were the yellow-lit buoys that marked the shipping lanes. The sea stretched gray to a horizon broken by the flicker of lightning. The wind had died in the night; the Monitor was disconnected, the engine was on, and the electronic autopilot was steering the boat east under power.

I sat huddled in my foul-weather gear in the cockpit, looking out from under the dodger at the rain, trying to decide whether to risk a quick nap or stay on deck to monitor the lightning. Two thousand miles to the Azores. I found myself vaguely off-balance, not quite computing how this damp and solitary dawn related to the passion I'd felt for this challenge a year ago.

I'd been through three eras in my twenty-year sailing career. In the first, I'd sailed on other people's boats, with a great deal of enthusiasm— at least initially—but without much say. In the second, I'd had a say on boats I didn't own. In the third—which overlapped the second—I'd become a boat owner.

My first passage had been nineteen years back, at the age of nineteen, from Spain to the Caribbean on a 57-foot steel ketch called *Zeelandia*. Awed by it all: the complex simplicity of ocean and sky, the boat propelled across thousands of miles by the forces of nature. A second passage in 1979, after finally graduating from college, when Steve and I made our starving-artist move to Europe; I left California ahead of him and sailed the 44-foot sloop *August Moon* from Florida to Bermuda to the Azores, then on to Portugal and Spain, a very similar route to the one I was embarking on with *Sonnet*.

I'd arrived in Spain in August; Steve joined me in November in England. We lived six months in Portugal, then two years in Paris, where I read books by singlehanders in our seventh-floor walk-up maid's room: Clare Francis, Naomi James, Robin Knox Johnson, and Florence Artaud and Bernard Moitessier in French. Solo sailing inspired me like nothing else ever had; someday, I told myself, I'd singlehand.

Steve took the quick route back across the ocean in '82—by plane. I walked docks for a week in Palma de Mallorca before securing a berth to Antigua on a Taiwanese-built charter boat which worked the summer season in the Med and the winter in the Caribbean. I rejoined Steve in

Southern California after the passage, with no idea how I planned to support myself, or keep sailing a part of my life.

As it turned out, I took a class at the Orange Coast College Sailing Center in Newport Beach and ended up teaching there; for the next six years I made my living primarily as a sailing instructor. I taught inside the harbor on Lido 14 dinghies and 30-foot Shields sloops, outside the harbor on the lovely 47-foot ocean racer *Saudade,* and offshore—across the Pacific to Hawaii, among tidewater glaciers in Alaska, down the length of the British Columbian and U.S. west coasts—on the 65-foot *Alaska Eagle,* which felt more like a miracle than a job. The boat had won the Whitbread Round the World Race in 1978 as *Flyer,* and now was run by OCC as a sail-training vessel. I learned like wildfire from my boss and skipper Brad, learned from the boat, loved the boat something fierce, but didn't always do well with all the people.

Gradually, over the course of years, I got the itch to kill—or at least disable—the Buddha. To do something of my own.

With nearly two years' lead time, I started seeking sponsorship for the 1988 Singlehanded TransAtlantic Race between Plymouth and Rhode Island, the granddaddy of solo races. I sent out nearly two hundred proposal letters, yielding three weak leads. I wanted this obsessively, continued to hope it might come together, but in the end the sponsor search was an unsuccessful and demoralizing process.

At virtually the last moment I shifted my sights to the more affordable 1988 Singlehanded Transpac from San Francisco to Kauai, trying first to lease a boat, then maxing out the credit cards seven weeks before the race to buy a secondhand Santa Cruz 27. The purchase was a tremendous milestone—it turned me into a boat owner, an offshore singlehander— but I was almost too harried to notice.

I was accustomed to big, solid boats. Mine was a sleek, fast mini-sled which only weighed three thousand pounds, half of that in the keel; she was suited to the race and my pocketbook, but not really to me. I named her *Colibri,* French for hummingbird, which was how she moved, hovering and then zipping so fast you couldn't keep track of her. I worked nonstop until the morning of the start to make her race-worthy.

Thirty-plus knots the second night out of San Francisco, waves breaking entirely over the boat, pouring below, pouring from each of the Plexiglas windows onto the big green trash bags draped on seats in an attempt to direct the water into the bilge instead of the food lockers. "Reseal the windows"—not being a speed or safety item—had never quite made it to the top of the pre-race work list. I lived in a salty rain forest until I finally reduced my sail area, dried out the fiberglass with acetone, and sealed the windows with duct tape.

There were moments of intense, emotional beauty in the Pacific with *Colibri*—steering for hours one night to the Brandenburg Concerti, the boat hitting eleven and twelve knots, the harmony of it all overwhelming—but I spent a good deal of time in exhausted, rebellious discomfort. As luck would have it, there was plenty of wind; I managed to land myself in tenth place of the hundred-odd sailors who'd raced since the Singlehanded Transpac's inception, and to break the women's record by two days.

1988 was a pivotal year, even before the solo passage. Steve and I were doing well in California. I was supporting myself through sailing. Steve was working on a novel in the mornings, writing freelance ad copy in the afternoons, earning good money for part-time work, his hard-won clientele growing steadily.

We decided—somewhat to our own surprise—to bag it all. It happened at the Crab Cooker on a warm summer night, under the influence of a cold pitcher of beer. Months before, Steve had taken the Foreign Service test, more to keep life options open than because he really envisioned himself as a diplomat. Some two percent of people who take the test pass. Steve passed, then passed all the clearances. By the time Uncle Sam offered him a job, we were happy enough with the way our lives were running that we planned to say thanks-but-no-thanks, but somehow at the Crab Cooker we got to talking.

Steve's novel—an environmental thriller set in the Himalayas—was almost finished. I was about to race alone to Hawaii. We'd done what we'd wanted with this stage of our lives, and were becoming—sacrilege to admit it—somewhat bored with the easy warmth of Southern California.

We said yes to Uncle Sam. I raced *Colibri* to Hawaii. We finished editing the novel and sent it off to a major New York agent. In March of '89, after we'd moved to D.C. for Steve's training, the agent took on the novel. In May we got married during Steve's lunch hour—after twelve years of happy cohabitation—to simplify governmental logistics. Then in July we moved to Abidjan, Côte d'Ivoire.

I loved the streets of West Africa, women in bright *pagne* fabric, rickety stands vibrant with fruit and tropical flowers. I loved the red-dirt upcountry roads, the towering flange-rooted rain-forest trees, even if they now only dotted the landscape above a lush low carpet of secondary growth. The sense of the swirl of life, a life I knew I'd never really understand, humid and mystical and colorful and cruel.

I hated the poverty, the *"patron"* mentality—pay me to guard your car, find me a job at the embassy—and the constraints of crime. Our two-bedroom house was surrounded by nine-foot walls, protected around the clock by machete-wielding guards. The house itself was wonderful, colonial-era, broad louvered windows, high ceilings with ceiling fans, shaded by huge mango trees and palms.

From the start, Steve's political and economic reporting won kudos from Washington. In December, HarperCollins bought his book. I was thrilled at his success. I was also debilitated by a lack of self-esteem— no job, no identity, little grace in the role of diplomat's wife—and floored by the enigma of Africa. Frequently bordering on clinically depressed, I lay for hours on the couch in our little house in Cocody, staring at walls as mangos thunked hollowly onto the roof.

The Buddha was still alive and well. I'd dipped into other realms of sailing—skippering a women's racing crew while we were still in California, training with the U.S. Women's Challenge for the Whitbread while we were in Washington, flying off to Uruguay from Abidjan to see the Whitbread boats after they'd rounded Cape Horn—but none of it came to much, so I went back summers to sail *Alaska Eagle*. I still loved the boat, but I also knew I'd grown past her and needed to break cleanly away.

Late in our second year in Africa, after learning our next post would be Bulgaria, I started thinking about buying a boat while we were studying Bulgarian in Washington, then sailing across the Atlantic to post. Not a little one-race boat like *Colibri*, bought and resold before the credit-card companies caught up with me, but a keeper. A boat to take with me into Steve's world of diplomacy.

As soon as I admitted the idea to Steve, he was behind me one hundred percent. Behind me emotionally and financially, as long as I didn't expect him to join me in the bilges.

I left Africa ahead of him in '91, had arthroscopic surgery in California for a problem knee and didn't recover as easily as I'd been led to expect. We moved back to D.C. I was swept into language studies, looking at boats when I could, driving up and down the East Coast, finally making an offer on a 40-foot Swan we couldn't afford, heart leading head, wildly infatuated with her—with the ways she felt like a little *Alaska Eagle* or *Saudade*—and turning a blind eye to her myriad flaws. After a disastrous survey, we withdrew the offer.

Running out of time, I contacted Sparkman & Stephens, the designers of virtually every boat I'd ever loved. A phone call, a fax, a trip to Maine in an East Coast snowstorm to look at the boat. Brokers, bankers, surveyors, shippers. Finally pacing alongside the car while Steve perused *The Economist* as we waited for the truck to round the final bend on Edgewood Road in Annapolis. He loved *Sonnet* the minute he saw her.

She was built of aluminum at the Derecktor Shipyard in New York in 1970, to a 1963 S&S design. For me, she was born in Africa, born on *Alaska Eagle*, born in a maid's room in Paris and on the foredeck of *Zeelandia* under star-scattered tropical skies. All the plans, all the precedents, all the dreams, all the mental images of the oceangoing boat I would one day own and sail boiled down, in the spring of 1992, to an extraordinary amount of work.

New standing rigging—stays and shrouds—to hold the mast in place, new bearings for the roller-furling headsail, a third set of reef points so the mainsail could be reduced by more than fifty percent in heavy winds, a new reefing system of blocks and winches for the boom, all the hardware off so the mast could be repainted, then all of it back on again, a new electrical panel entailing massive rewiring, the complex Monitor steering gear, a new wheel to accommodate both it and the Autohelm autopilot, a single-sideband radio with insulated-backstay antenna, a new VHF antenna, a masthead tricolor navigational light and strobe, new wind and speed instruments with their requisite new transducers, life raft repacked from valise into cannister, chocks built on deck to accommodate it, an abandon-ship bag complete with hand-operated water maker, a new 3,500-gallon-an-hour bilge pump, topside paint repair, bottom paint, welded mounts for corrosion-inhibiting hull zincs, new primary fuel filter, new engine mounts, on and on.

The toughest, in a purely practical sense, was the messy corroded section of keel the surveyor had missed. It was first immobilizing—everyone I talked to suggested a different solution, and I didn't know which way to turn—and then immensely time-consuming and expensive.

Tougher than anything, though, six weeks before departure, was the death of Oscar, my loving and exceedingly pure-souled cat, a death I could have prevented, a loss I felt at times was going to break me. Early on, deep in grief, overwhelmed by the work still to be done on *Sonnet*, I'd see images of the boat crashing over onto asphalt in the Annapolis yard and wouldn't care. I'd see images of her run down by freighters offshore, me aboard, and wouldn't care. I understood that not many people would fathom such despair over a cat, but that didn't help.

By the time I sat huddled in foul-weather gear watching my first Atlantic dawn, some of the grief had passed, though I hadn't quite reached the equilibrium I would have preferred for this passage. One mile at a time, one moment at a time; the lightning seemed to be going in the other direction, so I headed below for some sleep.

Fifty miles, sixty miles, seventy miles east of the Chesapeake. Thunderstorms with no wind in them, no ships and then a half-submerged submarine. I roused myself to chores between naps, still ticking items off the list.

19 July

1400 So changeable, rain and not, wind and not, powering with the Autohelm, sailing with the Monitor, stowing things, navigating; longest stretch of sleep in fifty-five hours is twenty minutes, if that. Need rest. Certainly don't need exercise, bigger boat like this there's always something getting your heart rate up. Doesn't seem too big, though; a good size. Motion is lovely; weather's been cooperative but I've never experienced so utter a lack of seasickness, start of a passage. Maybe from living on her ahead of time.

1515 Tired of the rain. Powered four hours; I can't power four hours every day or I won't have enough fuel to get me to the Azores. Exact same thing now as this morning: enough wind to sail very slowly in the wrong direction.

Tired of the rain, wary of the lightning.

1600 Couldn't keep my eyes open, writing that, headed into a seven-minute nap, couldn't even get seven minutes before awake from the bang and crash of too little wind in the sails. Up on deck in the rain to rig lines to prevent the banging, sailing at under three knots but I don't feel like listening to the engine, will slog along a couple of hours and get some rest, nap right here at the chart table with the radar on standby.

I'd discovered I could sleep almost as comfortably at the nav station as in a bunk. The padded seat faced forward to the desk-like chart table—the table's lid was hinged, with space underneath for charts and navigational tools—but if I rotated ninety degrees I could lean back against the curve of the hull and stretch my legs out on the engine cover. A pillow or two and it was bliss.

1650 Partway through my third seven-minute nap I wake to something "wrong." What's wrong is that we're sailing, and with a favorable wind shift. Back into foul-weather gear and onto deck, trim the sails, head up into the wind a bit, and we're presently sailing at over six knots in the right direction. In the rain, of course, but it's *warm* rain, I have no complaints.

I'd filled the last page of my previous journal a couple of days before leaving Cambridge. This new one had as its cover the grounds layout of some nineteenth-century farm, which had struck me as a suitable foil to the ocean. I'd filled blank books compulsively for nearly twenty years, writing in everything from rice-paper sketch books to palm-sized German date books (distributed by the Goethe Institute in French-speaking West Africa) when I couldn't find anything else. In some corner of my soul I feared I'd lose any phase of my life I didn't write down.

The heft of the new book was substantial, the sheaf of eighty blank pages daunting if I let myself think about it, stretching ahead of me like the seamless gray of the ocean.

On *Colibri*, my journal, the ship's log, shopping lists from the final days before the race, navigational notebook, and address book had been one and the same, a canvas-bound eight-by-ten-inch book Steve's mom had given me, a dense work-in-progress, journal entries starting at one end of the book, log entries after the shopping lists at the other, navigational sight reductions in the middle, even the actual times and sextant readings, nearly illegible, scrawled with my right hand as I clung to the sextant with my left hand and the little boat launched herself down waves. I scribbled more than fifteen thousand words between San

Francisco and Kauai. The book got moldy, the journal entries got petulant in my cramped, soggy world, but holding it in my hands was like holding my entire voyage. Ten days after the end of the race, in Honolulu, I'd left the journal in a phone booth and lost it.

On *Sonnet*, journal and log were two separate books; the latter lived over the radar at the chart table, the former over the VHF. I'd bought a printed ship's log, vowing to be more disciplined than I'd been on *Colibri*. I entered data in their designated columns: compass courses, boat speeds, wind speeds, barometer readings, coordinates. I kept my comments in the comment columns short; 1800, 19 July reads, "Not raining."

> *2000* Sailing along at night. Happy except that I'm so tired, hands ache, "good" knee aches badly, whole body aches to some extent.
>
> Now that I'm out here, it seems at once almost too natural and not at all real, like some amusement-park ride, like someone took *Sonnet* and me and stuck us into a virtual-reality machine.
>
> Cooking for the first time, heating water for instant soup. Maybe part of the unreality is that *Sonnet*'s so big, so different from *Colibri*. More like *Alaska Eagle*—a galley, a chart table— which makes it feel unreal to be alone on her.

I was in and out of my bunk innumerable times in the night, in and out of foul-weather gear, up on deck for sail adjustments and course changes. By morning the rain had quit and patches of blue had elbowed their way between clouds. The wind was light. The surface of the sea broke into shades of blue and gray, soft-edged facets reflecting a varied sky. I'd always liked the ocean when it looked like this, a paint-by-number sea in subtle motion.

My first noon-to-noon offshore run was 113 miles. Not humiliating, not impressive.

20 July

> *1820* Just went and sat at the bow for no particular reason, and it was wonderful, watching the boat move on the waves, black hull white deck bright blue water. Aware of how long it's been since I did something purely for the pleasure of it.

Sonnet is sailing. She's sailing very slowly but that's all right. I'm not going to worry about Monica waiting for me in the Azores. I'll have plenty of time to worry how Monica's doing once she's actually on the boat. I'll turn on the engine if the slowness of our sailing becomes more obnoxious than the engine itself, but otherwise no.

1900   There have been irritations, yesterday's rain, the windlessness of both yesterday and today, but I just stood at the stern, looking forward, the long deck, surrounded here by sea, cumulus and cirrus overhead, and it felt wonderful and peaceful. I've done the things today *Sonnet* needed of me, I needed of her, replaced the winch for the main halyard, ran the jack lines for my harness tether, rigged assorted preventers, tacked her and gybed her and trimmed her and powered things up and shut them down. Starting to get a sense now of the various worlds of her, to know which one to turn to in which mood, cockpit and foredeck and chart table and mast, worlds of this little world.

I'd had my hesitations, buying this boat, which made my growing affection for her—and my appreciation of her technical simplicity—all the more real. I'd balked, at first, at *Sonnet's* less than high-tech rig, her unbending mast, mechanical rather than hydraulic vang for holding down the boom, three-strand rather than braided halyards for raising the sails. I'd wanted fin keel, not full keel; I'd even told the yacht broker I was working with in Annapolis not to show me spec sheets of full-keeled boats. I'd imagined finding a retired aluminum race boat, maybe from the seventies, when racers still had wineglass-shaped underbodies and skeg-mounted rudders.

What I'd responded to from the start was her simple, traditional interior, white bulkheads, varnished mahogany trim, V-berths forward, salon berths and pilot berths—like staggered bunk beds—in the main cabin, galley at the base of the companionway to starboard, chart table to port.

1925   I love this boat. I don't really like her *lines* that much, the way everyone else does, a bit too classic for my taste. But the way she feels, the way she looks when you're on her, forward looking aft, aft looking forward. Run my eyes along the broad white stretches of deck, tactile detail of blocks and cleats and shackles, crisp transitions dark to light, hard lines dividing white and wood, wood and metal.

Monday. Going on three days off the dock, two days in the Atlantic, two hundred miles east of the Chesapeake. Steve flew this morning from California back to D.C.; tomorrow he would deal with the movers—I'd done it often enough myself to feel guilty as hell for leaving him alone to that—and Wednesday he would fly to Europe.

For over an hour Monday night I tried getting through to an AT&T High Seas Operator on the single-sideband radio. I was much too far offshore for the line-of-sight VHF radio I'd used in the Chesapeake. Single-sideband is far more expensive than VHF, but its range is vast when the airwaves cooperate.

Colibri, like a number of other boats in the Singlehanded Transpac, had only had VHF. We figured that if one boat with VHF contacted the next boat with VHF contacted a boat with SSB we'd all be accounted for, but we got so spread out that I was unable to contact a soul during my fourteen days offshore. Five other competitors had the same problem; Steve took comfort in the unlikelihood that *all* of us had sunk. Single-sideband went on the priority list for *Sonnet*.

SSB is expensive to use, as well as to buy. Five dollars a minute when you use AT&T, not to mention what it costs your batteries. It's tough when you burn up amperage and still don't get through.

Assuming I did get through, it'd be my last direct contact with Steve before the Azores. From here on, with him traveling and then in Bulgaria, his mom in California would act as go-between.

I gave up trying at 2300, figuring he needed his sleep, though it turned out he stayed up half the night prepping for the movers and then slept badly, worrying because I hadn't called.

21 July

0600 Went on deck at dawn to squeeze dish soap into a squeaky block and a single dolphin was swimming alongside the boat. Not joyful swimming the way they often do, just swimming along quietly, but it pleased me to see him. (I asked, "Are you a solo dolphin, come to see a solo sailor?") It occurred to me he might have been attracted to the squeaking. It occurred to me after he left that he might have been lonely or sad. Do dolphins feel loneliness?

0720   Sitting here waiting for whoever's on channel 1206 to get off, so I can try calling Steve. Extraordinary the loneliness I felt last night, after failing to get through.

At 0800 I got through to the operator, who put me through to Steve, who sounded so exhausted and seemed so far away. Our apartment in Glover Park—which I'd never see again—seemed surreal, a staticky apartment surrounding his voice. We talked only a few minutes; I was washed by an incredible love for him, and guilt, and a kind of helplessness.

The wind continued light. I'd gybed at seven—turning the boat so the wind moved across her stern, swinging the sails to the other side— and I gybed again at eleven, gybing my way to the Azores, back and forth slowly with the wind shifts. Ninety-one miles, noon to noon. Around one the wind veered and built, giving Sonnet and me the first smooth sailing of our passage.

1330   The boat is moving tremendously, right on course, cutting through the ocean.

Happy, but still a little wound up. Trained myself so diligently to keep asking "What am I forgetting?" that I keep doing it, but I can't think what.

1500   This would be a totally different experience with another person, and to a great extent I don't want that intrusion, want the purity of doing it alone. I'm comfortable out here alone, I'm not afraid of the solitude. What I'm afraid of is shipping, look at these pilot charts and it's just a crisscross of shipping lanes.

1515   I stand in the cockpit as my boat moves through the blue Atlantic and the feeling is strange: How is it that I know the things I needed to know in order to make this happen? Somehow I did it, somehow I've accumulated the knowledge over the years. Very odd.

1410 Slightly nervous feel to *Sonnet*, sails fiddling blocks, partly because the jib's cut wrong for off-the-wind sailing. Slightly nervous feel to her skipper; stakes are so different here, *our* boat, *our* investment.

Long way to go yet. Four and a half days on board so far. Long way to the Azores, *long* way to Greece.

My dreams are all extremely peopled; I should be writing them down. I dream of things I should do before leaving, and wake up a bit shocked that I've left, that *Sonnet* and I are offshore.

1715 It occurs to me that I enjoyed passages more before I knew much about sailing. Early passages, when someone simply told me what course to steer, and I steered as told, and looked out marveling at the elements. Now I'm more likely to beat myself up—why aren't you doing headsail changes, why haven't you replaced the leech cord on the jib—and less likely to stand in awe of nature.

WOO has reported an area of wind right where I am, twenty knots, eight-foot seas, and I'm seeing none of it.

1900 Just cheered myself by pulling out the #11 chart: *Look*, Lydia. You started in Annapolis. You powered over to Cambridge, then sailed down and out the Chesapeake, and here you are, five days out into the ocean.

If I look now at the chart of the North Atlantic, at the crosses marking my noon positions, those first five days are jumbled in my mind. Days of sleeping and waking, wind and then no wind, rain and then none. Beginning July 23, for better or for worse, the crosses jump out at me, the passage takes more form.

2023 There's a lumpy southerly swell, and a light five knots of wind from the west, and my only option under sail is to wallow along slowly with all kinds of wear on the gear toward either Venezuela or Nova Scotia. I've rolled in the jib and strapped in

the main and we wallow here adrift. I could hook up the Autohelm and take off under power but I'm not sure the Autohelm
could handle the swell and I've powered five hours today already,
I'm starting to worry about fuel consumption.

I think I'll sleep.

2

And now the STORM-BLAST came, and he
Was tyrannous and strong;
He struck with his o'ertaking wings,
And chased us south along.

With sloping masts and dipping prow,
As who pursued with yell and blow
Still treads the shadow of his foe,
And forward bends his head . . .
                    COLERIDGE, "The Rime of the Ancient Mariner"

                                                    23 July
0538   The sea is so calm it's oily-looking, the swell virtually
gone, sea and sky both pale in the sunrise.
   This could be a day for the *cafard* if I'm not careful, drifting
here completely without wind, nine hours already of no progress,
and Steve in Europe, flew over my head last night as *Sonnet* was
creaking to a halt.

0840   I don't really mind being dead in the water. Got some
sleep. Fixed the leech cord on the jib, even took a few photos of
the process. Not sure I'll feel the same after twenty-four rather
than twelve hours. Not sure Monica's gonna be thrilled with the
progress I'm making.
   The good news is, I'm making over a knot in the current.

0940 The wind has come gently around to the east-southeast and I'm sailing along quietly. I feel peaceful; glad to have stuck this out without turning on the engine. My evil twin, of course, is suggesting the bigger headsail to take full advantage of what little wind we have, but I'm content with myself for having done the leech-cord job, and have some grain of optimism that this might be a building wind. If we're still under four knots in an hour, I'll think again.

0955 I tiptoe around the boat, trying not to break the Monitor's concentration in this light wind. Nothing is banging, nothing is clanking, virtually nothing is moving as we cut quietly through this quiet sea. I close my eyes for a moment and listen to the slosh of water against the hull, this boat within the elements.

1018 Forecast low at 40°N 68°W, winds to 25 knots, seas to 9 feet within 360 nautical miles SE and S quadrants. Good excuse not to fuss with the big headsail, if I needed an excuse.

It was a pretty crappy first few days. So little sleep, so wound up still from the prep, a full day navigating the Chesapeake, then a full day of nasty rain, then assorted bouts of clanging and banging (it's Thursday, and I could no more account for the various days, summarize their personalities . . .), gybing and motoring, Autohelm to Monitor and back again. Right now I'm doing just fine.

I love being on the ocean, I love being on a boat, it's starting to come back to me why I went to the effort to do this.

1230 Substantial little scar on my thumb where I cut myself right after I told myself I knew better, stripping casing off electrical wire in Cambridge, cutting toward myself instead of away. Telling myself to cut away but toward was faster. A lesson scar.

Not being one hundred percent good about a safety harness, though I'm working on being better.

1315 Trying to eat up the fresh stuff, since the ice is long gone. Turkey ham and mini corn muffins; very tasty. Looking forward to sailing with Monica, not necessarily better but different.

Likely to have a higher caliber of cuisine with two instead of one.

Last third of a slice goes to Neptune.

Amazing though, the depth of superstition. I feel nervous as soon as I write that; what if Neptune doesn't like turkey ham?

1930 This morning was flat hazy calm. Late morning I was sailing peacefully close-hauled, afternoon with the wind farther aft, and now I'm surrounded with thunderheads and not too long ago (according to the SeaTalk) hit 8.2 knots hand steering through a squall. Might be a good night to sleep in foul-weather gear in the cockpit.

Long fruitless session trying to get through to Beth on the SSB, deeply discouraging. I don't like radios; I'm happier without one. And this one is doing things I don't understand: "If antenna VSWR exceeds 2.5:1 for ANY reason, at ANY time, the operating system will cause the transmitter to revert to the low power mode . . ." What does that *mean?*

2300 Staticky contact with Beth's answer machine, which leaves me feeling deeply depressed. Just such a totally different world I'm living, this boat so far from anywhere.

I'm still trying to decide how harshly to judge myself for not paying more attention to that predicted low-pressure system. I tell myself that the earlier forecast was inaccurate, reporting wind in my area when I was barely moving, that later predicted lows came to nothing. I tell myself the prediction was twenty-five knots, there was no way to know it'd blow forty. Still, I should have been reefed.

For the next twenty-four hours there are no journal entries, and only one log entry, a quickly scribbled GPS position fix at noon.

I remember struggling into my foul-weather gear, just after jotting my post-transmission blues. The boat had felt pressed during my radio labors, but I'd shoved it to the back of my mind. I now felt angry with myself for that negligence, angry at the radio.

The boat was more than pressed by the time I pulled my boots on; I got up on deck and behind the wheel just as the squall hit.

A boat, if conditions are wrong, if her crew doesn't serve her well, acts like an oversized weather vane. Her mainsail—like the blade of the weather vane—forces her bow up toward the wind; enough wind, hitting the mainsail broadside, can lay the boat on her side in a full-on broach.

Scared. As scared as I've ever been on a boat that first blast of the squall, with no reef in the main, and the boom prevented slightly inboard for the reach we'd been doing earlier. Hand steering in howling wind, the preventer rigged on the forward sheet winch, no way to reach it to let it off, the mainsheet rigged on its winch in front of the wheel, no way to reach it without tangling in the spokes, hand steering in dark and rain and the boat rounding up and me holding her down, holding her down, no turns left on the wheel and still rounding, yelling out to her in the dark, "You've got to come *down, Sonnet,* you've got to come *down,*" no turns left on the wheel and imagining the broach and holding her with everything I had, feeling her slowly slowly come back toward control as the worst of the gust passed, then gusting again, three or four times rounding into the wind like that, darkness and driving rain and no way to leave the helm to spill the wind from the sail. A flicker of lights—*too close*—off to starboard through the rain, and then the rain so thick I couldn't see the ship, talking out loud as my hands slipped on the wheel, "It's only a squall, squalls pass, it'll pass," wanting even the slightest of lulls so I could get the Monitor working again, spill the sail, and rush forward to reef. The lull came, the rain cleared, the ship was close by and frightening; throwing off the mainsheet, rushing to the companionway, flipping on strobe and spreader lights, rushing forward to the mast, the sail whipping violently as I hauled in the reefs, the world lit bizarrely by the pulsing of the strobe, the third reef in if not beautifully, the ship slipping past, and knowing I'd never felt so close to self-perpetrated disaster.

The squall had passed, but the gale was just getting its teeth into me. For the next twelve hours I lived behind the wheel, except for one or two lightning darts to the companionway to grab granola bars from a galley cupboard and cram them into the pockets of my foul-weather gear. I peed into a jar at the helm. I didn't sleep; the Monitor, linked to *Sonnet*'s too small rudder—a different rudder than the one on the design drawings—simply couldn't handle the waves, so I steered by hand. Big waves, breaking onto the boat, breaking sometimes in such a way to fill the baffled wind vents, pouring below.

Six years back, on *Alaska Eagle*, in our first gale off the Oregon coast, I'd steered toward dawn for three straight hours when three of the people on my watch had no desire to steer and the fourth had already slammed the boat through an accidental gybe. One watch mate sat next to me as I steered, grabbing the wheel with me when it loaded up so it wouldn't spin out of my hands; three hours became a kind of trance, an athletic, muscle-ache meditation, forgetting the last wave, focusing on the next.

Three hours four hours five hours six hours seven, alone in the wind-whipped North Atlantic night. Over and over I said to myself maybe it's easing off. It helped to think that. To think, with any small lull, that the worst of it was past, though the lull would pass and the wind would come back strong.

Trying to think how long the gales had lasted on the *Eagle*.

Steering through the dark, steering aching-shouldered through rain, wheel spinning out of my hands sometimes, no leather on the metal, another job that never quite got done. Thinking of Steve, thinking of my friend Deborah, thinking of Steve's mom Beth, thinking of my parents, thinking of my sister Layne, steering for them. Telling myself I could do this for as long as it needed to be done. Keeping the stern lined up to the waves. Keeping the boat safe.

Late that morning, the wind began to moderate, swinging into the north as the low swept past.

My noon-to-noon run was 192 miles.

In the early afternoon, with the wind still veering, I gybed to keep from being pushed too far south. Chicken-gybed, rather; I couldn't fathom handling alone both helm and lines through a regular gybe, so I swung the bow into the wind instead of swinging the stern, my heart in my throat, engine roaring to get us through the wicked waves, boat lurching, sails flapping, blocks banging; feeling, full-faced, the force of the dying gale.

I remember looking out at the water hours after the gybe, the Monitor managing the helm, rain and wind and the wild gray all around me, heaving rushing seas beaten down by the rain, ocean blending into sky. I looked at it with a kind of wonder, a kind of honor, to see it like this, in its state of impressive disarray, in my state of solitude, of exhaustion, to see this spot on the globe which no one would ever see in the same way.

25 July

0200   I have gotten some sleep, finally, and am about to get some more. Boat sails still triple-reefed on the outskirts of the infamous low.

The next morning the wind moderated and I shook out the reefs.

1205   Am I gonna get becalmed again? Isn't there a happy medium between gales and flat slatting calms?

Dropped a winch handle on my little toe and it hurts like hell, is puffing up like a sausage. When does this start getting fun?

1230   *Colibri* wasn't just a fluke, it wasn't just a matter of getting onto a bigger, more stable boat, I'm just not suited to singlehanding, I beat myself up mentally, I don't eat right (GOT TO EAT, Lydia!), I feel SORRY for myself. Christ I feel sorry for myself right now. I want to be with Steve and Butch in Italy.

Have been sleeping and sleeping. Sleep, get up and shake a reef out, sleep, get up and get a noon fix, sleep. Try to get caught up on sleeping, try to get caught up on eating, take it from there.

1500   Slight lull, wind shift to the south, tack back to starboard, sailing now great circle toward the Azores, and I feel much better. The constant changes wear me down; on the other hand I should learn not to agonize decisions since they'll probably be preempted in short order.

Sea charcoal-gray, sky light gray and white, horizon sharp as a razor.

Feels like there's more weather than in fact there is, because we're headed straight into a pretty substantial swell. East-northeasterly swell, southeast wind, where's this new wind coming from? What's it gonna do?

1919   This is starting to feel like some sort of cosmic bad joke.
I had—what—about four hours of sailing in the right direction
and now it's blowing like stink from right where I want to go
and I'm back to sailing close-hauled on a triple-reefed main.
On top of which I was in the middle of reefing and missed
my weather report, so I don't even know what's causing the
easterly.

Throughout the night the wind was against me, nasty and strong. By
dawn it moderated, clocking a bit to the south, favoring the starboard
tack, the wind coming over the starboard side of the boat. The early-
morning weather report, however, spread rumors of another low, so I
tacked back to port. The wind kept clocking.

26 July
0930   This is insane. Scuttling back and forth, north to south,
getting nowhere.
    It doesn't even make *sense*. If there's a low at 38°N 62°W why
have I been getting wind straight out of the east for all these
hours?
    I could be sailing more or less where I want to go, except that
everyone keeps telling me about this low. If it's where they say it
is, and I'm where I say I am, I'm within 150 miles of it but I see
no sign of its existence. I sail on the port tack to take me away
from it, and that's not even south, it's west of south, I'm sailing
back toward America.
    WHAT THE FUCK SHOULD I DO? Sail this way another
half hour, see if the next weather report says anything different,
and reconnoiter.

1020   Tired of sailing in the wrong direction, I tack to the east.
I do, however, leave in the reefs.

An hour later I shook the reefs out. The low, it would seem, was a
no-show. Between making very little way and running scared, my noon-
to-noon run from Saturday to Sunday was a rip-roaring thirty-nine
miles. At least I had pleasant weather in the afternoon.

1415   Hand steered for a while; in light air to windward in swells the Monitor fusses too much, interprets the swells as wind shifts. Boat's almost better off left to her own devices. Half steered, half left her to her own devices; sat there reading, glancing sometimes at the compass.

I still get unsettled, thinking about the blow. Hand steered the better part of twelve hours. People have done more; this was more than enough for me. Thinking in the midst of it: This is the most physically demanding thing I've ever done, but already it's like some kind of dream, something that never happened.

1910   Sitting in the companionway watching the sunset, wondering if I've lost my capacity for awe. Wanting to know myself, not the child who rode horses in the hills, not the college student who tried to touch the ocean every day, but this adult human being, this imperfect closing-on-forty human being, limited and talented, blessed and scarred.

Earlier, I looked out at the horizon with a kind of panicked dread, wanting a peaceful night so much, then realized whatever the night is, it is. Right now the boat's just right, more wind and there'd be leech flutter, less wind and the Monitor would be struggling, boat moving across the ocean, boat moving smoothly.

Not eating right, not brushing my teeth, not washing, not washing dishes. Steering through gales, handling sails, penciling positions on a plotting sheet.

We've got a long way to go, *Sonnet*, and then we'll rest a while in Greece, process this peacefully.

3

Sonnet *crosses the ocean.*
My *stomach hurts.*
Hurts *from worry, from inflicting it. Motion*
sick *(obliquely speaking) on the outskirts*
of *the low. Me, I crossed a line*
I *drew for myself in the sand, launched us both*
off *the edge of the continent. A fine*
new *resolution, an honest, star-crossed oath:*
I'll *leave off honing points I'll never prove*
(we *can't escape the world; what if we dance*
on *it?) . . . Sonnet! Partner in crime, we move.*
Two *hulls swirling slowly in vast expanse,*
two *names tugged by atmospheric tide,*
we'll *cross this stretch and touch the other side.*

From the Azores on to Greece I'd be sailing with crew. If Steve's response to my desire to buy a boat had been wholehearted support, his response to my desire to singlehand—which I hadn't mentioned straight off—had been disbelieving silence. I suppose he hoped I'd show a little common sense, that I wouldn't choose to risk our entire savings in order to be isolated and exhausted. Insurance for singlehanding is nearly impossible to come by; at least with *Colibri* the investment had been minimal.

He also knew I was still infected by the singlehanding bug, that the Solo Transpac hadn't cured it, and we arrived at a compromise: first leg singlehanded, the balance of the voyage with crew, and insurance.

I knew I wanted to sail with women, when I wasn't sailing alone.

Way back—as far back as Africa—I'd fantasized finding a soul mate to sail with. Not that I had the slightest idea how to find her. Advertise in the sailing magazines maybe: "Woman sailor seeks woman sailor . . ."

With time, I'd recognized that a soul mate wasn't likely to crawl out of the woodwork, that I already knew plenty of solid women sailors, from classes on *Saudade*, from offshore passages on *Alaska Eagle*, from the women's racing team. Maybe the lesson here was to look closer to home.

As soon as I made the offer on the Swan 40, I started making phone calls. Anne was getting married in July, and didn't think taking off to go sailing was the best way to launch her marriage. Tina had recently had a baby, and just changed jobs.

Andrea was between jobs, and very excited about sailing. Monica already knew about my boat project, since I'd been discussing electronics options with her husband, Brian (I've chosen not to use their real names). When I phoned her about crewing she said, "I was hoping you'd ask."

Andrea was the more aggressive sailor, more think-on-her-feet. Monica had a wider range of experience. She and Brian had recently bought a Valiant 40. They'd made a passage together from Fiji to New Zealand on a Swan 57—it was Monica's first offshore passage—and had belonged to sailing clubs for years. She'd taken sailing lessons—I met her when she took my Intro to Big Boats class on *Saudade*—and sailed extensively on a friend's Beneteau. The insurance company was looking for a solid résumé for the offshore leg from the Azores to Iberia, so I asked Monica to sail the Atlantic, and Andrea to sail through the Med to Greece. Both were enthusiastic. I could have made more phone calls, for backups, but I didn't. I felt that fate had settled things. I began to envision owning this Miraculous Women's Boat, a boat that a number of women, over the years, would sail on, and gain from.

The Swan 40 fell through. Weeks passed before I bought *Sonnet* and launched into intense preparations. I talked to both Monica and Andrea as often as I could, keeping them up to date on my progress.

In early June, Andrea got a job. She told me she'd taken it in part because of its flexibility, assuring me—and herself—she could get the time off for the Med trip, she just didn't want to ask her boss so soon after starting. She put off asking, and she put off asking, and by the time she finally found out she couldn't get the time off it was the second week of July. Her voyage wouldn't have started for six weeks; maybe it just didn't occur to her that mine was scheduled to start within days.

I spun out. I didn't have it in me to start making phone calls. There was the Monitor to finish mounting, and the electrical panel to wire; the to-do list was endless. I didn't want to *think* about it. I'd *wanted* to sail with Andrea, I didn't want to shift my mental image of the voyage.

I called Monica and said—half in jest, half simply as a way to vent, to tell her that Andrea had backed out—"You want to sail all the way through the Med?" I also asked if she had any ideas on crew, and she said there were a couple of women she could call. The next time I talked to her she said she *did* want to sail through the Med.

I told her we should play it by ear, see how both of us felt when we reached Gibraltar. I'd learned from previous passages that landfall—after the intensity of being offshore—was often the best time to part ways. She said she understood; we'd play it by ear.

In fact, a bigger conflict than what to do about crew awaited me at the end of the Atlantic passage. I'd be spending time in southern Spain, a place I hadn't seen in years, and the thought touched me with a little rush of pleasure. But spending time in Spain meant spending time at my parents' home.

I told myself it would be different this time, because of *Sonnet*.

27 July

0823   If I'd known the wind would die I would have powered my two hours now but instead I powered in the night. In the night the wind went from east to west, I went from close-hauled to nearly running, gybed, up on deck with stars overhead and lightning on the horizon, slept on deck awhile in foul-weather gear in case the weather went bad, slept again below, my body thick in sleep, rebelling against the alarm, the every forty minutes, sleeping through the alarm I'm not sure how, it beeps and beeps and beeps, going on deck to a ship which had already crossed us.

The boat wallows. The blocks and sails slam. We are going so slowly, not even close to the halfway mark not even close to a hundred miles a day.

From Roethke: ". . . Snail, snail, glister me forward / Bird, soft-sigh me home / Worm, be with me / This is my hard time . . ."

At ten in the morning on my tenth day out I got through to Beth on Whiskey Oscar Oscar 811, six in the morning California time, woke her up, but the air waves were cooperating and she assured me she was more than happy to be woken. She had talked to Steve the day before; he'd been in Italy, about to get on the ferry to Greece. I'd never been to Greece and had always wanted to; I tried not to remind myself I'd be there now if I weren't in the middle of the ocean.

Familiar voices never sound quite right on the SSB, flattened out. I'd told Beth's machine I'd be calling every four days instead of three and I now explained why, that I'd had to run my engine more than expected, that I was worried about fuel and needed to conserve my power, but in fact I'd stretched the time to four days mostly because the calls left me feeling lousy. Some singlehanders live for contacts with home on the radio; I'm not one of them.

1040 Still two sets of swells, one with one against. What does it mean? Should I not have shaken out the reef?

FOOD LOG, Mon 27th
2 yogurts = 200 calories
1 banana = ?
1 juice = 150
another banana
a Kudos bar
some too-oily tabouli
a raw green bean or two
cheese, with peanut butter

1540 Wind about the same all day, light, but getting lighter now, almost gone. Still the double swell, from east and west, which makes the sail slatting worse. Hot. I've told everyone how cold this passage would be and it's almost like the tropics.

Is there always this procession of lows across the North Atlantic? I guess I won't worry about today's since it's ahead of me and moving away from me.

1740   There's a thick overcast above the cumulus spreading from the west that I'm keeping an eye on. Slow day, though by the end I didn't much mind. Too hot below to sleep; I went on deck and put chafing gear on the bow pulpit where the sail's been chafing, allowed myself the luxury of no harness in the calm and it was liberating, the blue water, the deck somewhat to my surprise clean and white, whiter than I've ever seen it, washed by waves, rinsed by rain.

Something satisfying in the soft texture of the rag I was cutting for chafing gear, a rather ugly child's sweat pant, black with a stripe of orange, but the fabric of it soft and pleasing. Couldn't find the white tape, certainly didn't have leather ready at hand, so I used duct tape, enjoying a sense of rebellion, this is my boat, not Orange Coast College's.

Untangled the spinnaker halyard which yesterday seemed overwhelming, untangled it in about ten seconds. Sat and watched the water go by oh so slowly, thought of writing Andrea, thought of Monica spending so much time waiting for me and hoped it would turn into an adventure for her.

I frequently say it takes about ten days to get into the rhythm of being offshore and that might be the case. I still feel lonely, I still feel somewhat jumpy, mistrustful, but it's starting to feel logical to be here, logical for this boat to be on this ocean.

Borderline bored, a time or two today. I'd much rather be bored than terrified, or frustrated, or any number of other ways I've been, these last ten days.

1910   Sun down, still some light out. Sit in the cockpit munching corn on the cob (can't believe I forgot to buy butter). Boat moves slowly, has moved slowly all day and I'm fine with that. A bit of housekeeping, a bit of boat work, read a goodly bit of *Brazzaville Beach*, nap, munch this and that, write in my journal. At sea, horizon around me.

A hint of color now, behind colorless clouds in the west. Getting a bit too dark to write or read.

2000 Okay, one more entry, written by flashlight, like a kid under the sheets. I can't believe how good I feel out here, all of a sudden. This odd existence. Liking the way my skin feels, the softness. Living in nothing but underwear, not too cold, not too hot.

28 July

0800 On deck twice in the night, once at eleven, once at three, to trim sails and adjust course as the wind clocked and built, putting us on a reach, sending us on our way under a wide sky of stars. Sat for a long time in the cockpit as the boat sailed through the night, incredible sense of pleasure, incredible sense of rightness and power and potential. The possibility, in this simple world of boat and sea, for things to make sense.

Started, there in the cockpit, to do a sitting version of my Chinese stretches, which I've done so rarely for months, feeling I could do them for the good of how they felt, at the same time recognizing that the reason I'd stopped was because of Oscar, because of how they made me think of Oscar, the way he'd do them with me, be beneath my feet to be petted. I started to stretch, but all it did was bring back the cat, bring in the pain, bring in the senselessness, and I went below and climbed back in my bunk.

Such a fucking complicated world.

The ways in which I'm a sailor: with a certain restraint, a certain rebellion. In spite of myself. A sailor because I've been a sailor. A sailor who ends up way too thin.

1000 Radio contact on VHF with a somewhat snotty Norwegian on a big ugly freighter who wondered why I was calling if there wasn't any risk of collision. ("I am bearing 80. You are bearing 90. I don't see what the problem is.") Second contact, after he spotted me (we were four miles apart, and he had to search where I told him before noticing the little black-hulled sailboat on his starboard beam), I said candidly that I'd called partly to know if he'd seen me, partly just to hear another human voice.

They are headed to the east coast of England, out of Philadelphia. He didn't ask if there was no one else on board for me to talk to.

1225   Either we've still got some serious Gulf Stream with us, or the SeaTalk is underreading or both, because we've averaged closer to nine knots than seven since 8 this a.m. It's a rough ride, my stomach could feel one hell of a lot more settled, but it's a fast ride, the boat is going like absolute dynamite and I'm not going to complain. Wind settled out directionwise, able to crack off a bit, and we're blasting east on a beam reach, little jib setting perfectly, one reef in the main, blasting along, rough and tumble.

1545   I'm a hard one to please. Too slow and I bitch and moan, too fast and I'm on edge, nervous with the speed. We're not overpowered, just powerful. A lot less wear on the gear like this, with this constant pressure, than with the crash-bang of calms.

This thought, at one point: Next time I want solitude, load the boat up with food and go anchor somewhere. Seriously. Or go to a mountain cabin, somewhere you can sleep through the night.

I am flabbergasted by the likes of Tania Aebi, who simply went below at night and slept. My body wants that something fierce but it just seems monumentally irresponsible.

Should have called Monica before she left for the Azores, to tell her she ought to soak this up, she may never again be so vastly welcomed as crew.

1600   No wonder this has felt unnervingly fast—we've averaged 9.3 knots speed-over-ground for the past six hours. Some of it's current, but *Sonnet* she *moves*.

By 1830 the wind was well into the twenties, WOO was forecasting another low at 41°N 54°W—placing *Sonnet* less than a hundred miles away in the undesirable southeast quadrant—and I'd reefed all the way down to the third reef.

At 1930 I started the engine to charge the batteries. I made a stab, while the Westerbeke roared at me, at making myself some dinner, opened some Progresso Chicken Noodle, ate it cold from the can braced against boat motion, ate a tomato whole, leaning over the sink. Was it my imagination, or did something smell funny, from the engine? And didn't the lights seem slightly dim?

Then the awful clunking noise, and the lights dimming drastically, and I rushed to the cockpit, reached the kill switch, yanked. Silence. The masthead light brightened. The boat reached swiftly, almost violently, through the night. I sat there a moment, thought about trying the key but didn't have the nerve, went below and made an entry in the log: "We've got problems."

I was pretty sure—maybe fatalistically—that I wouldn't be using my engine again this trip. I made a quick assessment. My batteries were low, but not drastically. I'd called Beth yesterday; I wasn't due to call her again until Friday. I would shut down everything, use not one drop of power. Maybe, once I got through this spell of weather, I'd be able to figure out the problem and get the engine working again. If not, I should have enough battery power for one more call on Friday, to let her know I wouldn't be calling again.

The log entry was the last for more than a day, though I did manage some chores as the wind built. I got my nerve up and tried the key. Nothing. I shut down the entire electrical panel. I dug out the 9-volt emergency lantern and raised it in the rigging, hoping it would last through the night. I tossed a bottle of water in the cockpit and crammed granola bars into the pockets of my foul-weather gear. By 2030 the second blow was settling in with a vengeance.

Initially, it wasn't as violent as the first. I didn't hand steer nonstop, though I did spend the first night in the cockpit, sleeping in snatches next to the wheel with my harness tethers hooked in two directions. When the vane started losing control I was upright in seconds, disconnecting it, steering through the windy dark by hand.

I told myself it would end with the dawn, told myself the worst of the first one had lasted twelve hours, and this one wasn't as bad. By dawn it was getting worse. By ten I was hand steering in an oddly cheerful mood, telling myself it would end by noon, telling myself—or some companion—we'd simply hand steer through a two-hour movie and the blow would be over.

I remember asking myself, around noon, how the movie had been. I remember a lull around one, looking around, saying "See? The waves are definitely smaller." And then it started back strong. Short unpredictable waves, streaked with sargasso and foam, breaking right over *Sonnet*'s side, burying her deck, one huge one breaking right over the stern, I looked back and saw it and there was nothing I could do, bracing myself on the wheel, thrown into the wheel by the wall of water, water everywhere, water filling the cockpit, the cockpit taking way too long to drain.

Hours. Time meaning nothing. Wave after wave. Steering at the rougher times. Sitting at the more manageable times, looking out at the waves, images moving in and out of my mind, memories of Africa. Willing the waves to quietness, quieter, quieter, convincing myself of a lull, and then the waves building, breaking, filling me with irrational fury.

Low gray clouds, dark, rushing with the wind, all around the horizon. At one point, near sunset, I looked up. Above the flinging clouds were blue sky and alto cumulus, serene, unmoving. "I want *that* sky," I said out loud. "*That's* the sky I want." Aware that the wind was rushing only along the surface of the globe, sucking the ocean along with it.

Nightfall, odd currents mixing warm and cool air.

Twenty-four hours since the gale set in.

By 2100 the wind was lighter, the seas less crazed. I was able to sleep, below in a bunk, off and on for three hours.

30 July

0000   Twenty-six hours in the cockpit, three hours of sleep, then up to pull the main all the way down, *Colibri*-style, and put out the strobe, and now I plan a quick dinner at the chart table and tomorrow I'll plot our position (nearly to Greenland) and write all this up.

At 0300 I was back in the cockpit, lashing the boom in several directions, lashing the sail papoose-like to the boom, afraid the wind would tear something loose. The wind built more fiercely than it had in either blow, the Monitor losing all control, nearly broaching us on only the half-rolled-in jib.

Hand steering then, afraid of losing the sail, afraid of losing the rig, then struggling to roll it in, whipping and whipping, the rig shuddering, and the sail finally in, leaving it that way for hours.

It started raining in the morning, and rained hard in the wind through till noon; maybe the rain helped settle out the waves. My noon-to-noon run was around 145 miles, nearly half of that time without sails. The previous day's mileage—through the first of the gale—had been somewhere between 204 and 207, a hell of a run for a 42-foot full-keeled boat.

> *1330*   I keep toying with the idea of putting up the storm trisail, just to have done it, and so at least we'd be making some mileage, but the Monitor is steering us at nearly four knots in the right direction on bare poles and dodger, so maybe we'll keep up the time-out for a little while more.
>
> It's relatively noiseless below—I've got everything on deck so trussed up and tied down that you don't get the slam-bang of calms—but when I try to do anything at all—pump out the bilge, plot a position—I realize the violence of the motion.
>
> The Atlantic passage from hell.

In hindsight, I wonder why I didn't spend more of both gales on bare poles, or why I never tried heaving to, back-winding the jib, tying off the helm, letting the boat jog along slowly. I tell myself heaving to would have been nerve-racking, maybe even dangerous, waves breaking over the boat.

In fact, through both gales I was very aware of the mileage sliding under *Sonnet*'s keel as I hand steered. Something in me still regretted the solo race to Hawaii, that I hadn't put up a spinnaker on the windiest days and hand steered little *Colibri* at fifteen knots toward the finish line.

By the time I bought *Sonnet* I knew I wasn't really a racing sailor, but I hadn't quite figured out what I was instead.

Late in the afternoon the second day of the second low, with what seemed like willful perversity, the wind died almost to nothing. I rolled the jib back out, then raised the mainsail, exhausted to the bone, close to hallucinogenic. I thought of leaving in a couple of reefs, even though there wasn't any wind, but I couldn't get the second to go in right, so I raised it to the first reef and went below to sleep.

At first there was the crash-bang of too little wind and still-big waves, then slowly a kind of settling, finally a sense of utter bliss as the wind built to the perfect strength for beam-reaching, the wind at right angles to the boat, feeling that bliss in my bones, in my sleep, but the wind kept building and I was back on deck to reef again. This time, a bit renewed from sleep, I worked with crazed obsessiveness to put in the perfect third reef, with the second reef tied in ahead of it. Bear away from the wind to reduce apparent wind speed, second reef in, grind in the mainsheet to bring the boom centerline, safety line on the second reef's clew, sheet out, third reef in, sheet in, safety line on the third reef's clew, reef points tied in, believing if I did it perfectly the crazy weather would stop. Back to a beam reach, but the wind kept building.

On top of Mother Nature's perversity—or because of it—my stomach hurt.

2150 Tonight in darkness, in strengthening wind, I lay in my bunk, fighting hard against a kind of dread, fighting back images of disaster, gear failure, smashing into a half-submerged container, trying to recite poetry, trying to come up with affirmations ("I will listen to my instincts, not my paranoias"), not doing well at all. The wind kept building, waves crashing over the boat, so I struggled into foul-weather gear and back up on deck. I rolled in the jib, sat in the cockpit, dazed by the Chinese torture of the strobe, and then I looked up, and there were stars! All day it's been awful, dark gray skies and rain, and my spirit lifted, that response of hope.

By midmorning the wind had settled out and I was reaching triple-reefed at six knots. In the early afternoon I flipped on the electrical panel for the first time in three days, flipped on the single-sideband, and tuned in WOO in New Jersey. The traffic list on 1218 came through loud and clear; as soon as it was over I picked up the mike. Theoretically, if you can hear a station clearly, the station should be able to hear you.

I pressed the transmit button and held the mike an inch from my lips. *Whiskey Oscar Oscar. Whiskey Oscar Oscar.*

Twelve short syllables, trying not to visualize the amperage needle jumping on the electrical panel behind me. The High Seas Operators pan their antennas; the antenna might not have been pointed in the right direction on my first try.

I waited three minutes and tried again, waiting to be taken aback, as I had in the past, by a sudden clear voice asking my coordinates. Nothing.

I tried for fifteen minutes, knowing my batteries were getting weaker with each try, the chance of New Jersey hearing me getting slimmer. When I gave up it was for good; what power I had left I'd conserve for using the VHF.

31 July

Let's run through the list here. I'm weak, shaky, slightly dizzy, and my stomach's a wreck. The weather the entire trip has been terrible. I'm only two-thirds of the way to the Azores. I have no engine, no way to charge batteries, figured on using what charge I had left to call Beth but I ran them down trying and now there's no way—unless I can raise a freighter on the VHF—to make contact until I get to the Azores, which could be another week. I hate imposing this kind of worry.

On the positive side, my GPS uses its own batteries, I have a sextant if I lose the GPS, I have a tough boat, and we'll make it.

What else. The boat's a disaster below, everything damp. Water still trickling from distant hiding places into the bilge.

I tried to remind myself, since I wasn't having all that great a time, that there was more to the adventure of *Sonnet* than this voyage. There was also the destination, having the boat nearby while we lived in Sofia. I hoped *Sonnet* would provide a link—completely distinct from diplomacy—to the country where I'd be spending two years of my life.

The plan was to keep her in northern Greece for the first winter, then sail in the spring through the Dardanelles to Istanbul, through the Bosporus into the Black Sea, to the Bulgarian port of Varna. I'd been corresponding with a Bulgarian sailor for more than a year now, and knew quite a bit about the small but enthusiastic Bulgarian sailing scene. The country's coastline was limited to a few hundred miles of the Black Sea, but several Bulgarian sailors had circumnavigated the globe, and a Bulgarian woman hoped to race this year's Singlehanded TransAtlantic Race, though I hadn't heard if she'd made it to the starting line. Maybe she and I could put together an all-women team for next year's Bulgarian racing season. Maybe *Sonnet* and I could participate in some Black Sea environmental awareness program for schoolchildren.

Somehow the Black Sea seemed a long way away.

1512 There's another one coming, 41°N 49°W, they are chasing me around the Atlantic, maybe I'm far enough ahead of this
one, maybe *Sonnet* and I are rushing ahead and away from it.

Move *Sonnet* move *Sonnet* move.

Feeling slightly betrayed. I don't quite understand why I
should be going through this. Why I decided to go through it.
But I did, and I am, and *Sonnet* and I are sailing fast ahead of the
next one, maybe fast enough.

What can I eat? I know I need to eat, have barely eaten for
days, but I don't know what, my stomach feels awful. It isn't sea-
sickness, though I know it's some form of it, sick from the stress
and exhaustion.

1730 We aren't, in fact, sailing very fast, not even six knots,
though it has the urgent feel of the time we were reaching at
nine. Same heel, same waves breaking over the bow, but a
deeper reef, wind farther forward, trying to gain more to weather.

I did, at one point today, get the engine cover off, wrestled it
off against boat motion, but I saw nothing wrong, nothing I
knew to do.

Nighttime. Searching the horizon for ships. Until now I'd hoped
fiercely *not* to see ships, I knew they weren't looking for me, Big Boat
Has Right of Way, I'd imagine them appearing over the horizon just
after I went below to sleep. I *wanted* them now, I searched the horizon
for a link to the world, a means of relaying a message of my safety.
Perversely, I hadn't seen a ship since my engine failed.

Then came the rain, shutting off the horizon like a wall, and I didn't
want ships at all.

1 Aug

0146 Worried about the low and instead I have a slatting calm.
Sit in enveloping darkness on the bottom step of the companionway, flung back and forth by the motion, half in and half out of
foul-weather gear, crying, not knowing whether or not to go up
on deck and roll in the jib. Hour and a half of squally rain, bat-
tering the ocean into phosphorescent stars, and now nothing,
slop and roll, twang on the shrouds, I think I've got an ulcer, I

seem to have no sense of humor, no reference, no resilience.
Head spinning, boat rolling, stomach tied in knots, I have had it,
I have had it, I have had it.

Through the early hours of morning, graciously, almost imperceptibly,
the wind came back.

4

And a flushing wave sang backward from the bow
on either side, as the ship got way upon her,
holding her steady course.

HOMER, *The Odyssey*

1 Aug

1225 Oh *Sonnet Sonnet Sonnet* this is what we've been waiting
for: blue sky, blue sea, full sails, a gentle breeze.

1345 The incredible difference *environment* makes. This is the
same boat but it's *peaceful*, there's no violence from too much
wind, no nerve-racking noise from too little wind in waves, and I
have been moving constantly, doing things that have needed doing for weeks, even months, taking all my clothes off for a bucket
bath in the cockpit, then cleaning down below, all the floating
plastic bags out of the ice box, cleaning countertops, bagging
trash, attacking the mildew in the head which has been bugging
me since I bought the boat, putting things into the cockpit to
dry, back into the cockpit myself for a full ten minutes brushing
my teeth, none of this was doable without effort, or so much else
was more important, and now it's pure pleasure, the simple going-
about of life.

1700 Amazing, really, that I would be going the same speed—a
bit faster, actually—in this easy, quiet glide as I was—when? yesterday same time (a touch of fear as I write that; I have settled
into the marvelous conviction that the sailing I'm doing now

could last for days). Today the water is flat, the mainsail is full, the wind is on the beam; yesterday the wind was slightly forward of the beam and *Sonnet* was struggling double-reefed through waves. Twice as much wind yesterday as today, same speed.

I'm tired, but can't seem to nap. Hopefully (please) an okay night for sleeping. Stomach feels marginally better, I eat my bland foods, then open a bottle of green olives which taste spectacular.

My jaws ache; I wonder if I've been clenching my teeth in my sleep.

Maybe I should try napping here at the chart table.

I miss Steve. Easier since he's gotten to Bulgaria, is settling into his job, our apartment. Hardest was when he was traveling through Europe, because I wanted so intensely to be with him.

My shoulders ache, I'm not sure from what.

Still a long way to go.

Closer by the minute.

2022 Final project of the day was to brush out and rebraid my hair. It took forever, took me through to the first truly lovely sunset of my fourteen days, I stepped up into the companionway and not only the sunset but hanging above the horizon the perfect slender sliver of a moon.

The boat the ocean the sunset and this is why people do it. Sailing smoothly, sailing easily, three birds darting around in our wake.

2100 Remembering gathering for Hash runs, streets of Cocody, canopy of mango trees, lush lawns, coconut palms, day guards sitting on makeshift stools watching with detached amusement ("*Bon soir, patron*"). Cars parked, diplomatic license plates, Westerners in running clothes slamming doors and strolling toward the open gate of the designated driveway. Strange strange life.

Stomach's better, we'll see how it handles fresh grapefruit (it tasted wonderful).

Resisting going to sleep, writing by flashlight, not real bright (me, not the flashlight); need the sleep.

Familiar patterns of nighttime, with variations. Sleep, wake groggy to the alarm, look around, sleep, wake to the alarm, look around, sleep, wake doubled up in stomach pain.

Sleep, wake at three-fifteen, the alarm insistent as always, struggle out of the bunk as always, up the companionway as always, over the washboards, scan the familiar black-on-black horizon . . .

There. On my starboard quarter. A ship, going away from me. Quick down the companionway. Master switch on. VHF switch on. Instrument on to channel 16.

Vessel bearing 250. Vessel bearing 250. This is the sailing vessel Sonnet, Whisky Bravo Golf 6315, do you copy.

Sailing vessel, this is Aida, Sierra Charlie Foxtrot India. Channel 13.

Switching to 13. Blurting out my request and Beth's number without much *politesse,* afraid my weak batteries and the greater-by-the-moment distance between us would snatch away that staticky human voice.

Then settling down enough to communicate details. Explaining that I was sailing alone. That my electrical system was down, that I would not be able to contact America again before reaching the Azores. That I was entirely safe, healthy and well. That if he could pass this message and my position on to the number I would now repeat I would be eternally grateful.

Aida was a Swedish vessel, heading for the U.S. East Coast. Her radio operator spoke flawless English. He was professional and kind.

I told him *Sonnet* had an account with AT&T High Seas and he sounded vaguely offended. He repeated Beth's number. He repeated my requested message. He told me he would be standing by the VHF in case I needed anything more before our respective vessels were out of range.

2 Aug

0400   I'm not sure how often I talk out loud. Quite a lot, I think. Stood in the companionway after signing off with *Aida,* looking to the dark horizon where she wasn't even visible any more, shouting YES YES YES YES YES! *YES!!*

Contact made, Beth's number passed on, off comes the weight of worry. *Yes.*

Back into my bunk, with lightness. Familiar patterns of sleeping and waking, on through the night.

0855 There is a little *mrr Sonnet* gives of acceleration in this smooth sail, with each slight swell, when the heel is just right, and she pushes through the water. There's a restless feel she gets, jerky, when she isn't trimmed right.

Time to heal, held by the boat which sails so smoothly. Held by the globe, the blue symmetry of sky. Patterns of light through the interior, this vessel, starting to remember the whys, to know them.

Twenty hours now, sailing at six knots so smoothly you don't even need a handhold. No breaking waves no relentless rain no slithering forward leg-tangled in harness tethers to put in reefs no shaking them out no tacks no gybes no grinding in the Seafurl with the rig shuddering. Little adjustments of trim, that's all. Weak, so it's a lucky thing.

Now that I'd passed a message on to Beth, and especially since my world had become a livable place, I was secretly pleased to be sailing without an engine, putting silent, engineless miles behind me. I finally had time to read those back issues of *The New Yorker* stashed under the nav station seat. To read books. I finally had time to think, to let the ocean work into my soul.

1235 Weak, emotional, happy, worn. A bit wary, that this ease won't last, that I'll need to call up reserves I don't have.

Looking last night out at the black black sky and stars, thinking how everything is known, everything is charted and plotted. I know right where I am, or can, with about 30 seconds to pull out the GPS and request my position. It will never again be otherwise. Things have changed so much in sailing, even since I've been doing it, especially in the past few years.

Thinking of the explorers, that this ocean looked exactly the same. Crossing it on faith.

Thinking about sonnets, enjoying the long metered rhymed poem by James Merrill in the Feb 24 *New Yorker* ("A zipper's hiss, and the Atlantic Ocean closes over my blood-red T-shirt from the Gap").

Thinking of sleep, why I can't seem to do it very well. Or eat.

Had a pleasant fantasy that as soon as that radio contact was made my stomach would stop hurting but not the case, I still don't know what to put in it. Try some Top Ramen, simple and salty.

1330   *Two* big ships astern. Should I try to talk to them, or just assume *Aida* got the message through?

1600   A bit more of a reach, a bit slower. No complaints.

1715   Blue sky, cumulus scattered along the horizon. This looks like an ocean. Didn't look like an ocean before.

Amazing, that it doesn't more often strike me as strange, that I don't more often feel lonely, living this solitary life, sleeping and waking odd hours on a platform that's never still.

1900   Food today: Pretzels. Cookies. A whole big can of peaches. A whole package of Top Ramen. Third of a cucumber. Third of a beer. A mint or two or three. Stomach seems okay, with reservations.

Naps: Good thick naps at the chart table between about one o'clock and four.

New Yorker articles: The long one by Alastair Reid on the Dominican Republic. The sense that the disparities of the world are intractable; this isn't something I felt, that most people felt, twenty years ago. Roger Angell touched on this, too (feel like I picked out just about the best issue in the stack; a very different Roger Angell baseball article, "Personal History, Early Innings"; the tremendous, powerful story of Ireland by William Trevor): "These struggles continue to this day, God knows, but the difference back then was that men and women like my father always sounded as if such battles would be won in the end."

The birds that swoop in my wake, against reflected-sky light, as I stand in the companionway, the slid-aft hatch my desk, too dark below now.

Memory from Africa: The village where the Israeli vet and engineer lived, that huge circular house owned by their *métis* patrons, the porch, sitting there at night, men from the village

visiting, children from the village creeping up from the darkness
to sit on the periphery of light, listening.

The concept of privilege. How did it happen, that I ended up
with this boat? Nothing makes sense in the world. That people
are so selfish. That I am. It's what we are. Selfish with loyalties.

3 Aug

0545 I'll wait for this ship to get abeam and then crawl back in
bed. Big sucker, bristling with loading arms, big white ship with
colored containers. No ship for days and then this the fifth since
Aida, another in the night.

0920 The good part: A good night's sleep, caught up enough
now that there isn't the leaden oversleeping through the forty-
minute alarms. Able to get up, look around alertly, go straight
back to sleep.

The bad part: Hours of that sleep feeling like someone had
punched me in the stomach. How much blander can you get
than Top Ramen and canned peaches?

Sailing faster, a bit rougher, some white caps; I was perfectly
happy before. Closer to seven knots now than six.

1215 151 miles noon-to-noon, though I should have changed
the clock, crossed into another time zone. Changing it now.

Dreams: I was in a bizarre race, along a trail that ran beside
water. At first Steve was in the race with me, and then I was
alone. There was a deck of cards I scattered on the water, to get
rid of some weight, and then felt devastated to have done it, remembering this was a family deck of cards, we'd all played gin
rummy with these cards on Skyview Drive.

I was wearing a huge bright-red spinnaker-like suit, a cross between a nylon sleeping bag and a kite, and I was moving down
the trail in long soaring hops, almost like flying. By the end of
the dream I was more a kite than a person, my body the wooden
framework of the kite; there was a news report about me, how I'd
worn my feet down to wooden stubs with the hop-flying but had
done extremely well in the race.

Another dream, in a station wagon, traveling with Madonna,

and Tina from OCC. Oscar was in the car, I reminded them not to leave the doors open at gas stations, he was sleeping, I petted him, he rolled over luxuriously, loving it.

A dream a few days ago about Angelica Huston. A bit of a shock to discover she was intellectually shallower than I expected. Spectacular body, though; telling her that.

Want this to be over and don't. Want my career as a single-hander to be over and don't.

Last night I watched the sun set, like I used to try to do every day, watched the slow sink, from touching the horizon to disappeared. Moon a bit bigger, a bit higher than the night before. Spinning globe, shifting satellite.

Up a few times in the night, so gorgeous out, the enormous sky of stars, shooting stars, Scorpio early on lounging on the southern horizon, the Milky Way.

And then dawn, the sun coming up again, the pure, quiet wonder of it, spinning globe, fiery globe, spinning and circling.

That sort of thing used to be enough for me, used to be the most of it. Less now, but it was lovely, a kind of necessity.

Plenty more to go of this adventure. Plenty more.

Boy, though, do I feel like shit. It's not appendicitis—no nausea, no fever—but it isn't good. I have no idea what to put in my stomach. Latest tactic is Red Zinger tea with plenty of honey and lemon. Not many calories, but maybe there's some medicinal benefit.

1400 I just did something I haven't done in too long: sat in the cockpit and meditated. There are things which serve you, have and should. Meditated a strong body, a healthy stomach. Long slow healing breaths.

The sky is blue, the ocean is blue. I haven't gazed out at them as much as I would have nineteen years ago, half a lifetime, but that's okay. Feeling for the changes, feeling for what's right and what isn't. Feeling for some form of optimism, even if it isn't the same as before. Needing it. Feeling for my adult self.

A kind of affirmation while I meditated, which I may or may not ever use again (already I've forgotten the exact words). The world does not make sense. I won't try to make sense of it. It does have love. I'll try to give and receive it. It does have beauty and harmony. I'll try to see and hear them. This sounds empty and silly as I write it, but it made sense.

1810 Well, we'll see if appetite has anything to do with reality. In a sudden craving for the harsher foods my stomach's been warning me off, and rebellion against opening a can of chicken soup, longing for Real Food, I started chopping cucumber, tomato, jack cheese (hope it's okay). Olive oil, vinegar, oregano, a sprinkling of Parmesan. Sat in the evening warmth of the cockpit, eating my dinner. Hope I don't regret it.

The wind is back down to a pleasant 8–10 knots, *Sonnet* right on course. I have started reading *The Strong Brown God*, about the Niger. So far the jacket copy and preface are more inspiring than the book, but we'll see. I like the book, even if just for the length of it, and because Deborah gave it to me. Gave me *Brazzaville Beach*. Gave me Roethke.

The neat, penciled crosses which marked each noon fix had marched their slow way across the chart; I could no longer look at them without my eyes sliding farther, to Faial.

The islands of the Azores—a volcanic archipelago spanning three hundred miles—rise from the sea in a surprise vision of greenery and dark stone. Faial is part of the central cluster of islands, separated from its eastern neighbor, Pico, by a narrow channel. Pico soars to 7,600 feet only a stone's throw from the water.

I'd fallen utterly in love with these islands thirteen years back, hooked from the morning of landfall aboard *August Moon* when the top of Pico emerged from a blanket of cloud. My first afternoon on Faial I'd walked a hilly neighborhood south of Horta harbor, looking at vegetable gardens through fences choked with bright lantana, eating from the half-kilo bag of small sweet strawberries I'd bought in town. We'd planned to stay a few days; we stayed eighteen. By the time *August Moon* sailed out of Horta I was fantasizing about coming back, buying land, and settling in.

By dawn on August 4, *Sonnet* and I were 90 miles west-southwest of Flores—the westernmost island of the Azores—and 230 miles from Faial.

0850   Thick overcast of clouds in the west, still the westerly
swell. I really don't want any funny stuff, I just want to get there.

Slept close to ten hours. What does that amount to, if you're
getting up every thirty-five minutes, how much do you lose each
time?

Three ships last night.

Stomach feels fine. Good good good. Things to eat in Horta,
wonder how different the place will be, how hard it'll be to see
the changes. Remembering Graciosas, long tables, a handful of
yachties mixed in with Azorian regulars, the elderly waiter shuf-
fling along between tables with platters of food—no menu, you
ate what he brought you—and ceramic pitchers of red Pico wine.

0915   Definite degree of grouchiness in me. Feel I should be
there, not just almost there. Mixed with a wariness, be nice now
Lydia or the weather will change. Mixed too with a very legitimate uneasiness about a singlehanded landfall without an engine.

Strive for serenity these next couple of days.

1030   Feel myself starting to get wound up, emotional, in a way
I didn't quite expect, certainly didn't feel on *Colibri*. This landfall, my own solid boat, singlehanded which who knows if I'll
ever do again. Twenty years exactly since I first got hooked on
boats. Thirteen since I sailed into the Azores, extraordinary islands rising up out of the sea, someone else's boat, so much I've
learned, so much I know, islands, ocean, earth sea sky, I am trying with regularity to stop and breathe, three deep breaths, for
the oxygen into my body, twenty seconds in, twenty seconds out,
then five more for serenity and health, quiet the brow, quiet the
heart, quiet the gut.

Seventeen days alone so far, nothing compared to some, a
lot compared to most. No contact face-to-face for all that time,
talked to Steve, talked to Beth's machine, talked to Beth, talked
to two Scandinavian radio officers. Talk to myself, to the boat.

1445   A peaceful, unplanned, untimed nap at the chart table
and I feel more settled, freed a bit of the cabin fever that was

starting to come on. Do a bit of housekeeping, boat sails along
sedately.

1650   Seems like it takes forever today for an hour to go by.
Tough, to be on the same quadrant of the chart (finally) as the
Azores, and still have two days to sail. More like a day and a half
now.

1810   A flurry of weepiness—I haven't experienced what I
could have, of this—and then it subsides. This, to a huge degree,
was the Big One. Want to believe—do believe—that I'm moving into a slightly different era, more accepting of myself, not attempting to be something I'm not.

   Sinking in how important this is, to have set this goal and
achieved it. Something I needed at this stage of my life. Something I'll be taking to Bulgaria, taking into Steve's next novel,
taking on forward.

5 Aug

0450   I come up on deck, grouchy loggy achy from bad sleep,
and it is extraordinarily beautiful out. The hush; the boat moves
just fast enough that nothing is banging (banged a lot last night),
just the quiet whoosh of her movement through the water (two
sounds, really, a slightly higher whoosh from the stern than the
bow, tiny breaks in the crests of the stern wake), fabric sounds
from the sail filling, reef lines slapping. The wind like a touch on
my skin, cool through my shirt, cool on the bare skin of my
thighs, light filling in now, less luminous; squat solemn cumulus
ringing the horizon.

   This light brings out something in the stainless steel, breaks it
into dark and light facets, brings out the orange in the wood.
Makes me wish I could paint, the color even of this white page
with a pen moving across it. The sail with sunrise light from behind.

0815   Is the wind gonna die? Do I put up a bigger headsail?
Would it be worth the effort? Get me there tomorrow in daylight?

And then the dream comes back at me: on the boat, but with a crew, they're getting the pole ready, big spinnaker bag on deck, Brad's here but he's not really important. I come on deck, point out that the sail they're readying is a gennaker, not a spinnaker, they don't need the pole, and then my small pillow with the African cover goes overboard, some GQ-looking guy makes an obviously halfhearted grab at it then sort of snaps his fingers shucks and it's floating behind us, and I'm screaming TURNTHEBOAT- AROUND, and finally they do, we go back for the pillow, drag it soaking on deck, I'm furious, GQ is pretty noncommittal, says look if the truth be told it smells pretty awful, I say a lot of things got wet and smell awful and then I'm sobbing, somehow away from them all, on a street somewhere, sobbing in the awareness that I haven't even had the chance to talk to anyone, to tell anyone how hard it was, at times how terrifying.

1020   Would I get more speed, or would it just be a bigger sail to slam around on the rigging?

Dug it out of the cockpit locker, dragged it to the foredeck, haven't put it up.

I seem to be able to gybe through about 70° and keep up about four knots. This is not going to cut it. Put up the gennaker? The gennaker would be a pain in the butt to gybe.

This wouldn't cut it even if the wind shifted enough for me to steer a straight course.

Fuck this. I could be out here another two days, was worried not that long ago about getting there tonight, in darkness.

1130   Switched to the big genoa. Gennaker would have been even better speedwise, but maybe a bit ambitious. Genoa is better not worse than the little sail, slapwise. Big soft sail slapping around, rather than a little irritable one.

1330   Poor *Sonnet* looks like shit. All the varnished surfaces are peeling, parts that were fine three weeks ago, looked first-rate three months ago.

I HATE THIS. Even another knot or two of wind and we'd be sailing slowly, rather than barely sailing. Sailing slowly at least you can concentrate, read write whatever, not driven crazy by the lurch and slam and bang THIS ISN'T FAIR.

Is anything fair? Nothing's fair. But I'd just gotten back the health of my digestive system.

Crash. Slam. Lurch, roll. Steering 50° now; it'd make sense to gybe.

1430 Try to be optimistic, the wind could come up, I could make it by tomorrow evening (crash! slam!). Heat myself some water in the sun for Red Zinger, quit eating junk food (nice little lunch of BBQ Pringles and dinner mints).

Is this totally unfair to my boat, to let her bang around like this?

1845 There's another sailboat out there, tiny on the horizon, no headsail up, under power probably, which if she's going to Faial should bring her closer to me as the evening wears on. Tried VHF to no avail, makes me feel wistful to see her, a kindred soul.

An hour or so ago, on deck, I was hit by an immense sadness. My parents; wishing I could have had a boat at a time my father could have worked on it with me, a project he would have loved. I've cried before on this trip but this was different, from a deeper slower broader place, not tears of frustration just sadness, finally just curled up on the cockpit seat to cry, deep aching, of lives that go by.

I've hardly thought at all about going to my parents'. Better maybe to go through some of this now. It's been six years, and things have changed immeasurably. Thinking of what Dad always wanted to do with me, a tour of Spain by horseback. We'll never do it.

Sailboat bears 320°.

Poor *Sonnet*. Steering has gone extremely stiff, I've gotten down inside to try to figure out where the problem is but it's tough without someone on deck to turn the wheel. The Windex is loose, jerks drunkenly from side to side as the boat rolls.

Could all be depressing—there's always *something*—but it's not. I know there's always something, the boat will never be perfect, on the other hand she's proved herself, I can fix the things that have to be fixed, I can sail with the other things, prioritize and work on the rest as I can.

Thank you, Steve, for this boat. Thank you for being who you are. I'm sorry if you're worrying right now, I hope the message got through ungarbled and you're not, though it's taking so long to get the rest of the way that you may be worried again.

Two ships out there, in addition to the sailboat. A big one and a small one. Sailboat is getting bigger but is dropping behind me, bearing 310°.

Maybe I should sleep on deck tonight. Pleasantly—with a sleeping bag and a real pillow—so I can simply stumble upright to look for ships. Worrisome, the trouble I've had getting myself out of the bunk when the alarm goes off.

Not sure the Monitor's going to be able to turn this wheel, stiff as the wheel is, light as the wind is. I've been hand steering for a while.

Tried calling again but the sailboat isn't listening.

I limited my VHF attempts to every fifteen minutes, trying to conserve what little battery power I had left. *Sailing vessel bearing 310, sailing vessel bearing 310, this is the sailing vessel Sonnet, Whiskey Bravo Golf 3615, near 38-15-north, 25-42-west, do you copy.*

An hour went by; the boat kept getting closer.

Sailing vessel bearing 310 . . .

They copied. Barely. The English that responded to mine was very rusty, and the connection was awful. I said I'd try again when they were closer and signed off, hoping they'd understood. When I went back on deck the boat appeared to have altered course straight for me.

It's an odd thing, seeing another sailboat on the ocean. Slightly eerie, very silent. Very slow. For hours the triangle on the horizon gets larger agonizingly slowly. Then suddenly it all accelerates, you can see details, you can see the line of horizon past the hull.

I remember reading an account of 12-meter class racing. The reporter was in a photo boat as the race boats swooped down on the windward mark. He wrote about the intensity of concentration, the impressive teamwork; these are the best racing crews in the world. The Australians whooshed by, lines hissing, the spinnaker crackling open. The Japanese whooshed by. And then the Italians: waving arms, everyone yelling at everyone. They made it with great efficiency around the mark, but the

noise.

My sailors were Italian. The triangle I'd been watching for hours was approaching now, still silent in the deepening twilight. And then, in the space of seconds, I could hear them: first the dim rhythm of the motor, next the voices, increasingly loud and clear. Gabbing in Italian, laughing. I could see individual forms, discern every roll of the hull. This eerie shape had been transformed into a manifestation of good cheer.

It was a little boat, smaller than I'd realized, with a big identification number on the bow. They'd altered course to come visiting, and now they were here. It was nearly dark as we rolled along, chatting, the two boats side by side, the Italians' motor chattering, *Sonnet's* sails slapping, too dark to discern their faces, even to know how many there were, how many men how many women, or maybe it was just my disorientation, after nineteen days alone. Still, it was wonderfully warm, wonderfully human, the contact.

The boat had raced the Singlehanded TransAtlantic Race; the solo skipper had flown home and his friends were making the delivery back to Italy. They were going to Faial, like I was. I explained that I had no engine. There was a big Festival of the Sea going on there, did I know that? Beginning yesterday, going on all this week. And of course they would take a note to my friend.

I scribbled two quick notes to Monica, one which they'd give to the harbormaster, the other which they'd leave at Café Peter Sport. We held the boats apart at the shrouds and passed across the notes.

They asked if I needed anything else. I said only wind. I said, "Thanks for dropping by" as the two boats pulled apart, but it seemed to lose something in the translation.

The engine noise and boisterous voices faded out as they'd faded in. For hours I could see their masthead strobe to starboard, a tiny intense heartbeat of light in the darkness.

I set up camp in the cockpit that night, sleeping less than an hour before it became the right thing to do to gybe. The gybe—by the time I got everything reled and retrimmed—took more than an hour. As I tidied up lines, something caught my eye to port: the loom

of the light of Flores. Not the light itself, but enough to confirm the
reality of land.

The wind picked up just slightly, and *Sonnet* sailed on slowly, no
lurch, no slam.

6 Aug

0550 Didn't sleep much at all, hope I can sleep today, that I
won't be too wound up.

Need to sleep, and to organize the boat; need to be rested for
landfall.

I wrote very little the rest of the day, channeling my need for pen-
between-fingers toward making myself a Portuguese courtesy flag, indelible felt pen on one of Steve's white handkerchiefs. The only flag I'd
located in Maryland had cost $39, and I'd rebelled; I now painstakingly
reproduced the elaborate shield from a photocopy.

1610 Fingers of cirrus emanate from the north, streaking overhead. I try to sleep and can't; maybe simply resting is good for
me. Figure I'll sail straight toward the island, gybe, then sail parallel to shore. I almost expect to see it now but I can't.

Came close to pulling the big sail down a while back, when I
was starting to get some whitecaps and we were charging right
along. Didn't want to start an artificial slowdown too far ahead,
decided we were still well within control, I'd rather get close and
reduce way down than end up not using wind and then losing it.

A lot to fight, this next half day. Weepiness, fatigue, over-
eagerness to get to land. I'm no longer thinking about entering at
night; no moon, a foolish move, will wait until dawn.

It was my final journal entry of the passage.

I had dolphin visitors that day; the first group had come around two
o'clock, staying only a few minutes, but somehow welcoming me back
to a life among other living creatures. The second group came around
five, and played joyfully around *Sonnet*'s bow. I leaned over the pulpit—
calling out to them as they streaked around the shiny cutting hull—
filled with pleasure, filled with awe. I was just thinking, *This is almost a*

cliché but it's wonderful anyway, when I saw something I'd never seen in twenty years of sailing: a baby dolphin.

She couldn't have been more than a foot and a half or two feet long—I decided without basis that the baby was a she—and moved in perfect synchronization with her mom. The group stayed and stayed, shifting and changing; I watched all those weaving, streaking, surfacing shapes—all more or less the same size—and then just when I was afraid I wouldn't see them again I'd spot the one with the miniature reflection.

I found myself wondering how something so small could swim so fast, so effortlessly, though I knew intellectually that *Sonnet's* four or five knots was no challenge at all.

I found myself wondering if *Sonnet* was the first sailboat for this little dolphin to play around the bow.

They stayed—my initiated dolphin and her family and friends—and then they were gone. At 1840 I made an entry in the ship's log, no bolder than the others: "Land ho," faint mountains among clouds.

Toward sunset I changed the headsail, wanting the control of the smaller sail for landfall. It was harder than I'd expected to haul down the big sail alone; I was glad not to be doing it in a building breeze, and enjoyed the physical work of it.

I wrestled the sail down inside the lifelines, dragged the whole thing aft by the clew for easier folding, folded it (in a fashion: flake the luff, secure it with a sail tie, flake up the full length of the leech, middle's a bit iffy but it fit in the bag), bagged it, then dragged the bag aft to the cockpit, feeling somehow like a lioness hauling a wildebeest back to her young, or maybe a young lioness hauling her first wildebeest.

Dragged the smaller sail to the new leeward side, reled the sheets, shackled on the halyard, winched the sail up. Through the whole maneuver I felt—in a positive sense, not a negative one—like I was playing Boat, playing House, or—what—having my picture taken in front of a backdrop of Singlehander. Then no: No game, no backdrop, just the marvel of having crossed this stretch of ocean alone.

It was dark by the time the new sail was trimmed, quarter moon and stars. With *Sonnet* up to speed I sat on the cabin roof, looking up at the pattern of mast and sails on sky, immersed in the contrasts of the universe, tactile boat, swirling sea, familiar constellations in a fathomless sky. As I sat gazing upward—almost as if my eyes knew where to watch for it—a meteorite streaked through Cygnus. I took a breath and held it there, holding the faint silver trail, feeling the most pure, the most extraordinary sense of achievement.

That something can be Absolutely Right, having felt Absolutely Wrong at points along the way. That you've got to honor your core impulse, be tough enough to keep pushing, maybe even accept that it all might end up only Kinda Right, for all the pain. Like *Colibri*. Though *Colibri*, just now, felt more right than ever before.

I was back in the cockpit less than an hour later, looking aft at small waves on moonlit water, and I half heard half saw a splash but didn't think much about it. A few minutes later another splash and I thought wait, those aren't waves, the waves aren't big enough to be breaking.

I clipped my harness tether to the jackline and started moving forward just as they all zeroed in. I lay flat on my belly way up at the bow, head and shoulders under the pulpit and over the cap rail, arm dangling down, close to the dolphins. Sometimes, at night, the shapes of dolphins are like luminescent torpedoes, but tonight there was very little luminescence, and I made out their forms by moonlight and moonlit bubbles. At one point a dolphin leapt straight up next to me, splashed straight down, making me jerk back and bump my head, gasping and laughing, drenching me but I didn't care, I no longer needed to ration my salt-free clothing.

I have no idea how long I stayed there, soaking wet, soaking them in, their energy. Soaking in the reality of their world, a world existing past man, past land, in the dark, in the water, joyful and purposeful and beautiful. Always out there, through riots in L.A., traffic on the Long Island Expressway, African coups, Roman conquests. Out here now as *Sonnet* closed the gap to land.

At 2330, according to the GPS, I was eight miles off the western end of the island. The 15-mile Ponta Comprida light didn't seem to be working, which made me nervous, so I gybed.

I saw, off and on, a strobe which *wasn't* on the chart. It took a couple of hours before I figured out it was the Italians, slipping into Horta ahead of me.

I sailed along southeast—more or less parallel to the coastline—and by 0230 I was abeam of the gap between Faial and Pico. I gybed again. At 4 a.m., three miles off Ponta da Cabra south of Horta, the wind came up. Hard. With a sense of amused disbelief I found myself on deck, reefing yet again to the third reef. Not so amused when I lost the winch handle overboard; two thousand miles and I lose it within swimming distance of Horta.

By the time I'd finished reefing we were a mile and a half from land. No light yet in the sky; I could sail into the channel between the islands and bide my time there in the dark, but it seemed wiser in this blow to head back offshore.

I tacked out to sea, sailed for fifteen minutes, and tacked back. The wind began to die. It quickly became apparent that giving myself sea room in a blow hadn't been such a brilliant idea; three miles to go—again—and Horta was looking farther away than ever.

Sonnet sailed along slowly. More slowly. Black outlines of islands against a lightening sky—the distinctive peak of Pico to the east, the more rolling silhouette of Faial to the west—with light on the channel between them.

Sailing slowly toward the entrance of the channel as the wind died; I left the triple reef in the main, silly as it seemed, knowing I would want all the control I could get when I made my engineless entry.

More light, the islands emerging green. White buildings of Horta, the land rising behind it to the west, lush green pastures bordered with dark green hedges, dark green acres of trees. Two dark rocky hills to the south of town, volcanic.

Slow slow sailing, into the channel, seeing the seawall, less than a mile from the entrance. Then no wind.

None.

Drifting.

Horta to the west, Pico to the east with streaks of clouds across its upper slopes. The wind did not pick up. I kept looking toward the harbor, hoping maybe Monica had seen me out here, that she'd met some cruising couple with a nice little dinghy with a powerful outboard and they'd come rescue me, but it didn't happen.

I tidied the boat, though I would have preferred to get some sleep. Removed the myriad secondary dinghy lashings, loosened the primary lashings, moved the dinghy enough to free the larger of the Danforth anchors stowed underneath it, lugged the anchor to the bow. The thing seemed impossibly heavy; I hoped I'd be able to get it over the pulpit when the time came. I settled it at the bow, secured it with a quick-release sail tie, attached the anchor line. Forcing my muscles to keep moving.

When *Sonnet* started drifting with the trashy current back toward the Atlantic, as well as in toward the rocky coast south of Horta, I finally gave up and shook the reefs out of the main, giving myself a whisper of boat speed.

Around 0830 by my watch the racing dinghies started coming out of the harbor, slowly, on the nearly nonexistent wind. I was amazed at how many there were. When I'd been here thirteen years ago, sailing had pretty much been something done by foreigners; if Azorians had owned boats they'd been fishing boats, or whaling boats.

A bit of breeze filled the sails of the dinghies, then stretched its lazy fingers out to *Sonnet*. Finally we were moving. In fact, after ten minutes or so, we were moving quite nicely. In fact, this seemed to be a building wind.

It filled from the north. I hauled in the sails and pointed *Sonnet*'s bow to the end of Horta's outer seawall. The wall ran north and south, opening at the north; without the current, I might just have cleared the wall close-hauled, but with the current setting south it looked as if I'd have to do some tacking. Never had it seemed so clear that tacking a 42-foot boat alone was a *lot* of work. I sailed for a while, hoping the wind would shift or the tide would change, but neither did.

I was tired. But I tacked. Self-steering disconnected, wheel over, jib sheet thrown off the winch on one side to free the sail, sheet on the new side hauled in. Sailed away from my destination again. Maybe I should just visit Pico. Fifteen minutes, to be sure. Tacked back. Barely staying out of the way of the racing dinghies.

The wind kept building. I figured I'd sail around the end of the seawall, take a look inside, get a sense of the anchorage area, and tack back out to think things over if I needed to.

I managed to clear the seawall but not by much. Still steering straight, I looked left down into Horta harbor. *Cripes* but the place was small. I'd have the wind dead behind me once I headed for the anchorage; no way was I going to do this on a full main.

Another tack. Flogging sail, snaking sheets, grinding it in. Sailing back away from the harbor to put in the reef. Directly toward the dinghy fleet, and not even on starboard tack, but there was no way at this point I'd detour around them and then have to claw my way back to weather. I figured this was a clear case of Big Boat Has Right of Way.

Release the mainsheet to spill wind from the sail. Up to the mast to drag down the whipping Dacron. A dinghy approached me, falling off around me; I saw a hint of what might be disgruntlement on the faces of the crew until they saw I was alone. They smiled and waved.

Back to the cockpit, grind back in the mainsheet to bring in the boom. More dinghies tacking back and forth, the Monitor steering *Sonnet* merrily through their midst. I bundled loose sail and tied red sail ties at reef points.

Sonnet was now sufficiently upwind of the harbor entrance to beam-reach back. I rolled in the jib, took over the helm from the Monitor, tacked, and headed once more through the racing fleet, waving politely at the committee boat. The wind whipped up whitecaps; dinghies flying spinnakers scooted across the water like crazed butterflies.

I cleared the breakwater for a third and final time, peeled off to port, eased out the mainsheet. Committed now. Moving fast downwind on a triple-reefed main. Thinking fast, assessing things, seeing the new inner seawall to my right and past it the masts of boats in the marina, seeing the few moored boats ahead of me. That's where it would have to be. There, in front of that barge, outside the last of the moorings. I'd stay to port a bit like this, reach over to the right when I got abeam of the moorings, then shoot up into the wind.

I was on the reach, heading toward the moorings, mainsail luffing, when I noticed, on the wall in front of the harbor office, upwind of two boats, a space for a third. *Shit.* Should I have prepped for that, instead of the anchor? Gotten out dock lines and fenders? Could I still go for it? Reach back and forth in this narrow space while I dragged some fenders out?

And then it was as if my decision were made without the benefit of words, of intellect; was this how animals made decisions? Just the sense of the weight and balance of the boat, the rush of wind on our beam, the existence of that spot *right there* where we could come to rest at anchor. Sense those things and act, no thinking.

I swung her straight into the wind, centered the rudder, pulled ten more feet of mainsheet free, sprinted forward, freed the anchor, heaved it over the pulpit (the thing seemed impossibly light), judged how much anchor line I needed purely on adrenaline (this seems *just* right), cleated it, sprinted back aft to the main halyard, noticing, for the first time, the fleet of swimmers heading straight for the boat, evidently in a race from the outer seawall to the town. All but two wraps off, handle the halyard with the right hand, haul the sail down with the left, how often had I done this reefing in a blow?

The boat had not stayed obediently head-to-wind, was almost beam into it by the time I got the mainsail down, drifting quickly—swimmers detouring around her—back toward that ugly moored barge. *Shit.* Was the anchor dragging? *What now?* I looked around frantically, mind spinning, utterly incapable of any more thought, any more decisions.

At which point, with a tug, the rode went taut, the anchor dug in, and *Sonnet* straightened bow into the wind.

II

Interdependence

5

Every twenty minutes: wait to get
the operator, wait to place the call.
No go. Three minutes can't compete with all
those hours, can't kiss his collarbone or let
us read in bed, knees touching. Still, I'm set
to hear his voice, not buzzes. Cruise the hall,
install myself back at the table, fall
to watching an unnerving tête-a-tête.
The local (straight-backed, smooth) supports the bar
while I long for connection, nips a cool
blonde's ear. Alas, I'm not a blonde. Alas,
I play with pencils, link the near and far
frustrations, draw this sonneteer: a fool
for both an alter ego and an ass.

"Two Men: Love from Bermuda," 1979

I pulled in the mainsheet hand-over-hand, bringing the swinging boom under control, shaky and weak, feeling so pumped with emotions that I could hardly take it, exhaustion and amazement and sadness and overwhelming pride. *We did it,* Sonnet. *We did it.*

Swimmers still churned the water all around the boat, heading for town. I was making a hell of an entrance into Horta's Sea Week. An organizer in an outboard passed close and I called out a babbling apology in I'm-not-even-sure-what-language. He waved, no problem.

The wind howled; above it I could hear the pulse of music. Crowds of people strolled the waterfront. Brightly colored flags whipped in the rigging of sailboats in the inner marina. The marina hadn't existed when

I'd been here thirteen years ago. The harbormaster's offices and fuel dock hadn't existed, or the big new blocky yacht club. The old yacht club still existed, hovering there in my memory, shaded tables in a tiny quiet courtyard. I felt disoriented, like some female Rip Van Winkle.

I went to the boom, flaking and tying the sail. Looked toward the dock. A woman's figure, waving. Monica. I waved back.

She clasped her hands in front of her in congratulations. I collapsed my arms down onto the boom, miming my exhaustion. She was trying to yell something to me over the rush of wind.

I yelled back, "I can't hear you,"

She pointed to the harbor offices. A lull in the wind. "They're closed till one."

I yelled, "What time is it now?" pointing at my watch.

She looked at hers. "Twelve!"

Mine said ten. Portuguese time, plus daylight savings.

She was yelling something more complicated now, and I couldn't hear it. Pointing away from herself.

"I'll see you then." Some such. Another clasp of congratulations, a final wave, and she walked away.

The swimmers had all reached the shore.

I went below. The boat still moved, but not forward. I went into the head and looked at my face in the mirror, an unfamiliar face, thin and worn. I stepped back into the level cabin, the boat jerking slightly at anchor, light pouring in the starboard side windows, this world where I'd lived alone for twenty days.

I was exhausted, but there was no way I'd be able to fall asleep. I straightened up below, got my papers in order, went on deck every few minutes for a look around, hoping again that Monica might have met some friendly cruisers, might be lining up a dinghy to come take me ashore.

I straightened up on deck.

At one-thirty I freed the remaining lashings on *Sonnet*'s dinghy, dug out fenders, bailer, oarlocks, oars, and somehow managed to heave the sixty-pound *Couplet* over the lifelines, not a job I'd envisioned attempting alone.

Made a mild spectacle of myself, rowing ashore against twenty knots of breeze in a seven-foot dinghy I'd never before rowed, oars popping out of the oarlocks in the chop. Made it to the wall, tied up, and ventured onto solid land that seemed to buzz and buckle under my feet. Walked across to the harbor office in a kind of disbelieving haze, clutching my yacht documents. Did I really own a yacht I'd sailed to the Azores?

Entrance formalities. Customs, immigration. Filling out forms, talking face-to-face with real live human beings. They told me *Sonnet* was the two thousand and first boat to arrive this year in Horta. There couldn't have been more than a couple of hundred boats total in 1979. They told me I was the second woman to arrive this year singlehanded, and I felt both deflated and pissed, not the most admirable reaction, not the most gracious to my fellow singlehander, but instantaneous. They told me the harbor office would provide a tow to my space on the marina wall.

I went back outside, looked at the classic black sloop anchored in the channel, and felt confused. I wasn't used to seeing her like this, from a distance. Maybe some part of me hadn't forgiven her for not being a Swan 40. I climbed back in *Couplet* and rowed out to the classic black sloop. I'd barely gotten aboard when two men powered up in a launch. One helped me set up the towline and haul up the anchor. The other drove the tow—not too fast, not too slow—and deposited us neatly against the wall.

A couple of teenagers from a big American ketch—six or seven people on board and at least two dogs—took *Sonnet*'s dock lines, then sat on the wall to chat, asked me about my passage, told me there was another singlehander in at the moment, Reiner on *Snow Goose*, he was away on the race to Pico but should be back tomorrow. Their boat was leaving later in the day and I felt a flush of panic, my first contact with fellow cruisers and they'd be gone.

I futzed with my fenders and dock lines, adding spring lines, hopping up and down off the seawall to get it right. I kept expecting Monica to appear, but she didn't.

I sat for a while in my cockpit and looked across the marina to the town, the square two-story colonial-feeling buildings—white or pale gray or pale pink—with tall windows and tile roofs, the spreading shade trees juxtaposed with pine trees and palms. Sloping behind the town were hydrangea-bordered pastures—quintessentially Azorian—though it didn't look like the flowers were blooming.

I finally headed down to the marina bar-and-laundry complex. The marina was only eight years old, and already the vertical surfaces of its seawall were virtually covered with paintings. Hundreds of them, ranging from the simple to the sublime, hundreds more on the less desirable horizontal surfaces underfoot. Boat names, crew lists, dates, routes, illustrated in endless variations. A patchwork of color and pattern against concrete gray; a huge, cheerful piece of cooperative folk art.

In '79—back in Horta's pre-marina days, when you anchored out and rowed ashore, or rafted off fishing boats—I'd painted *August Moon*'s name on the outer seawall where this tradition originated. You could walk that wall for a history lesson in sailing, *Pen Duick* and *Robertson's Golly* and *Gypsy Moth*. A few years back I'd heard from a friend that a lot of the paintings had been covered over, but *August Moon*'s had survived.

I changed money at the bar, and found the phone in the shower-and-laundry building.

It took four tries to get through to Beth. She was thrilled to hear from me. *Aida*'s radio officer had called her as promised after talking to me on the VHF. She said, "I told him, 'You don't know how many people you've made very, very happy with this news.'" I tensed at the effusion; this isn't how you're supposed to talk about self-sufficient sailors. She told me she and Steve had notified the Coast Guard and I was mortified, I'd only been a couple of days past our contact schedule.

She asked if I'd ever felt in any real danger, and my first instinct was to brush it off, tell her no, at which point I recognized that she not only cared a great deal for me, she had an uncanny sensitivity, could very well have sensed something from me while I was out there, so I told her yes, told her briefly about the gales, realizing how grateful I was for her deep, honest interest in Steve's life and mine, and our adventures.

She gave me Steve's number—our number—in Sofia. We signed off and I tried calling, even though it was only five in Bulgaria. After six or eight attempts I finally heard a ring but he wasn't home.

I tried my parents in Spain, dialing with some nervousness, and got through easily. Dad, as usual these past few years, mostly listened. Mom was happy to hear from me, though she showed no particular sign of appreciating what I'd just accomplished. Also no sign of the fit she'd had when I'd first told her my plans. She said, "I was starting to wonder. You said three weeks, and that's tomorrow."

I told them—for Dad's sake—how soon I'd be seeing them, as I'd told them every time I'd talked to them for months. Dad seemed pleased, but I couldn't tell if he remembered I was coming.

There was a message board near the phone, which I checked, thinking Monica might have left a note, but she hadn't. I wondered if maybe she'd told me the name of the hotel where she had reservations here in Horta before I left the States. If so, I'd forgotten. I wandered back to the boat. Still no Monica. I wondered if she was trying to give me space to adjust to being ashore. I didn't need space, I needed someone to talk to.

I left her a note on the shrouds, telling her to come aboard and meet *Sonnet*, or to come to the showers and find me if she wanted, then went back to the harbor complex to wash my hair. By the time I was done, it was seven o'clock in Sofia. I tried getting through to Steve, dialed for fifteen minutes straight, getting several different variations of dial tones at varying points in the number, and finally he picked up the phone.

We talked for twenty minutes, depleting my supply of escudos. He told me about his plunge into the tumultuous world of Bulgarian politics. He told me about the drive through Europe with Butch, Butch riding comfortably in his open cat case on the passenger seat, taking the whole thing like a champ, checking out the corners of each night's hotel room. He told me about our apartment in Sofia, god-awful Stalinesque from the outside but inside airy and bright, with a view, if not of the whole of Mount Vitosha, at least of the slopes and peak around the edges of the god-awful block next door. He was swamped already at the embassy, and trying to write at night; our shipment had arrived but he hadn't attempted to unpack.

I told him about the storms, the engine problems, the days of glorious sailing and then calms. I told him about the final night alone, seeing the meteorite, feeling that extraordinary sense of achievement, and he said, "I'm glad." Those two words, the affirmation in his voice, brought home what I'd done. He was sitting in an apartment surrounded by boxes, he'd driven four days alone skirting ex-Yugoslavia in the company of a cat, he was dealing alone with all the details of settling into a new job, a new home, a new culture, and I believed from the depth of my soul that he supported what I'd done. Not that my project hadn't been tough on both of us, on the two of us. Not that he didn't know full well

that my sense of achievement would falter a time or two before this
adventure was over. But he lauded that one pure moment when everything was right.

I headed back to the boat. Fatigue was starting to hit hard. The sensory input, the *colors*, the *people*, the wind whipping through the fluttering flags of the marina. I felt that I needed sunglasses twice as dark.

A pink backpack rested brightly in *Sonnet's* cockpit. My note was
gone. I swung from the seawall down to the deck at the shrouds, moved
the familiar path to the cockpit.

Monica was below, sitting on the port berth, looking extremely
happy. Her hair was shorter than when I'd last seen her, which looked
good. I slipped down the companionway to join her.

We hugged. She told me she'd just gotten to the boat, and really liked
it. She'd been on a tour of the island, she was sorry she'd gone off like
that, but she'd already made the arrangements and figured I wouldn't
mind if she went ahead with her plans. Some part of me was surprised
they gave tours of the island—they certainly hadn't in 1979—but I
didn't think that much about it.

The next few hours blur. I know I told Monica war stories, more
stories than I'd habitually blurt out. I know I talked at times in a very
disjointed manner, stopping midsentence for no reason at all. We went
to dinner at a restaurant she'd gone to with some friends from her hotel.
I felt unbelievably tipsy—that marvelous fresh fish, those marvelous
fresh vegetables—after the first of two spectacular, ice-cold San Miguels.

She had war stories of her own. Her luggage had been lost; her first
week had been miserable, trying to track it down, here in a strange town
where she didn't speak the language, knowing no one, trying to locate
replacement gear in case the luggage wasn't found, sitting in a quiet
Azorian church and crying at one point when she just couldn't take it.
Calls every day to Brian, who jollied her from afar, telling her to see
this as an adventure. Calls every day to the airlines, trips to the airport.

In time, people had come through for her. The desk clerk at her little
hotel was wonderful, she and Monica taught each other words in their
respective languages, the woman would pass over the phone when Brian
called then quietly retreat when Monica's eyes began to fill. Two couples
in the hotel—Azorians by birth, Americans now by nationality, back
home in the Azores for Sea Week—had taken her out to meals, to the
homes of relatives. A man she worked with in California had a brother

here, who had helped her immensely. The luggage showed up just two days ago—it had traveled to Rome—and she'd finally been able to relax and enjoy Faial.

She had a spare bed in her hotel room and suggested I sleep there, which felt simultaneously like a massive disloyalty to *Sonnet* and like a good idea. I'd always slept better on boats than anywhere in the world, but for some reason I never woke from a full night's sleep on my own boat without a backache, and tonight I needed a full night's sleep. Maybe, too, I needed a little distance.

We swung back to the boat for my gear. I whispered an apology to *Sonnet*.

We made our way through the crowded square, past the stage set up for nightly live music; headed up the street to her hotel, mosaics on the sidewalks; passed through the little sitting room where guests were watching TV, Monica introducing me proudly, the friend she was waiting for had finally arrived.

I was shocked, up in her modest room, by the volume of her luggage. Two huge bags and several smaller ones. I mentally started rearranging the boat to give her space.

She showed me things Brian had bought her for the trip, a calculator with large numbers since she had trouble seeing at night, a battery-operated fan in case it got hot, a compact tripod for taking pictures on time delay ("He told me, 'You've got to clamp it to the shrouds, and take pictures of you and Lydia . . . ' "). She showed me the present he'd wrapped for her forty-second birthday, clearly three cassette boxes, she'd even known when he was recording the tapes. I nodded as she talked. I'd felt ready to incorporate another person into my solitary world, but I suddenly felt that I needed to incorporate two.

Brian: highly intelligent, primarily in the realm of computer technology. Highly insensitive, with a sincere, hyperactive generosity; I'd been a grateful recipient of that generosity, most notably when he helped me format and print a sailing manual I wrote for the OCC program, giving me his and his laser printer's entire Saturday, his mouse darting at a dizzying pace. Thick-skinned. The day they'd arrived in Fiji after their passage from New Zealand they'd gone ashore, and toward dinnertime Brian had said we'd better get back, they'll be expecting us for dinner, and Monica had said I think they might want their boat to themselves, maybe we should eat ashore.

He'd insisted on going back, and they'd found the owner and her daughter and the skipper sitting down at a table with only three place settings. The skipper had said to Brian I guess I could share my steak with you, and Brian had sat down and eaten half the steak. Monica had been mortified.

When she'd told me this story on the phone I'd said, "Didn't you *talk* to him about it?" And she said, "You don't talk to Brian." I suppose I imagined getting to know her well enough on our passage to ask her how she lived with someone she couldn't talk to.

He'd already given her "Action Items" to pass on to me. He wanted the exact coordinates of Horta harbor. He wanted me to try contacting him ship-to-ship on the SSB on Friday and Saturday nights, when he'd be down on their Valiant 40 *Macroskiff*. He'd supplied a schedule, frequencies and times—a new frequency every five minutes—scribbled in his slanted script on a three-by-five card.

I'd been the one who'd suggested radio contact, a couple months earlier, but that was a lifetime ago, back when I was intrigued by the ionosphere, before I'd learned to hate my SSB for every amp it stole from my batteries.

Right now, I didn't want Action Items. I wanted to sleep. Monica and I talked a bit more, and then slept. Outside, the festivities of Sea Week went on long into the night.

8 Aug

1025 and I seem to be awake. I feel like I have a massive hangover, the whole world, all day yesterday, feeling slightly distorted, too loud, too bright, too detailed, too sensory.

Headache, nausea, eyeballs ache. Body aches; not a good bed.

Tired, still emotionally overloaded. Take the day slowly.

Monica had gone off on a walk to let me sleep. I was glad for some time in the stillness of the room, reliving dolphins offshore before I lost them.

She was back by eleven, animated, excited about getting started—finally—on this adventure. As we walked down to the boat she laughed and said, "The first thing I thought this morning was: 'I'm going to be going to the bathroom in a bucket.'" Maybe I hadn't needed to tell her my offshore toilet policy the very first night.

By noon we were at work, pulling up all the floorboards, rinsing them and setting them out to dry, running fresh water below. We scrubbed the hull, me in the dinghy, Monica on deck manning the hose. She wasn't sure whether to be irritated or pleased when people who'd looked right through her from their own decks smiled at her now in recognition.

She'd walked these docks every single day, the ten days she waited for me. She was familiar with just about every boat, every face in the marina, but had talked to hardly anyone. It seemed funny to me that she'd made friends with hotel guests, but not with sailors; maybe it was more that the hotel guests had made friends with her.

I guess I expected her to be more like I'd been when I was eighteen and first sailing. Expected her to talk to people as they arrived, ask them what the weather had been like, how long their passage had taken. Explain that she was waiting for a friend who'd left from the Chesapeake eighteen, nineteen, twenty days back. Make friends that way. Learn some things. I hadn't really *liked* walking docks—especially by the time I was twenty-four, then twenty-eight, then thirty-five—but I'd disliked it because I'd been in such a position of vulnerability, hoping like crazy I'd be offered a berth. Monica already *had* a berth; she had nothing but positive to gain from dock walking.

She was pretty sure that one boat, the Chris Craft across the way, only had women on board. It was news to me that Chris Craft even *made* sailboats. I said, "You should at least have talked to *them*, then. They might have been buddies to you." She said, "No. I just wouldn't do that."

We talked a lot as we worked. I learned that she'd gone to her boss and said she was really sorry, she appreciated so much the month he'd given her to sail across the Atlantic, but she guessed she'd have to quit completely so she could sail through the Med. Her boss had said don't worry, the job will be here when you get back.

The story unnerved me. First, she'd told me how much she liked her job, and I didn't want even hypothetically to be the cause of her losing it. Second, we hadn't decided for sure that she *would* sail through the Med. She seemed to remember this, as I rinsed Atlantic salt out of *Sonnet's* bilges in silence. "Of course, we'll *see* if I end up sailing through the Med, but I had to talk to him . . ."

A number of people stopped by to chat, Judy and Marc off *Australe*, a gorgeous custom 50-foot sloop registered in New York and built of aluminum in France. Judy was American, Marc French. Then came Richard, drawn to *Sonnet* because she was designed by Sparkman & Stephens—he'd spotted that from across the marina—as was his *Annual Hope*. He told me the Chris Craft was also an S&S design, which surprised me. He said the Chris Craft Caribbean 35 was a solid comfortable cruising boat, quite sought after.

Then Reiner. He was in his fifties, very fit, with a rough, tanned, slightly flattened-nosed face and a hint of a German accent, though he'd been an American citizen for thirty years, defected from East Germany on a soccer tour. His 42-foot fifty-year-old Alden-designed *Snow Goose* was tied now behind *Sonnet*, low black sloop, low forest-green yawl, an elegant double portrait.

He was one of those solo sailors, to my amazement, who slept through the night. He talked about coming on deck one dawn to a huge Panamax freighter not a hundred yards off, looking like a block of urban apartment buildings. The experience shook him greatly, but not enough that he quit going below at night for his seven hours of shut-eye.

He talked about Herb, alias South Bound II, a radio operator in Bermuda who provided a weather service for cruisers. He talked about his any-vessel VHF call when he was approaching Horta, asking for someone to be ready to take his lines since he was alone, how a small crowd had welcomed him in, knew him from South Bound II though they didn't know him from sight, they all had become a family.

Funny, to hear about a net, a family, when I'd been so utterly alone out there.

I asked him if he knew anyone who might be able to help me with my engine and he suggested Tom on *Proud Rosie*, he was young but he seemed pretty smart, might have some ideas, he was helping the girls with their engine problem. Did I know about the girls?

I said no, and he motioned across at the Chris Craft, told me how the girls—Lisa and Bridget—had lost use of their engine a few days out of Bermuda, saltwater in their oil, and he could hear them calling South Bound II but getting no response as their batteries got weak, so he came in as relay, and for days they stayed in contact with Herb that way, getting support and advice on their problems. Seems that everyone was pulling for them, worried about how they were doing. They'd been totally becalmed just off the island, called him on the VHF—he'd already arrived in Horta—to ask if he knew anyone who could come out and tow them, so he and the folks on *Elaphonisos* had gone out in *Elaphonisos*'s dinghy, which had a nice little outboard, but by the time they got out there the breeze had come up, so they offered cold beers and congratulations instead of a tow and puttered alongside as the girls sailed in.

"And they sailed her right onto the dock," he said, his hand swooping like a sailboat onto a dock, his face suffused with pride.

Funny, to hear about these women sailing their boat onto the dock, to feel that wash of regret.

He told me I should introduce myself to the girls, and I said sure, I'd do that.

p.m. Letdown after the victory of all this, maybe. Beating myself up because I didn't get on the VHF, arrange to have someone take my lines, sail onto the dock. I made the right decision, dropping the anchor. I don't know how this boat handles around a dock, have docked her only once, less than impressively. The sense of rightness when the anchor bit was enough for me at the time (or actually, it wasn't; as I came in I eyed the dock, I thought about it).

I'm afraid this kind of regret is getting worse not better as I grow up. (Am I growing up?) Is it a perfect, closed creation I'm looking for? Nah, the regret can be at a screwup in the middle of something just as easily.

This wasn't a screwup. At the end of it *Sonnet* and I were still alone, still surrounded by water, but hooked to the land. Overwhelmingly exhausted, overwhelmingly emotional. *We did it.*

I need to respect the anxiety involved with a landfall, the fatigue. I could have rammed into the dock. I could have blown back into another boat. All a successful docking would have gained me was glory, the people I'd called on the VHF there to take my lines, admiration at my accomplishment. I left the dock at Cambridge with no fanfare, no one to see me off. I came in with Monica watching, proud of me. This is enough.

Monica went off at three to receive a call from Brian at her hotel. She asked what she should tell him about the radio contact. I told her I had no charge in my batteries, there was no way we could call.

In the evening we went for a walk. I wanted to walk as much as I could here, to get some strength back in my knee. When I'd been here in '79 I'd taken long walks, five, six hours into the interior. I remembered horse carts filled with metal milk cans, a roughly whitewashed house with empty cans outside the door. It had been July, not August, and the hydrangea had been in full bloom, miles and miles of blue-blossomed hydrangea hedges bordering lush green pastureland, placid black-and-white cattle fenced in by flowers.

Monica said there were still a few hydrangea blooming in the interior, but mostly they were finished.

We walked through town, then along a little beach, skirting Monte Queimado, the smaller of the two rocky hills I'd seen from sea. Monica said she loved this beach, since she didn't know how to swim, the water was calm, you could walk way out, not like the breakers of California. I hadn't realized she didn't know how to swim. She promised she'd wear her safety harness offshore every single second she was out of *Sonnet*'s cabin.

We headed up the switchback road of the second and larger hill, the round volcanic peninsula of Monte da Guia. It felt exceedingly good to walk. Monica was getting winded as we neared the top and said maybe she'd wait for me, I only had a little ways to go to the church and a viewpoint. I asked when she'd been up here, and she said with Carlos, the brother of the co-worker in Palo Alto, he was such a nice man. I said oh, so it was Carlos who took you on the tour yesterday, and she said no, he drove me around the island last week. She peeled away with a wave to sit on a low white wall, and I kept moving, loving the feel of my pounding heart, ignoring the ache in my knee.

From the church I looked out to the sprawling blue Atlantic—amazed that I'd crossed it on *Sonnet*, aware of how small she'd look out there from up here—and straight down to a small round bay, the Caldeira do Inferno. Two big sloops were anchored in the bay, toy boats on the still dark water.

I rejoined Monica and we headed back down, talking as we walked. We didn't know each other well; she'd taken some of my classes on *Saudade*, and gone on two *Alaska Eagle* Channel Islands cruises, and we'd sailed together a number of times on other boats. As we walked down the Monte da Guia I asked how she and Brian had met and she told me about her first marriage—barely out of high school—to another man named Brian, through whom she met the Brian she was married to now. Brian One was in the military—they lived in Germany for a while—and then was a ski instructor. He had a job at a ski resort in Canada—the marriage really wasn't working, she didn't feel he took things like finances seriously, but she was still trying to give it a go— and she temporarily took a job herself when a woman quit unexpectedly with no one to replace her. The immigration people found out she was working without papers and deported her, twenty-four hours to get on a plane. She enjoyed telling the story. "Can you believe I got *deported?*"

She'd pretty much left Brian One for Brian Two, turned to the latter at the deportation crossroads, the former still back in Canada, a sticky transition period, married now to one Brian or another for over twenty years. She believed fate had worked in strange ways, things had worked out for the best, she'd ended up with the security she needed.

We skirted Monte Queimado on the west side this time, and cross-countried through weeds to the outer seawall to seek out *August Moon*. This wall was like a warehouse of yacht paintings, a haphazard repository compared to the bright new gallery walls around the marina. Shipping containers blocked some of the paintings, boxes and huge brackets for wiring had covered others for good, but those remaining—weathered and encroached upon—were wonderful.

Two-thirds of the way down the seawall we found it: *August Moon*, 7/79, faded but intact. Green serif letters on a white rectangle, a portion of the mast in black, and behind the mast a round rising moon. I had photographs of this from the day I finished it, the colors sharp and new. Photographs of my *August Moon* shipmates standing on this spot, Jim and Dee and Jim's nine-year-old son Chris, who'd be twenty-two now.

We made our way back to *Sonnet*. A couple of the mid-Atlantic Italians stopped by. They told me how nice my boat had looked offshore. They told me they'd been the two thousandth boat to arrive this year in Horta—arriving just a few hours before I did—and were getting all kinds of special treatment because of it. I invited them on board, but they were off to a dinner in their honor.

Monica and I cooked, sharing our first meal together at *Sonnet*'s ma-hogany table. She suggested she'd maybe start moving her things on board tomorrow, then move on board herself on Monday. I appreciated her making the transition gradual.

She slept in the hotel, I slept on the boat.

Reiner stopped by in the morning, told me there was a race today at noon, said he would invite me to race on *Snow Goose* but his crew was pretty full-up, he'd already asked the girls, and Tom. Had I met the girls yet? I said no, and he motioned across the water, said look, they're having breakfast in the cockpit. I said then I shouldn't bother them, and he said why not, looks like they already have visitors. So I got in *Couplet*—easier than walking—and rowed across.

Antelope Medicine, Mammoth Lakes, CA. A Monitor wind vane, like *Sonnet* had. The wheel outfitted exactly like *Sonnet*'s, rings for both the Monitor and an Autohelm 3000.

A blond woman, a brunette—both in their early thirties—and two men. They waved an invitation.

As I tied up *Couplet* I asked, "Do you want a fender? I'm not sure how good the rub rails are on my dinghy . . ."

The blond woman laughed. "The whole boat's a fender."

I climbed on board. The brunette was Lisa; the blonde, Bridget. I couldn't remember if Reiner had told me which one of them owned the boat, so I asked Lisa, "It's your boat?"

She smiled, shook her head, and motioned to her friend.

I have scores of journal entries, over the course of the next three months, talking about Bridget, and the word looks wrong to me, because the skipper of *Antelope Medicine* no longer has that name. She'd never liked it, she'd tried a time or two to change it, but hadn't come up with a new name that stuck. I know her now only as Skyli, so it's Skyli I'll use in these pages.

Her hair was short and sun-bleached and not very well behaved; her eyes were green; she was slender and strong. Lisa's hair was collar-length and glossy; she had extraordinarily lovely skin, even her hands, even after an Atlantic passage. They were both tanned, relaxed, at ease with each other and their boat.

Ken from *Moonspinner* dominated the early part of the conversation—the younger man was Tom from *Proud Rosie*—but I don't much remember what he said. I remember the presence of these two women who'd sailed together from Bermuda, Skyli sitting to starboard of me in the cockpit, Lisa standing in the companionway.

I learned that first meeting that Skyli—like me—had put her boat together herself. Like me, she had a husband named Steven—I later learned they weren't married, but she called him that for simplicity—who, like my Steven, knew little about boat maintenance and left the decisions and the work to her. Like me, she'd poured her love and sweat into a boat which someone else's salary, for the most part, had paid for.

Lisa talked more, at first, asking questions about my solo passage, about *Sonnet*. At some point she put her hand out to shake mine and said, with simple sincerity, "Congratulations," and Skyli did the same.

They had a third friend—Amy, a.k.a. Liebchen—who'd sailed with Skyli from the Bahamas to Bermuda. The three of them planned to sail from Europe back to the Bahamas in the Columbus 500 Rally, though Skyli now was feeling disinclined toward doing the Rally and thought it might be more fun to sail somewhere like Brazil. I asked Lisa what she thought about that, and she said, "I want to go through with the Rally. It's what we've been planning for." She'd taken a leave of absence from her teaching job for a year to do this.

The men wandered off, Tom promising to come by *Sonnet* to look at my engine. I asked Skyli about her sailing background, and she said, "Purely literary, I learned what little I know from books," which I suspected might be a bit of an exaggeration. I asked about the name of the boat, and she mentioned the Medicine Cards, a process based on Native American belief systems, in which you learn which animals speak to you. I told her I'd heard about the cards, but I didn't know what the Antelope had to say, and she said the Antelope tells you to go out and *do it*.

Lisa asked about *Sonnet*'s name, and I said she'd had the name when I bought her, and I'd been pleased since I used to write sonnets, years back.

We talked about *Antelope Medicine*'s engine failure. Skyli and I had essentially the same engine, the 4-107, hers a Perkins and mine a Westerbeke. Her repairs were on hold right now while she waited for a head gasket to be shipped from England; I told her I was pretty sure I had one she could use.

We'd been born in neighboring communities of L.A. County. We'd both gone to school at UC Santa Barbara, though not at the same time. I mentioned—I can't remember why—that Steve had kept our Macintosh PowerBook, and she said that her Steven had kept their

PowerBook, too, at which point I had to laugh, saying, "Okay, wait a minute, what does he look like?"

Mine was blond, and close to six feet; hers was no taller than she was, light brown hair, a professor of biology, and in fact hers always went by Steven, mine mostly by Steve, though Skyli that day and thereafter usually referred to hers in the longer form: "Sweet Steven Morgan."

It was after ten. I looked over, saw that my crew had arrived on *Sonnet*, and rowed back across.

Monica had brought two of her bags, a big one and a small one, which now rested prominently on the starboard pilot berth. I showed her which lockers I'd cleared out for her, then said we should maybe get the sails off before she unpacked, I'd talked to a sailmaker yesterday, he was coming by at eleven. We worked together to get the main off the boom and the jib off the headstay; both sails needed repairs. The sailmaker arrived with a handbarrow and wheeled them away.

As race time neared I decided to go rowing. I headed out of the marina and up the main harbor entrance in the wind and the chop, watched the start of the race and through the first mark, then rowed back, taking my time, knowing Monica was in the process of stowing her gear, figuring I'd let her get a jump on it before I ventured back on board.

She'd barely started. I felt claustrophobic, seeing all her things spread around the boat, then guilty for feeling that way, since she was clearly enjoying making *Sonnet* her temporary home. She'd brought her own pillowcases at my suggestion, pointed out to me how nice the pillows looked, plumped and propped on the bunk, adding color to the boat.

I decided the better part of valor was to take a walk, headed into town, found a pleasant bench near the post office and pulled out my journal.

9 Aug

Stressed. Wanting what I've said I've wanted: for Monica to feel this is her boat as much as mine but in reality I can't come close to it, burgundy is my least favorite color, there isn't a color I would have wanted less than burgundy (maybe pink). Demons to fight, always.

Appreciative of her, her patience through all of this, all my delays. Feel she is precisely the right person to be doing this with me, and at the same time not, I long for more of a soul mate, visited *Antelope Medicine* this morning and felt, there, the kind of rapport I'll never have with Monica.

All in good time, plenty of phases to *Sonnet*.

Sad, stressed, doing fine. I've always been moody, I'll always be moody.

I own this boat. This lovely boat.

Wanting to accept how each friendship will have its gaps, its strong points and weak. Deborah is the closest I have to a soul mate, my gratefulness for her is immense, and the one point I felt disappointment in her was when she was terrified of sailing. How can a soul mate of *mine* not feel which way the wind is coming from?

Goddess, thank you for Steve, thank you for Deborah, thank you for Monica, thank you for *Sonnet*. Thank you for Skyli on *Antelope Medicine* (I seem to be finding my way back to talking to a deity). Thank you for my sister, watch over her through this fifth birth of a child.

Thank you for this life, for this island, this spirit in which I feel the toughness coming back.

On my way back through town I bought a *Time* magazine in a tiny bookstore, and wondered, flipping through it as I walked, if I'd even be able to read it, if I'd be able to absorb these words and images after the Atlantic's simplicity. The cover showed emaciated men, smiling inexplicably from behind barbed wire in Bosnia. Inside were articles on inner-city gangs, Rodney King, the U.S. presidential elections. When I got back to the boat Monica was happily reading a novel in the cockpit, wearing a short shocking-pink jump suit. I felt a wash of clarity and affection; mine were not, in fact, overwhelming challenges.

Marc and Judy came by and invited us tomorrow for drinks. Tonight they were going to the awards ceremony, the windup for Sea Week, we should go too.

Tom came by next. We looked at my engine, and discovered that the insulation on the wire from the solenoid to the starter motor had heated up and melted. We then did some current testing, and determined that the solenoid was shot. Tomorrow—Monday—I'd try to find replacement parts.

Monica and I headed in the evening up to the Sea Week ceremony, in a school in the center of town. The room was packed, the food tables overflowing, the presentations good-natured and largely incomprehensible. I saw the *Antelope Medicine* women and Reiner across the room, but when the crowd began to break up they slipped out before I found them to say hello.

We headed back down to the waterfront, split up at the road to Monica's hotel.

I was gone in the morning before she got to the boat with the rest of her things.

10 Aug

I'm sitting here with my back against old ramparts, my hiking boots planted on grass, open ocean to my left. Enjoyed wandering the aisles of the little supermarket next to the electronics store (no solenoid), struck by how much I love it, being in a version of Europe, packages in Portuguese, familiar and not.

Last night, in my bunk alone on *Sonnet* for the last night in a long time, I sobbed for my cat, sobbed and sobbed and sobbed, my cat I loved so much.

On my way back to the marina I ran into Skyli, who was on her way over to *Sonnet* to check out my gasket supply. Together we ran into Greg, the skipper of the Nonesuch 38 *Peryton* docked two slips down from Skyli. He and his Dutch girlfriend Sascha were en route to Europe to meet the owner of the boat. Greg had curly dark hair, a thick dark mustache, a loudmouthed Louisiana accent, and a couple of suggestions on where I could find a starter solenoid.

Almost to *Sonnet*, we ran into Monica—she'd finished her second round of stowing and was on her way into town to check out the produce market—and I introduced Skyli to my crew.

I then introduced her to my boat. She looked around the brightwork-and-white interior, the simple classic layout, shaking her head. There were people who didn't respond to *Sonnet*, found her somewhat spartan, but Skyli, it was clear, thought she was beautiful. *Antelope Medicine*, if truth be told, wasn't beautiful. She was comfortable—far more space below than *Sonnet* in seven feet less of length—but her high freeboard and wide beam didn't make for a breathtaking silhouette. Skyli would have preferred a beautiful boat.

She'd boat-hunted for months, up and down the East Coast. Steven Morgan was working at NY State University at Stony Brook; they'd been living for two years on Long Island, which Skyli hated. *Antelope* *Medicine* had presented herself in Fort Lauderdale at the right price at the right time, roomy enough for three women, safe enough for the challenge of the Atlantic.

Skyli had done massive amounts of work to make the boat even safer, commuting back and forth between Florida and New York; there'd probably been a point we'd crossed paths on boat missions, she on I-95 between New York and Tampa, me on Highway 50 between Washington and Annapolis. She adored her boat, had been proud of her almost to tears on the offshore passages, found in that 35-by-11-foot space an intensity of refuge.

I found her a head gasket for the Perkins. Our conversation veered into deeper waters than either of us might normally have been brave enough to enter, so early on. She mentioned how, a time or two alone in the cockpit at night, hundreds of miles from anywhere, she'd thought how easy it would be to slip out of the safety harness, do a back flip over the side, and tread water as the boat sailed away.

I told her how I'd gone through a period, before departing with *Sonnet*, of thinking yes, I could die out there, but it wouldn't really matter if I died, the planet would sail through space without me. Gone through that period and then moved into the next, recognizing the hugeness of the world, the unfathomable suffering, recognizing the pain I would cause in my own tiny corner of the world if something happened to me, and vowing—within, granted, the framework of doing this in the first place, the fact that my temperament seemed to insist on doing it—that I would fight while offshore with everything I had not to contribute, even infinitesimally, to the universal wail.

She listened, looking at me rather strangely.

Monica came back, wanting to help me on my afternoon engine-parts hunt. Skyli headed with her gasket back to her boat. Monica and I found a lovely little solenoid in town, then knocked a few of the smaller to-do items off the list back at the boat. At six we went next door to *Australe*.

Monica responded to *Australe* in completely different ways than I did, would have killed for that mini-dishwasher in the galley, the washing machine in the forward head. I liked *Australe* because she was spectacularly thought-out and built; the creature comforts were fine but you couldn't have paid me to have them on *Sonnet*, I felt far more compulsion to yank such things out than to put them in.

As we took the tour I tried hard to keep Monica involved, pointing things out to her, asking her what decisions she and Brian had made on *Macroskiff*, but as soon as we got settled down with drinks—which evolved to staying for dinner—it was harder. I was immensely happy, sitting in the comfortable salon of this impressive boat, talking to these fellow sailors, plunged back into a world I loved. Marc and Judy and I talked about the French singlehanded sailing scene, and aluminum maintenance problems, and Mediterranean ports. It turned out Marc had spent years in West Africa working in real estate, and then we were off on Africa, talking about the wildness of the place, the addictiveness.

When Monica and I got back to *Sonnet* I told her I was sorry if she'd felt left out and she said it wasn't a problem at all, she was used to that with Brian, there'd be these evenings where she'd have to sit around for hours with a lot of computer types, trying not to seem bored. She said the worst, with Brian, was that sometimes from the blue he'd try to include her, lean forward and say "What do you think, Monica?" about some esoteric software subject she hadn't a clue on.

I wasn't sure I liked being compared with Brian.

I slept in the forepeak, port bunk, where I usually slept when I wasn't under way. Monica chose the main-cabin pilot berth to starboard. A new adventure: two women sharing a 42-foot boat.

I spent a good part of the following day on my engine problem, bought a hefty new solenoid-to-starter-motor wire in one store, terminals in another, and finally—after suggestions and maps and gesticulated directions—left them to be soldered at an old warehouse by the outer seawall.

In a way, this felt like a replay of Annapolis, job after time-consuming job just to get the boat out to sea, and an undercurrent of restlessness ran through me. In other ways it was wonderful to be learning my boat, learning new aspects of her, slowly coming to the point that my heart caught when I saw her across the marina. Wonderful to be on this lush island, with views across to the steep-sloped Pico, a slice from my past.

It had been a different era, my last time here. Our crew had hung out nightly at Café Peter Sport when Peter himself officiated. The postmaster—who'd known every sailboat in the harbor—would spot me in town and tell me there was a Poste Restante letter for *August Moon*.

There were more brightly painted hand-rowed whaling boats in Horta harbor, those days, than yachts.

At times I felt torn, looking back thirteen years. I missed my mar- velous long walks, the bond I'd felt with the island, the intensity of discovery. But I didn't have the same knees now, I *couldn't* take long walks. I now had different priorities, different responsibilities.

Through Richard on *Annual Hope* I met Stan on *Mustard Seed*, who came over with his trusty multitester and helped me figure out the true culprit of *Sonnet*'s engine problem. Stan was retired, cruising his little boat with his wife, and always willing to lend a hand to other cruisers. He wasn't satisfied that my solenoid had failed, wanted to know *why*.

Half an hour of sleuth work led us to the key switch in the cockpit. Designed to engage the solenoid when you held the key counterclockwise, then spring the key back upright when you let go, the switch was sticking. When it stuck on that windy Atlantic night, the starter motor had run continuously, drawing vast amounts of electricity (no *wonder* I hadn't been able to get through to Beth on the SSB), finally burning out the solenoid.

At Stan's suggestion, I took off the key switch and lubricated it. The next day I got the new solenoid wire on, and reinstalled the lubricated switch, though I still didn't trust it. When I finally turned the key, and the engine roared to life and exhaust water began belching out the stern, a cheer rose up from *Antelope Medicine*, across the marina.

The next day they got *their* engine running, and Monica and I cheered them, too.

The day before Monica's birthday, while she was in town, I made a banner—each letter of HAPPY B'DAY MONICA drawn with bright felt pens on a half sheet of notebook paper and taped to a string—and after she'd gone to sleep I quietly strung it athwartships so she'd see it first thing when she woke up.

She waited until I was awake to open her present from Brian. Two of the casette boxes contained tapes, the third a solid-gold dolphin pin with a diamond eye, which she unwrapped with shaking fingers—he'd wrapped it in tissue, and put the tissue in the cassette box, so she'd think she was getting three tapes—and literally started jumping up and down when she got it far enough unwrapped to see what it was; she'd seen this in a jewelry store, and mentioned it to him, but thought he'd forgotten.

I pretty much disliked this type of jewelry; was it false of me, to pretend to be impressed by the pin?

For the most part Monica and I were getting along fine, with flashes of legitimate intimacy. She told me things about her past which took both courage and trust. She told me stories about Brian which didn't much endear him to me, how he'd told her she had to finish all the varnishing on *Macroskiff* before she left to sail on *Sonnet*, and she'd run herself ragged. How he'd made virtually every decision when their boat was under construction, including the installation of a button in the cockpit which sounded an obnoxious buzzer right by her head when she slept. Her one unilateral decision had been to order secondary sheet winches while he was crossing the Pacific on someone else's boat; she'd told him about the decision over the SSB, and said you could just about feel the disapproval over the airwaves; he'd finally said well, if you've already ordered them I guess there's nothing I can do about it.

She told me how she suffered stomachaches from stress, and how pleased she was that she hadn't taken a single stomach pill since coming aboard *Sonnet*. I told her she should start thinking of ways, in her life with Brian, to do things for Monica. She said she wasn't entirely sure who Monica was.

I showed her my Chinese stretches one night, which was maybe a bit hypocritical since I hadn't done them myself in months. I'd learned the Eight Pieces of Embroidery—reputedly used as healing exercises in China—from a Tai Chi instructor, then adapted them a bit to fit my own body, then come up with words to focus on as I stretched (the arms-over-head stretch was *celebration*, the punch stretch was *power*, and so on), turning the whole into a kind of personal pep-talk and therapy session. As I showed the exercises to Monica I thought this is ridiculous, there's no way she'll ever do these.

She started talking to Brian less often, using the excuse of no longer being in the hotel. She got a kick out of relating to me the times she weaseled out of Action Items.

15 Aug

Dream: Monica and I were visiting Steve in Bulgaria, for a short time only, then had to get back to the boat. Mount Vitosha rose precipitously a stone's throw away, literally just past the next apartment building, brown and barren and volcanic-looking. The slope dropped away from the balcony; in the river below I saw sailboats tacking, then realized my perspective was wrong, they were model boats being let out on strings.

In the dream, Monica could swim. We were down by the water, there was even a current, and she was swimming with confidence, upstream.

I got back to the boat from the showers that afternoon—my second Saturday in Horta—and Monica was packing a daypack, barely containing her excitement. Carlos had come by and suggested they go to the beach together, he'd pick her up in ten minutes down at the main road. I rather enjoyed the afternoon alone on *Sonnet*, getting projects done without distraction. When Monica got back she was flushed but rather coy, downplaying the beach trip.

On Sunday, Skyli and I took a walk, north out of town, cross-country up a slope toward the ridge with windmills. We'd seen each other a couple of nights ago, when I'd wrangled Lisa and her a tour of *Australe*. She'd declined the drink Judy offered, saying she had a little headache, and I'd cheerfully told her she ought to take an aspirin, I used to avoid the likes of aspirin but in fact they helped. Only later did I learn that Skyli got real headaches, vascular migraines, a lifetime affliction.

On our walk, I learned about her sister's sought-after artwork. I learned that their father had died when Skyli was twelve, that he hadn't lived with the family in years and she'd disliked him intensely. She said, "I remember standing at the funeral, thinking I should cry, thinking maybe I wanted to cry, but I didn't."

I learned about *Yansa*, her previous sailboat, a little green Montgomery 15 she'd sold to help buy *Antelope Medicine*. She'd written the boat into a grant when she was in grad school, sailed her every day in Monterey Bay to look at sharks, sailed right up to them, wrestled with them, leaning over the gunnel. She loved that little boat. She loved sharks.

We sat at the top of the ridge in the lee of a monument—my knee wasn't happy with walking—out of the wind, in the sun, talking, then walked back down.

Lisa came over later that afternoon and invited Monica and me to have our Medicine Cards read after dinner; by nightfall the four of us were sitting around the table on *Antelope Medicine*. In all my years sailing I'd never sat on a boat in the evening with only women. I'd taught all-women classes on *Saudade*, I'd taken *Alaska Eagle* five miles up a British Columbian inlet for fuel once with an all-female crew while the voyage's male crew members went fishing, but those were boats which soon returned to their mixed-crew modes, boats which men maintained. This was a boat a woman had poured her soul and smarts and elbow grease into.

Skyli explained how the Medicine Cards worked. Monica went first. She stirred the cards spread face-down in front of her with the most wonderful expression of anticipation, a kind of hope. It pleased me to see her lighting up like that.

Skyli read from the book as each card was chosen. Lisa wrote down notes.

16 Aug

We did our Medicine Cards tonight on *Antelope Medicine*. I've resisted it from Derek and Jackie, the way I resist Tarot or visits to psychics or any number of other things, and tonight it seemed the absolute right thing to do, a willingness to start trusting intuition again, start allowing in religion, in whatever form. A softening of pessimism. Recognizing the incredible number of belief systems, recognizing that I'll never really believe in any one of them, and at the same time accepting that certain things fall into your life.

Four women on a boat, the presence of the boat around us. The more I see *Antelope Medicine* the more I like her, for what she's done, what she'll do.

Horse and Hawk both tell me to claim power, to balance my strength, perceive, receive. Opposum tells me to expect the unexpected; Lizard tells me to listen to my dreams. Monica's cards were predominantly "contrary"—Lisa and Skyli kept assuring her this was fine, it just means you have things to learn—and overwhelmingly about change.

I want this next portion of the trip to be for Monica. We aren't very much alike, but maybe we don't need to be. She may not gain what I'd like for her to gain from this passage, may not thrive on it, may not come out changed, but might. I can't control her experience, and shouldn't try; *can* control my generosity, strive for that. Wanting that. Not writing this well at all.

The howling wind unsettles me. Hard to concentrate, hard to act. Patience, patience.

Monica will pretend to understand something when she doesn't. I was punching in the ship-to-ship stations, tuning the antenna, talking through it while she watched, did 16A and 16B, she was making understanding noises, I stood up and said why don't you do 22A and 22B and she froze, totally lost, close to panic. Sat her down, talked her through it with the book in front of her and radio at her fingertips and she did okay, but she hadn't been following me at all.

I need to write postcards but my nerves are on edge when it blows like this.

I spent two hours at the post office that afternoon, needing so much some contact with Steve, dialing Bulgaria every five minutes without getting through. I finally got a ring, and a pickup, and the voice of a Bulgarian woman who told me—as my mind rummaged frantically back through my Bulgarian language training—that Steve was out of town on a business trip.

Late that night I got it in my head to make inroads on my *Sonnet* painting. I'd resisted doing a painting at all, knowing how time-consuming it could be, and met protests from all sides, you *have* to do a painting at Horta, it's bad luck not to.

Lisa had finished *Antelope Medicine*'s painting, after days of work. It was a marvelous multicolored creation from a design by Skyli's sister, a stylized antelope standing on a globe, encircled by a geometric border. Under the dates of their passage were Skyli's and Lisa's names, and also Amy's and Steven Morgan's; Amy hadn't sailed this leg, and Steven wouldn't be sailing at all, but this was their voyage, too.

I'd decided on a simple painting, just the name of the boat and the date—gray and white on black, like on her stern—on the horizontal surface next to where we were docked. I'd started the previous day, drafting out the letters with a straight edge, and at eleven o'clock got impulsive, up on the seawall in the dark with a battery-powered lantern.

Marc and Judy stepped up onto the wall from their cockpit while I was working, planning a walk, which they never quite took. Marc figured I needed a better light, and set about rigging a powerful twelve-volt light from *Australe* on an extension. They then sat down to watch for a bit and chat, and then Reiner came by, and then a young man from the Argentinian boat, and then Judy went back to *Australe* for a bottle of wine and some wineglasses, and Monica popped her head up from below where she'd already gone to bed and decided to join us, and by midnight we had eleven people sitting around my two-foot-long *Sonnet* sign, four Americans, a Frenchman, two Germans, an Argentinian, and three Poles. A few candles came out from other boats, another bottle of wine. The wine flowed, the twelve-volt light shone pleasantly, and I worked methodically along my boat's name, listening to the conversation, focusing downward, surrounded by good cheer.

On Tuesday, Monica and I had dinner on *Antelope Medicine*. Lisa and Skyli told Bermuda-to-Horta stories. How the folks on *Elaphonisos* had blasted them over the VHF with a rap written in their honor, complete with rhymed references to saltwater in the engine oil. How the skipper of a British boat had referred to them over the South Bound II net as "two brave girls on a rather small yacht," which they'd modified slightly, referring to themselves now in mock British accents as "two brave girls with rather small breasts."

Lisa and Monica faded early, and Skyli and I talked. She learned I'd lived in Africa. I learned she'd felt a strong draw to Africa ever since she was a kid, and that her only trip to the continent had been cut short. Africa, sailboats, and sharks; she said if she ever saw both Africa and a shark from a sailboat she wasn't sure she'd be able to handle it.

She was a biologist, an ichthyologist, though she insisted on calling herself an *ex*-biologist, adamant that there was no place for women in science. She'd had a shattering professional experience while doing research for her master's thesis and never quite came out the other side of it, finished and presented the thesis but never went through the final hoops to earn the degree.

Her Steven had surged forward in his field—also biology, in his case larval ecology—since she'd been with him, earning his Ph.D., winning grant after grant, making a name for himself.

I learned how she'd lost her dog—a beautiful Siberian husky—a couple of years back, hit by a car, how she'd withdrawn for two solid weeks, hadn't gone to work, hadn't talked to a soul. She had a new dog now, a Queensland heeler named Chainsaw.

I managed to tell her how Oscar died, crushed between a wall and a fence in a freak accident. How his death still caught me unexpectedly.

She told me about *ogbajis*, African deities who appear in your life for a short time only, when there's something you need to learn. She saw Alyosha Tess—the dog she'd lost—as an *ogbaji*.

I asked her what the Ali-*ogbaji* had to say. She answered, "Accept love where you find it."

I said, "Did she have to die, to tell you that?"

19 Aug

Another down-day. Monday it blew like stink. Yesterday it settled down a little, not a lot, and today it's blowing again, raining hard, boat soaked. Part of me knows that it's fine, this too will pass, another is restless and stressed, wanting to be moving, not at all wanting to be moving in nasty weather. Part of me feels a deep gratefulness, an important person has come into my life, another is exhausted by it, even a bit spooked.

Lisa dropped by to tell me a little yellow Bulgarian boat had arrived bearing a race logo. There were a number of solo race boats—which everyone still called OSTAR boats, from the years when the *Observer* had sponsored the Singlehanded TransAtlantic Race—in the marina, on their way like the Italians back to Europe, and it was with a kind of detached fascination that I realized I felt no tug when I looked at them. No regret that I'd never raced across the Atlantic, that I never would.

I'd been watching, though, for the Bulgarian boat, hoping that Petya Christova had in fact raced, hoping that she might be stopping off in Horta and we could meet. I headed, excited, over to where the little yellow boat was docked, and was surprised when a man emerged from below, not a woman.

The man told me yes, Petya Christova had sailed this boat—named *Nord*—in the Atlantic Race. He himself was Nedelko, the owner and builder of *Nord*. He and a friend had sailed here from Newport, and he and the friend and Petya would cruise the Azores a bit, then sail on to Gibraltar; from Gibraltar, a Bulgarian freighter would take them back to the Black Sea.

Petya was helping a Frenchwoman deliver her little Beneteau and should be in within a few days. The two of them, a Dutchwoman, and the well-funded Florence Arthaud had been the only female starters in this year's eighty-odd-boat fleet. I'd learned from Marc and Judy that Florence had capsized three hundred miles from the finish.

Nedelko and I talked a bit about Bulgaria, about Petya's experiences in the race. I felt torn; should I put off leaving, in order to meet Petya, when I could meet her in Sofia, and when I was so restless to leave?

On Thursday morning Sascha came by, off *Peryton*. She and Greg were leaving later in the day, lousy weather or no, and since both *Sonnet* and *Antelope Medicine* were planning to get off within a day or two they proposed a nine-o'clock radio date daily. We all exchanged phone numbers of people to contact in an emergency.

I was ready to be gone, Petya or no, emotionally if not technically; I figured we could crank on the final tasks and be ready by tomorrow. As soon as I decided for sure to leave tomorrow—weather permitting—the woman on *Wizard* said there was no way we could leave, tomorrow was Friday, it was bad luck. I'd forgotten that old sailor's superstition, and wished I hadn't been reminded.

Monica had been oddly resistant to leaving—saying how much she liked this place, she really wouldn't mind getting stuck here awhile longer—which wasn't helping my mood any. When the Friday issue came up she said if we're going to wait until Saturday we should wait until Sunday. I was working on something at the time and the suggestion didn't quite sink in, but a bit later when she repeated, in a slightly joky voice, "Maybe we should leave on Sunday, Lydia," I asked why Sunday. She said Carlos had been away for five days, he was coming home on Sunday, she could say goodbye. I asked her something it hadn't occurred to me to ask before: if he had a wife, and she said he did, but he hadn't really wanted to introduce them, and I asked doesn't that seem a little strange to you and she shrugged.

I decided—with the help of Lisa and Skyli, who were also in the countdown stages of preparation—that the Friday proscription didn't apply to boats with all-women crews. A lot of superstitions, after all, had their origins in a fear of the power of women, so certainly they didn't *apply* to women.

When I got up on Friday the weather was still lousy.

21 Aug

Realizing: (1) My sense of feeling crazed is as much from Monica, from the fact that as soon as I'm awake she's talking to me (why

don't morning people understand that you can't talk to night
people in the morning?), as from the weather. Or from the two
combined. (2) It's really not all that awful out, it's raining but no
longer all that windy.

A lot of this craziness bounces off Maryland, finish half of
what needs to be done each day and you never leave. Also
thinking, Christ, if it's a race, you just go on the day of the start.
If it's an *Eagle* trip, you go on the scheduled departure day, why
can't we *leave*, why can't we get out of here?

In fact, little by little, the jobs on *Sonnet* had been completed.
Around nine o'clock on Friday the rain stopped, and reality hit me with
a little rush: Today we would head for Europe.

At ten I walked over to the harbor offices to check *Sonnet* out of the
Azores. The immigration officer was checking someone in, so I stepped
over to look at the newly arrived boat and started chatting with the
young man in the cockpit about their passage. At some point he said,
"My father's Bill Butler. You've heard of him?"

Something in his tone suggested I *should* have heard of Bill Butler,
but I admitted I hadn't, and the son said this is the Bill Butler who was
adrift in a life raft for sixty-six days. The third crew member, an older
guy, stepped from below and verified how phenomenal it was they'd
survived. Turns out Butler and his wife had written a book about it, *Our
Last Chance*. This new boat was named *Another Chance*. His original
plan, before the previous boat sank in the Pacific, was a circumnaviga-
tion, culminating with the Columbus 500 Rally. He now planned to sail
in the Rally as a kind of comeback; his wife had apparently decided he
could do it on his own.

Bill Butler himself—a solidly built man with a salt-and-pepper
beard—strode purposefully from the harbor offices, having checked *Another Chance* in. I took his place and checked *Sonnet* out.

As I walked back to the marina, I ran into Nedelko, who told me
Petya had arrived this morning, and what dock I'd find her on. I found
the little Beneteau, and woke Petya up, which she didn't seem to mind.
She was amazed I spoke some Bulgarian, and disappointed that I was
within hours of taking off. I liked her instantly, her animation.

We sat at the bar by the showers and talked. She'd been thirty-five
days at sea between Plymouth and Newport; her 25-foot Folkboat had

been so incessantly wet that she called it her Yellow Submarine. *Nord* was the same hull design as *Jester*, which Blondy Hasler had sailed in the first OSTAR (*Observer*) in 1960. Numerous Folkboats had raced over the years; Petya had broken the OSTAR Folkboat record by two days.

She told me how the little plywood *Nord* had been docked in Plymouth right next to the high-tech *Pierre Premier*, Florence Arthaud's 60-foot trimaran. A French television crew had a heyday filming the two boats, and Petya felt upset, as if they were gloating over the contrast between East and West. I said, look who *finished*. What you did is more impressive, in its way, than what the front-runners did. Twice as gutsy. They were out there under two weeks. You were out there over a month.

I was proud of her, impressed. She'd done something—on a shoestring budget and with grace—I no longer had any desire to do. Or so I claimed; she started talking about the Two-Star—two years from now, right when I'd probably be taking *Sonnet* back across the Atlantic anyway—and I felt the old tug again, maybe a *double*-handed race . . .

Running out of time. We exchanged Sofia addresses and phone numbers, and I headed back to *Sonnet*.

By just after noon, Monica and I were ready to get off the seawall and power over to the fuel dock. There was a bit of a send-off party, more people helping us with our lines than we really needed, and I laughed, said if you want to do a send-off do it when we're leaving the island, not just heading over for fuel.

I'd been told the fuel dock stayed open through lunch but it was closed, so we were stuck there for a while. Lisa and Skyli checked several times to see if there was anything they could do for us. They hoped to get off that night; I liked the idea of our two boats out there together.

Sonnet was heading for Gibraltar, *Antelope Medicine* for Cadiz. I wouldn't see Lisa again. She planned to leave as soon as they made landfall and fly to California to take care of some business; she would either return to Cadiz for the Rally's start in October or meet Skyli and Amy in the Canaries before the main crossing. Skyli would stay with the boat; Sweet Steven Morgan was attending a conference in England next month and would fly down to spend some time with her. I told Skyli I would drive my parents' car from Marbella down to Cadiz to see how she was doing, and meant it, and she was pleased.

The fuel pumps opened. We put on fuel. I paid, and got a receipt;

the State Department was actually going to reimburse me for fuel, since it hadn't had to pay my airfare to Bulgaria.

Ready to be off.

I was wound up, only just now noticing how tightly. Monica was on deck, excited, chatting with Lisa and Skyli. I went below alone, sat down, closed my eyes, took a slow deep breath, and talked with my animals. I asked for grounding from Lizard, strategy from Opossum, wisdom from Hawk. I then took one last slow deep breath and went on deck to start the engine.

Skyli and Lisa cast off our lines.

6

We remain the center of a circle of
horizon, counting on a circling sky
to place us on the chart, make headway by
those pencil marks marching on. I love
such order, court it, steer by stars above
the spreaders, watch the sun move north, still shy
of summer by a measured day. Rely
on sense, decision, fly wide sails and dove-
tail dark Poseidon's stomping ground with light,
logic with illusion. The night reveals
a dreamer's noon, a white-backed wave's a dune
at sea, no time, no heading, heeled at night
and wheeling underneath a moon that wheels,
a monthless moon, an August moon in June.

"On the Yacht *August Moon*," 1979

We powered off the fuel dock—past the spot where I'd dropped
my anchor alone two weeks back—and headed for the harbor entrance.
I turned the wheel over to Monica, pulled in the fenders, and went
to the mast to haul up the pre-reefed mainsail, grinding it home
as we passed the crowd gathered atop the marina wall to wave us off.
Marc and Judy, Reiner, the Argentinians, the Butler crew, whistling,
blaring air horns, raising glasses; I was glad to provide an excuse for a
party.

I moved aft, trimmed the main, rolled out the jib, throttled back and
pulled the kill switch to the engine. Under sail by the time we rounded
the outer wall; not bad.

One last wave goodbye. Ease out the sails and bear off to the east. At sea again.

It was windy and beautiful, pale blue sky, white clouds. Monica continued to steer as I coiled dock lines, put away fenders, and tidied up sheets and halyards.

Faial behind us. Pico ahead and to port. Monica was exhilarated and emotional, steering this new boat on a smooth clean reach, tears streaming down her cheeks as she looked back over her shoulder at Horta. I let her settle in a bit, settle into the boat, the wind, the lovely receding island, then started commiserating, said how I'd come to this island the first time and fallen in love with it, apparently our mutual friend Brad had too, it was that kind of island, but she waved a hand to silence me, looked back at Horta one more time.

"The last few days before you came," she said, "were the most wonderful days of my life . . ."

I waited a bit, thinking she'd say more, but she didn't.

"What," I said finally. "You had an affair with Carlos?"

She shook her head. "It wasn't an affair. It didn't go that far. But, Lydia, do you know what it's like to have a man kiss you, and have him trembling?"

She summed up their time together, for herself maybe as much as for me. He'd helped her with the luggage fiasco. He'd driven her around the island. They'd gone to the beach together twice. I later learned from Skyli that the first beach trip had been the day I arrived—Monica had gone to the beach with Carlos, not on a bus tour of the island.

The second trip to the beach, last Saturday, was after they supposedly weren't going to see each other again but he wanted to see her one more time. That was the day he finally kissed her.

"He wasn't just trying to sleep with me, Lydia. It's just that we really got along. We have so much in common."

I wasn't sure how to respond to this. I felt stupid—and insensitive—not to have put things together, her excitement about change, the look on her face as she stirred the Medicine Cards, her resistance to our departure, her subtle rebellion against Brian. I remembered something Skyli had said, about my crew not being truly honest with me; it struck me that Monica must have been telling Skyli and Lisa about Carlos all along, and I felt the odd guy out.

I knew my role as a friend was to listen to her on her own terms, not mine—to provide a non-judgmental ear to her giddy flush of attraction—but I wasn't doing very well with it. She wasn't in love with Faial just for its being Faial. She wasn't caught up in change for the sake of change. She wasn't pulling away from Brian better to know Monica, this was all wrapped up in an attraction to another man. Why the hell did so many women define themselves by the men they were involved with?

She opened up, talked a lot as the afternoon wore on. He was such a gentleman, he hadn't pushed anything. If anyone, it was she who would have wanted to push things. He didn't love his wife, hadn't for years, but he cared enough about his wife and their children that he hadn't wanted things to go further with Monica. This was the first I'd heard about children.

If we'd stayed until Sunday she would have gone to the airport and met his plane.

"With his wife and kids there?" I asked.

"Only his wife. And she wouldn't have had to know anything."

I let her talk. Whatever we were to each other, whatever our relationships were beyond this boat—with each other, with men—we now were sailing together, with nine hundred miles to go to the mainland of Europe.

By late afternoon we were sailing along the southern coast of Pico in a building wind. We reefed *Sonnet* more deeply.

The wind blew hard through the night, then died at five in the morning. Monica was sleeping, I was on watch. The engine wouldn't start when I tried to crank it up, the starter motor turning without response, air in the fuel lines maybe. I waited until dawn, *Sonnet* rolling in the slop, then bled the fuel lines, back and forth between the engine and my Westerbeke manual. I'd never actually *done* this, on this boat.

I wondered, as I worked, if it wouldn't have been easier to wait until Monica was up, if it wouldn't have been more generous, something for her to learn from, but I wanted to be alone in those early hours, so I bled the fuel lines myself, cracked the secondary fuel filter and pumped with the primer pump, same with the injector pump (which bolt?—aha!), cracked an injector, up on deck to turn the engine over, back below to tighten the injector, back on deck and somewhat surprised—

also somewhat queasy, from the swell, from the diesel fumes—when the engine started.

Monica slept peacefully through all of it.

She was up an hour later. At nine I talked to both *Peryton* and *Antelope Medicine* on the SSB, 6 Alpha as planned. Greg and Sascha were about three hundred miles out; Sascha had been miserably seasick since they left and was only now starting to feel better. Skyli and Lisa had left this morning at dawn, and had taken the route north of Pico. Greg had suggested we all head north, almost to the latitude of Lisbon, said there'd be stronger winds there, plus the Portuguese trades and current would set us south. I didn't really care if I had stronger winds—lighter winds would be fine by me—and planned a course not much north of the rhumb line.

The Westerbeke was running fine. I'd been pleased for the first hour it ran and now felt grouchy at having to listen to it. I turned the fort over to Monica and slept for a while, wearing earplugs.

A southwest wind came up by early afternoon and *Sonnet* was back to sailing.

22 Aug

More than twenty-four hours out, and this is the first I've written. We sail peacefully as the sun sinks; I feel no particular inclination to make the boat go faster, though we've talked about putting the gennaker up in the morning if the wind stays so light.

I've concluded that I'm not a very tough sailor, or not in certain realms. I detest motoring; I can't help it, I detest it, the noise, the heat, the smell. I get seasick, especially going to weather. How'm I supposed to get through the Med, if I don't like it flat and I don't like it rough?

Sun sinks slowly, Monica sleeps below. I realize I hesitate writing about her because I'm afraid she might seek out and read this.

The wind died around ten at night and we powered until it came back up at two. In the early morning we put up the gennaker, the first time I'd seen the big light colorful sail except stretched through the dining-room and living-room floors in Glover Park. At nine I talked to *Peryton* and *Antelope Medicine*, plotted their positions as well as our own.

At noon, the GPS gave me a fix but refused to shut off when I punched the on-off button. I dug out the manual and got it shut off by removing the battery pack for a few seconds, then popping it back in. When I turned the unit back on, it agreed to give me my last fix, but not my present one. I loaded the backup clip with fresh batteries, switched clips, and got a dim screen and no readouts. Some buttons beeped when I punched them, others didn't. I decided to deal with it later.

Light breeze, easy sailing.

Jupiter and Venus were in conjunction that night; I showed Monica how you could find this sort of thing in the *Nautical Almanac*. We located them at sunset, two bright planets low on the western horizon.

At 2100 I tried the Magellan again, initializing it as if I'd just taken it out of the box. It accepted the coordinates I entered, and the altitude, then froze. The manual suggested I leave the batteries out for a while and I complied.

Nighttime. Not having to get up at an insistent alarm, sleeping a full three hours. On deck in the dark for watch. Back below again. The cycling of sleeping and waking within a single cycle of the sun. The nature of passage making.

Pushing back quiet waves of discontent.

In the morning the GPS spent forty minutes in sky searches without finding any satellites. I officially gave up on it, and pulled out the sextant.

Another 0900 radio show. *Peryton* was caught in high pressure and no wind; they'd been motoring for thirty hours. *Antelope Medicine* was having engine problems. Same thing as before, water in the oil, after all that work.

24 Aug

1450 Sailing easily with the gennaker up, southwest wind, our third day out, I write less when I'm not alone. A bit tired.
Pleased that I can sleep for hours at a time and not worry, also feel constrained, should be sleeping if Monica's up. Or long for the daylight hours she's sleeping, so the boat is mine alone again. Not many of them.

All in all, not sleeping enough.

She says how happy she is and I'm glad for that, days go by

easily.

Monica wondered why I didn't have a name for my Monitor—Skyli and Lisa called their wind vane Max—and I said maybe it was because I didn't know if it was male or female.

I said I would give her the honor of naming the wind vane. She decided to name it Pat.

1930   Peaceful peaceful sleep at the chart table, only about an hour but so pleasant. And I sit up now to write and Monica starts talking to me; she talks to me the moment she sees my eyes are open; there's got to be a way to make this work.

I need silence, to be alone and listen to I'm not sure what. Right now I need to go on deck and figure out what the wind is doing.

1945   The ocean looks exceptionally huge, no whitecaps, hardly any swell, the textures of two-tone blue, light and shadow. Sun low, sky pale at the horizon, deeper overhead, boat moves slowly, not sure what I'm looking for, not sure.

Certainly not dinner for two, or deciding if powering would be the responsible thing to do, though these are realities, these are part of what comes with the peaceful naps, the four hours' sleep at a stretch in the night.

We should turn on the engine but I don't want to.

2244   Did, after gybing, but that was no better, wind on the stern, light, steer to Africa or steer to France.

Nighttime, stars, a strange formation of cloud spreading from the northeast. Thoughtful tonight, needing time to think, sitting at the stern after Monica went to bed, engine on, autopilot driving, noise and silence, nothing but this boat, this ocean.

Thinking of *Colibri*, feeling that *Colibri* only becomes a complete experience through *Sonnet*, remembering *Colibri*, looking down into the dimly lit interior of *Sonnet*, so different, more solid, more complex, a home. But loving my little ultralight, her swift surges downwind, *no moon, no stars, no instrument lights, nothing . . . steering into nothingness, steering into the universe . . .*

Recognizing the two solo passages as crucial in my life, alone on a sailboat in the middle of an ocean. Completing each other, though I'm not entirely sure how.

I'm never fully at ease with the engine on, fearing bad things, not doing overwhelmingly well in my resolution to think better of it. Diesels *like* to run, prefer to run. Truck drivers leave their engines on in parking lots. So relax, Lydia. Just too many experiences in my sailing career with misbehaving engines.

Monica and I gybed the gennaker at sunset, she was on the wheel, I was handling the sail, and I yelled at her when she didn't keep the boat dead downwind. Feel bad for yelling at her, *was* important, can't gybe the sail with it filling back over on the old side, certainly didn't want it wrapping around the headstay, but the whole maneuver, seemingly from nowhere, left me thinking of Brad for the first time on this boat. It wasn't being yelled at I was remembering (or maybe to some extent it was, in that I learned so incredibly from my mistakes) but just the poetry of maneuvers, the number of times I steered the *Eagle* under spinnaker during gybes, *feeling* it, holding her steady, ten people hustling with lines and poles and sails, steady downwind then head up easy onto the new gybe, Brad standing near the shrouds, orchestrating. The teamwork. The extent to which I knew the boat. Missing it.

25 Aug

0113 For some reason I don't mind powering right now, I'm almost enjoying it. Futzed with the radio, contacted South Bound II to explain about *Antelope Medicine*'s engine problems, no worries about power consumption of a nav shack light. No catnaps this watch, which probably isn't the smartest, but I'm not really tired.

Used to write poetry. Don't now. Don't know why.

The wind came back in the morning, gently out of the west-southwest, partly cloudy skies. We turned off the engine and put up the gennaker. I talked to Skyli and Sascha at nine, telling Skyli not to talk back, except for coordinates, not to waste amperage.

Antelope Medicine was making better time than *Sonnet*, more wind. *Peryton* was still powering, slowly emptying out those huge backup tanks Greg had lashed on deck, working north gradually rather than early like Skyli had done, hardly following his own advice, getting up to the latitude of Lisbon just about in time to drop back down.

Fourth day out.

1015 No ships, little speed, blue sea and sky, happy. Leg exercises, book to read, slosh of water.

1440 This is more than a little unnerving; I'm confident in our position only within about fifteen miles, and this is with a chalkline horizon and no waves. Glad in fact that the Magellan went out sooner rather than later if it had to go out; I've got time to work out the kinks. I'm enjoying the navigating—just not enjoying how it looks when I plot it on a plotting sheet. Hopefully there was a major blooper in the Sirius sight and everything else was pretty close.

Also a bit unnerving that the only how-to celestial guide I have on board is the one I wrote myself. Is there something major I've been doing wrong for years?

It's hard, in fact, to call up the individual days. I worked on navigation. "Pat" steered. Monica and I took turns on watches, no set watch system; we cooked we stood watch we slept we ate we washed dishes. It was good, to have someone else to cook and eat with; the cuisine on *Sonnet* improved immeasurably. We established our little *politesses*, found varied routes around the cabin so as not to run into each other, chose discrete times to use the bucket in the cockpit.

We learned a lot of each other's stories. I learned things about Brian that made me like him more than before. He always encouraged Monica to come with him when he went to conventions, and to use the trips as jump-offs for adventures. She'd been into the interior of China, the Australian outback. In Hawaii she'd been intrigued by tandem parachute jumping, and he'd encouraged her to do it; it was one of the things in her life she was most proud of having done.

She listened to her Walkman a lot, on watch. Danced at the dodger during night watches. Worked on her suntan. I know I wasn't always easy to sail with, but I look at photos and we both seem relaxed, photos we took of each other beneath the brightly colored gennaker, photos of Monica sitting cross-legged on her bunk, looking girlish and pretty, wearing prescription sunglasses rather than contacts, having just woken up. Wearing the rust-colored silky pajamas she wore every time she slept.

26 Aug

1300   Such a different experience than the first leg. Day after day of southwesterlies, five knots, six, flew the gennaker off and on for—what—three days? Took it down today when the breeze picked up but in fact could have left up the bigger sail.

No particular rush.

So it's peaceful sailing but I find myself wondering why I'm doing it. Who I am and what I want. (What's new?) Doing it I suppose because it's the thing I know how to do.

Not peaceful in that I'm totally baffled by the celestial problem. All I can think of is there's some sort of problem with the sextant itself, got banged around when I left it on *Alaska Eagle* last year for students. Sun positions seem to be working fine among themselves, but any star sight is way out of line. Am I working them wrong? SHA star plus GHA Aires; it's perfectly straightforward, search my brain for something big I might be missing and come up with nothing.

Monica had told me, early on in Horta, that she really had no desire to learn celestial navigation, joked about getting a GPS surgically implanted in her thigh. She'd told me that Brian, surprisingly enough, had taken a celestial class and hadn't done very well with it; at that point I'd told her she definitely should learn it herself, something she'd know that he didn't, and she'd started getting excited about the challenge.

I had every intention of teaching her celestial, offshore. I got as far as showing her how to make plotting sheets and how to handle the sextant. I gave her a quick overview of the almanac. And then I stalled. By the fourth day out I was spending enough time poring over sight reduction tables myself not to want to do it with her. I'd spent enough time as an instructor on *Alaska Eagle* to rebel against being one on my own boat. There wasn't much willing instructor left in me; that's part of what the break away from the *Eagle* was all about.

Maybe I owed more to her, celestial lessons and patience, for what she'd done, flown to the Azores to meet me. Maybe she owed more to me, to be there for me when I sailed in alone.

The way she said to me, in a somewhat too sweet voice, "It's so good to see you sleep well," one time right after I woke up. Repeated it when I didn't respond, making sure I heard. Why did that irritate me? Why did I sense she never quite said what she meant? Why did it feel like she was self-conscious about how easily she slept, how hard a time I had waking her up, and came up with "It's so good to see you sleep well" almost as a way of saying, "Ha, you're human, too"? Was I a total louse, to be irritated when she was trying to be nice?

I stared at charts; the distances were starting to feel huge to me. I wondered if I should modify my goals, focus on sailing the boat only as far as Malta, head to Bulgaria for a month or so, send Monica on home, find someone in Sofia to sail the rest of the way with me, maybe Petya, if she didn't have to go back to work.

I broached the idea of Malta with Monica, and she seemed fine with it.

27 Aug

Feeling so astronomically low. Long night watch stretching ahead of me; told Monica I wanted her to get five hours' sleep so she could then let me get five hours. My soul settles slightly in the darkness, alone on the boat, alone awake on the boat, finally got a halfway decent nap, trouble sleeping, trouble dealing, trouble quieting myself.

I'll never feel about this boat the way I felt about *Alaska Eagle*. Grow to love it; I didn't need to grow to love the *Eagle*. Afraid of life. Christ Christ Christ afraid of life, that those powerful pure moments become fewer and fewer, that my father can't even tell the story anymore of his survival at sea, can't write a postcard, can't plant a garden. That my mother is no longer beautiful.

Turn the flashlight off for a while to look for ships, stand in the moonless night, stand under stars, *Sonnet* pushing through the water. Afraid of owning my solo passage only by what I write of it.

Sense of failure, that I'm not a singlehander, not a doublehander, not at all patient with Monica.

I'd tried, in the past few days, to raise several ships on the VHF, and none had responded. That night—Thursday—I finally got a response from a Portuguese freighter, and a position fix, which calmed a bit of my celestial discontent.

In the morning, as expected, only *Antelope Medicine* came up on the SSB. Greg and Sascha had been forty miles off Cabo São Vicente at 0900 the previous day; they no doubt were now snug in a slip in the Algarve marina of Vilamoura, sleeping in.

Sonnet was 280 miles from the Cape, three days or so from Gibraltar. *Antelope Medicine* was 65 miles north-northwest of us. Skyli, in spite of the impressive performance of little *Antelope Medicine*, was sounding roundly discouraged, not at all looking forward to another engineless landfall. She'd decided to go into Vilamoura, get the engine squared away sooner rather than later, she'd have plenty of time to get to Cadiz before the start of the Rally. We agreed to talk again at one o'clock.

As soon as we signed off it hit me: we should meet mid-ocean. Skyli was concerned about her engine, I was fed up with navigating; if we met, she could navigate, and if she was willing to go on to Gibraltar I could tow her into port.

I was antsy for the next few hours, just wanting to get back on the radio, to see what she thought. When we did make contact it turned out she'd been thinking exactly the same thing I had, but hadn't wanted to be the one to suggest it.

We talked it through. Our strategy—since *Antelope Medicine* was so far north of *Sonnet*—was to stay more or less on course, and meet to the east, both boats closer to Portugal. Skyli and Lisa would sail at speed, and Monica and I would slow *Sonnet* down; as we got closer to converging we'd figure out how to find each other. I commented that once we did find each other we'd be a catamaran named SAM. I could hear Lisa laughing in the background; they'd thought of this, too.

By nighttime, the wind had built. It was more than a little discouraging to hold *Sonnet* back when there was good wind for sailing but I did it, jogged along on triple-reefed main and no jib.

In the morning, the wind shifted from southwest to northwest and built further, so we gybed. I decided to sail upwind for a while, partly to help slow us down, partly to see how *Sonnet* handled herself to weather in swells. The plan would take us north of *Antelope Medicine*'s course, but it didn't really matter, we could drop back down.

Sonnet, it turned out, handled herself better than I did; the seas were confused by the wind shift, and I started feeling decidedly queasy. I got a ten-o'clock sun sight as clouds moved in, plotted it fighting nausea, told Monica to wake me at noon if there was a sun to shoot, and curled up on the starboard cockpit seat.

When I woke two hours later we were sailing 30° farther east than when I'd gone to sleep. I asked Monica how long we'd been on this course and she didn't know. She'd always been very good about keeping the boat on a given heading, adjusting helm and sails if the wind shifted, but today we were simply heading into the wind to slow down and it hadn't occurred to her to keep an eye on the compass. She hadn't made a log entry while I slept; we could have been steering this course for five minutes or we could have been steering it for two hours. We could have been steering *any* course for two hours. I explained to her, nicely, that when you don't have a GPS to tell you where you are you've got to pay attention to where you're going. I knew how far we'd gone, from the distance log, but I didn't know in precisely what direction.

We eased out the mainsail and fell off onto a broad reach, a more comfortable angle to the wind for creative thinking than smashing into big seas. I told Monica to maintain a course of 170°, went below, and pored over the plotting sheet.

Our ten-o'clock dead-reckoning position, brought forward from last night's freighter fix, had been seven miles west of my ten-o'clock sun line, a line achieved with a dubious sextant in substantial swells. Not that it made much difference if I knew where I'd been at ten, since I didn't know where I'd gone between ten-thirty and twelve-thirty.

I picked up pencil, dividers, and parallel rules, and launched into the fine art of naviguessing. I plotted where we'd be if the dead reckoning had been correct and we'd been steering 40°, plotted where we'd be if the sun line had been correct and we'd been steering 70°, drew a course of 170° from each dubious position, and ended up with parallel lines, ten miles apart. I figured we'd steer slowly in this direction until the two lines were equidistant from *Antelope Medicine*'s course line, then get onto the same course she was on and take it from there.

The sun made a late-afternoon appearance. I got a 1718 sun line which seemed to agree with the more easterly of my plot lines, though I wasn't going to put money on it.

I talked to Skyli every hour on the SSB, plotted her positions neatly among the spider's web of my own calculations, the hypothetical DRs, the APs and Zns and LOPs of celestial navigation. We'd been trying the VHF radio, but still couldn't hear each other.

By sunset I'd reached *Antelope Medicine*'s course line—more or less— and both boats were steering 110°.

By 2000 we started hearing each other faintly on the short-range, line-of-sight VHF. *Sonnet* was maybe fifteen or twenty miles ahead of *Antelope Medicine*, and hopefully no more than five miles to the north or the south. According to my brilliant calculations, they'd catch up to us sooner if to the south, later if to the north.

We agreed to watch for ships, weird cloud formations, anything we could use to confirm our relative positions; we would monitor channel 72. I had a crappy little VHF with a nonfunctioning squelch dial, one of the pieces of equipment I should have replaced but didn't; if you wanted to monitor a channel you had to listen to nonstop static. Somehow, I didn't mind.

Monica and I sailed as slowly as we could, strapping the triple-reefed main in to centerline. I didn't want to heave-to or we'd drift off to leeward.

We talked with *Antelope Medicine* every hour on the VHF. Our reception kept getting better, which was a lucky thing since I was starting to look at my plotting sheet and wonder who I was kidding. Every hour, once it was dark, I put on *Sonnet*'s strobe for a minute, and Lisa or Skyli scanned the horizon. Nothing.

Around 0200 I looked out and saw the lights of a plane. It was flying nearly due west, slightly to the north of *Sonnet*. I got on the radio post-haste and reported its existence.

Seconds later Skyli was back on the VHF. The plane was approaching, passing directly overhead.

Yes. We adjusted *Sonnet*'s course a bit north, and sailed that way for two hours. At four we straightened back out to the same course as *Antelope Medicine*. I told Skyli I would flip on my strobe for twenty seconds, starting twenty seconds from now.

I looked at my watch, flipped on the switch, flipped it off, went back to the radio. A brief pause, then Skyli's voice: "Will you get out of my way?"

We'd actually pulled this off.

Monica retired below. It had been a while since either of us had had any bona-fide sleep, and it would be hours before *Antelope Medicine* caught up. I catnapped in the cockpit, setting the alarm for every fifteen minutes, getting up and looking hard behind us. Skyli was using an emergency strobe for a navigation light, but I couldn't see it.

Nap, get up, look behind us, nap again. When I got up in the brightening dawn the horizon behind us looked empty. The next time I got up the sky was fully light.

I looked and saw nothing. Had we somehow screwed this up? I looked again, carefully. I'll be damned! Tiny little triangle, straight behind us, just where she belonged. Long straight horizon and one tiny boat.

Monica and I breakfasted in the cockpit, watching *Antelope Medicine*'s steady approach. She seemed so small, seemed to be gaining so slowly, and then Skyli and Lisa surprised us, closed the final distance before we knew it. By the time we scrambled to get the sails up and trimmed, it was *Sonnet* chasing *Antelope Medicine*.

At 0900 I plotted the first position of SAM.

It was wonderful fun, sailing the two boats together out on that deep blue sea, under blue sky and clouds, sailing so closely we could chat in normal voices. Monica and I sailed circles around *Antelope Medicine*, just for the hell of it, blocked her wind to windward and pulled ahead, fell off across her bow, trimmed in and slid into her wind shadow, reached up across her stern and started again; the boats were like two graceful animals, playing.

After a while we put in *Sonnet*'s second reef and the animals separated to a somewhat more sensible distance, pacing each other, content just to be in each other's company.

Skyli and I pulled out charts and got on the VHF, discussing whether to go inside or outside the shipping lanes around Cabo São Vicente, now some fifty miles to the east. We decided on outside, and adjusted course accordingly.

By 1730 we were twenty miles south of the cape, some five miles south of the shipping lanes. I asked Monica to start the Westerbeke to charge the batteries. The engine had been running for about five minutes when it started making a horrible noise. I yelled to Monica, who pulled the kill switch.

What *now?* I opened up the engine cover, saw nothing. I went on deck, turned the key. The engine made a horrible noise again, so I let go.

At that point I realized I should have noticed the position of the key before I turned it. We'd been careful, every time we started the engine, to make sure the key was back to vertical, though in fact it seemed to be springing back okay on its own. I asked Monica if she'd remembered to check the key, and she was pretty sure she had.

I contacted Skyli, told her *SAM* was two engines down.

At 2000 the wind came up, still northwest. Skyli called, said she and Lisa were planning to reef.

By now we were keeping track of each other by nav lights in the dark. Monica and I weren't close enough to see what was happening on *Antelope Medicine*, but the reefing project was taking longer than it should have. We sailed closer. The strobe traced an arc, the boat wallowing. A brighter, steadier light came on, moving around on deck; Skyli's rechargeable spotlight, which she'd no doubt been reserving for an emergency.

Lisa called. The topping lift which supported the boom had broken. They were getting together the tools they needed to fix it.

The night was pitch-black, the wind building. Monica and I rolled in *Sonnet*'s jib and beam-reached back and forth near *Antelope Medicine*, sailing away until her spotlight and strobe grew small behind us, heaving between waves through a tack and heading back, drawing closer in that blackened night until the light regathered into details, pitching deck, shadowy figures working against the roll. Sweeping past, sailing away, tacking back; the healthy animal keeping watch over the faltering one.

The repairs took nearly an hour. By the time we were ready to get back under way we had twenty-five knots of wind. To head in a blow into the narrow Strait of Gibraltar—without an engine between us, in strong currents and some of the busiest shipping in the world—seemed injudicious. I called Skyli and suggested we head for Vilamoura—thirty-five miles to the north-northeast, close-hauled across the shipping lanes—and she sounded relieved.

Monica and I reefed *Sonnet* to the third reef. We rolled the little genoa back out to half its normal size, sheeting it inside the shrouds. Lisa and Skyli rigged their second headstay for the "gust-buster" heavy-weather jib.

It was exceedingly tough to stay together, with two such different boats in that kind of wind; we finally agreed to make our own ways through the shipping lanes, and *Sonnet* pulled ahead.

Within an hour Monica and I were seeing three eastbound freighters, one behind the other. White range lights and green side light on the two that hadn't passed us, a blossoming of white lights on the stern of the one that had. Beyond them, seeming smaller, white lights and red on two ships traveling west.

All three eastbound freighters crossed ahead of us; we got through their lane behind the last of them, looked left at another, distant but bearing down. I could no longer see *Antelope Medicine*, just hoped she was doing okay out here in the wind.

Three vessels ahead of us now in the westbound lane. No way to thread between them, no way I'd feel comfortable risking it, and I didn't want to lose ground by bearing away behind the final ship. We tacked into the protection of the two-mile-wide separation zone, tacked through some 150°, but at least we were safe in here, parades of freighters on either side of us, stern lights receding, side lights and range lights approaching, ships to the north and ships to the south, out there in the windy dark.

I was not happy in the shipping lanes off the coast of Portugal. I found myself fighting resentment, aware that we could have been nearly to Gibraltar if we hadn't slowed down, trying to remember why meeting and sailing with *Antelope Medicine* had sounded like such a great idea. Soaked and salty from deck work, exhausted, way too short on sleep. Doubtful, not feeling resilient and not wanting to feel resilient, not wanting to figure out what was wrong with my engine, not wanting to be where I was, not enjoying it, not remembering enjoying hardly any of this passage. Not believing in anything, not in adventure not in life, sailing exhausted in the dark with ships everywhere, on a highway of ships in the wind.

And then, off to starboard, I saw a tiny blinking strobe—dim among the bright lights of freighters—and instantly everything made sense. *Antelope Medicine* out there in the night, vulnerable and tough. That other person out there in the night, that other person with whom I had connection, the tiny pulsing light, and everything was right, the changes of plans were right, the resentment was gone, the discomfort bearable.

I don't remember how long we stayed in the separation zone; our log-keeping by now had deteriorated. I barely remember cutting through the westbound ships when a reasonable gap presented itself. By the time we cleared the shipping lanes the wind had started to moderate; we rolled out the jib and shook out the reefs, Monica went below for some sleep.

By dawn we were virtually becalmed, and my exhaustion was catching up with me. This wasn't a single night with hardly any sleep, a single night cold and wet and faced with big decisions. This was one night on top of nine nights on top of months.

30 Aug

Drifting off the Algarve coast of Portugal. *Antelope Medicine* is the tiniest of sails off my stern, two birds with clipped white wings.

The night Skyli and I talked I felt strong, I felt focused, I felt purposeful. Saw her doubts about herself—Skyli who has every reason to be confident—and related to them, but felt I'd taken an onward step, somehow clawed my way clear and could maybe even help her do the same. This morning, last night, the depth of my doubt has been fathomless.

But I'm not the same person I was when I first crossed this ocean. This is not the same world. This boat is not the answer to all of my dreams but neither is it a mistake.

Tough passage, in a totally different way than sailing alone. Fighting demons, not big seas.

This adult self does not feel those moments of awe as often but occasionally she feels them. She doesn't feel hopeful about the world hardly at all. She's who she is. She's who she'll be.

Monica is up; harder now to write.

That one moment, then, in the shipping lanes, even though it was followed this morning by utter lows. That one moment when nothing existed but darkness and ships and wind and I saw the tiny blinking strobe. At some point I'll try to write it better but there it is.

And here is this: I need exhaustion sometimes, I need crises, I need them because my mind finds its way to a different kind of clarity.

I turned the boat over to Monica, told her we wanted to steer 035° magnetic, explained that she might not be able to keep that course— I'd been steering anything from 035° to 050° close-hauled on port tack— but should try. We were hardly moving; I went below to try to sleep.

I slept, but not well. At some point we started to sail. A while after that I heard Monica adjusting the sails and the Monitor; I thought about going up to see if she needed help, but decided against it, decided this was good for her, she was taking initiative, feeling in control, feeling good about herself. I went back to sleep.

An hour later I heard her on the VHF, talking to *Antelope Medicine*. She sounded relaxed, happy, saying Lydia will be amazed when she gets up, we're moving right along, it's a totally different boat. Then saying, same cheery tone, Do you have any idea where I am?

I pretended to sleep a few minutes longer so it didn't look like I'd leapt up because I didn't trust her, then stretched, climbed out of my bunk, wandered up the companionway, and looked around.

We were moving at a good four knots. She had her Walkman on, dancing a bit in the cockpit. We seemed to be sailing well to the west of the direction of Vilamoura. I looked at the compass. 355°, forty degrees off-course. *Antelope Medicine* was nowhere to be seen.

"What've you been steering?" I asked, trying to sound casual.

She took off her earphones—I could hear their tinny beat—and looked at the compass. "355. But it's varied. I was steering 45 for a while after you went to bed. The wind shifted, so I followed it around."

Followed it around? Our course was supposed to be 035°...

Maybe it's a complicated concept, if you've never navigated. Say you want to steer north. If the wind's coming from the north you won't be able to steer that way, you'll have to steer northeast. If the wind shifts to the northwest that's great, you can steer where you want to be steering. If the wind keeps shifting, goes to the west, you can steer northwest but you don't *want* to, the whole idea in the first place was to steer north. If the wind shifts to south you can steer north. If the wind shifts to east you can steer north. Change the sails, but steer north.

And this: whatever you steer, if you don't keep track of it, at the end of the day you'll have no idea where you are. After a couple of hours sleeping, I had no idea where we were. I thought Monica and I had been through this, the day we were waiting for Skyli.

It was hard for me to process how little Monica understood about sailing. She was comfortable on a boat, at ease at the helm, at handling sails, and it seemed that she *should* understand about sailing, she'd been doing it for years. It was hard to process what she did and didn't know because she was extremely good at covering, saying yes she understood when she didn't, as if appearance were more important than comprehension. I supposed it was a common female defense mechanism, fine-tuned to avoid criticism from men, but it seemed out of place on a boat with only women.

I tried not to make a big deal about the course thing. I figured if we found Skyli, she could help us find our way in; if not, I could determine our position once we got closer by taking bearings on charted details of the coast. I set a course somewhat east of what I'd calculated earlier and left it at that.

We started sailing a bit better, and before long spotted *Antelope Medicine* angling in on our right. As we got close enough to shore to see details I got on the radio with Skyli, who walked me visually along the Algarve until I was pointing my bow the same place she—with the aid of GPS—was pointing hers.

By 1400 we could pick out, with binoculars, the striped towers at the entrance to Vilamoura. The wind had filled in substantially. Skyli had fallen behind. At 1500 I switched the VHF to channel 16, planning to make an any-vessel call and request information about the marina from someone already inside. Before I could pick up the mike I heard a woman's voice—very American—say, "Vilamoura marina, this is *Cardiff*."

The marina requested she switch to channel 12. I switched when they did, and listened in. *Cardiff* was given instructions to come onto the reception dock. As soon as the marina signed off, I clicked on the mike. "*Cardiff, Cardiff*. This is *Sonnet*."

Cardiff came back. We arranged to talk in five minutes, once they were secure on the dock.

Back on deck. Sail past the harbor entrance, take a look inside, as I had with Horta. An outer harbor, a narrow neck where the reception dock was, an inner, cramped marina. Dicey. Good plan to stay outside until I talked to *Cardiff* and decided on a strategy.

Back below for my radio date. I explained our situation, asked what the wind angle was like inside, how high the dock was so I knew how to place my fenders, whether there were bollards or cleats. The woman on *Cardiff* was marvelous. She described the dock in detail, told me the wind would be behind us on our approach. *Cardiff* was the only boat just now on the reception dock; she'd let me know as soon as they were off, so we'd have plenty of room to work with.

Back on deck. Dock lines out of the lazarette, main halyard ready to go, wind approaching twenty knots and building. Working in wind and spray. I figured the best plan for slowing us down on the dock would be an aft spring line; I set up a block amidships and led a line aft to a winch I could handle from the helm. Monica would hop off with this spring line, get it on a bollard, then deal with the less crucial bow and stern lines.

Dock lines ready to go. *Cardiff* called to tell us the reception dock was empty.

By now we'd sailed well past the marina entrance to the west. I pulled down the main, furled it somewhat messily, and took over the helm from Monica. We gybed back around, beam-reached on jib alone around the end of the breakwater, then turned and headed down through the harbor with the wind on our stern.

Fishing boats moored to port, reception dock and main marina ahead of us. I was astonished at how fast we were moving, and rolled in most of the jib. We were still moving too fast, so I rolled it in the rest of the way, holding the wheel with one hand, hauling in the furling line with the other. Monica was stationed at the port beam with the dock lines, looking nervously from me to the long dock some five hundred yards ahead of us.

Bare poles. I started swearing, just to release some adrenaline, out loud and full-force, cursing the wind, cursing our speed. "We're moving too fucking *fast* . . ."

I tried to slow the boat down by steering a serpentine course, but it didn't work as well with *Sonnet* as it worked with fin-keeled boats, she responded too slowly, too sluggishly, you risked losing control.

Closer, straightening out for the approach, slow but I wished it were slower, wind pushing us hard, a man on the dock waiting, Monica handing him the spring line rather than hopping onto the dock, me yelling to him which bollard I wanted the line on, him tossing the line on the bollard, realization spreading over his face that we had no engine, that there were only the two of us, me slowing the boat with the spring line, easing out the wraps on the winch, easing, easing, trying to keep the boat straight with the wheel as the line went out, almost to the end of the line as we slowed to a stop.

7

He catches early light there by the stream,
flips the first trout out, its mottled skin
glistens. He holds it, doubting refuge in
a world where what you leave behind won't seem
to stay there. Finally real, his long-time dream
of camping with his daughter wavers when
he's victim to this moodiness. The wind
is light. The sun touches wet rocks, lets steam
ease off them. Zipped into the morning, their last,
she thinks of times when she was small, the way
she'd wake up early, hurry, dress, to walk
with him. She doesn't want to hurt him, lock
his child away, but can't quite seem to say
the words he longs for. Static, she watches him cast.

"Backcountry Camping," 1978

Sonnet had crossed the ocean. I had sailed her—this, my own boat—
from the New World to the Old. Monica had completed the most ambitious passage of her sailing career.

Somehow those achievements weren't registering. I was exhausted,
bone-deep. I was busy putting off the assorted Vilamoura officials and
their assorted official forms, explaining that some friends were outside
the harbor, also on a boat without an engine, that I wanted to help
them come onto the dock, I'd clear customs and immigration as soon
as they were in.

I raised *Antelope Medicine* on the VHF, described what the harbor
was like, described the spring-line setup we'd used, said there was

plenty of room for them on the reception dock right now, we'd be waiting to help.

The wind was still building. A sloop came in behind *Sonnet*. A bit after that, a big square-rigger came in, in front of us, nearly taking out *Sonnet*'s headstay with her bowsprit, her engines nearly useless in the wind.

Monica and I helped get her straightened out. I paced the dock. Where was *Antelope Medicine* supposed to go? There was room behind the sloop, but not much, no margin for error.

I talked to the skipper of the square-rigger, explained about my friends, asked if they could go along his starboard side. He said of course. I talked to a marina man. He shrugged; the square-rigger idea was as good as any. I called Skyli again and explained the new scenario. She and Lisa were still getting dock lines ready, getting the mainsail down. It was nasty out there. It'd be a few minutes yet.

I was like a caged animal, prowling the dock, prowling the deck of the square-rigger, organizing people to take lines, waiting to see a boat with a yellow-bordered jib enter the harbor. The skipper of the square-rigger finally gave me a glass of wine, which didn't much help.

And then she was on her way in, scooting along with a little scrap of headsail. Monica had wandered down the dock a few minutes before and hadn't come back to her post. I yelled, "What's going on?"

"They're going to put them on the end here," she called back. "They have a boat out there to help."

If they'd told *her*, why hadn't she told *me*? I flung myself off the square-rigger and down the dock, irrationally furious.

Watching them come in, a bit too fast, a bit too far to port, risking ramming the dock rather than coming alongside it. Feeling helpless; nothing I could do, no way even to yell suggestions over the wind, assuming I'd had any.

A launch out there, receiving a line from *Antelope Medicine*, slowing her down at the last moment. Monica and me fending off the bow. A bit of shouting, bit of maneuvering, and they were alongside.

Dock lines. Fenders. Skyli and Lisa spilling, finally, onto the dock.

Skyli was high and exhausted, ecstatic at having sailed across the ocean, at having done this thing she'd set out to do; also furious at herself, in hindsight, for risking her boat on the lee shore of the breakwater, for not just waiting offshore when the wind kept building.

·

At which point I was struck by a new reality, all my advice on how to come in and the best advice might have been not to come in at all.

Lisa, who until now had looked windblown but more or less composed, inexplicably burst into tears, then assured us it was wonderful to burst into tears, just what she needed after such incredible pressure, like an orgasm, a marvelous release. Crying, laughing, the tears intensifying the blueness of her eyes.

We'd all been short on sleep a bit too long.

Skyli and I headed up to the offices. I made it part way through my paperwork—almost to the point of being assigned a slip—and then completely and utterly fell apart. I think I even said to Skyli, "I think I'm about to fall apart," went back down to *Sonnet* and didn't reemerge for nearly an hour.

There've been three or four of these in my life, these major cries, which start in one place but won't stay there, and won't let me go.

It was somehow not being there for Skyli, though that certainly wasn't her perception.

It was having crossed an ocean without feeling a flush of success. It was doing this thing I'd wanted so intensely to do, without really feeling I'd done it.

It was my parents, being on the same continent, the same peninsula as my parents. It was everything their problems had meant, my entire life. It was everything new, the past few years, my dad's slipping memory, the shift of emphasis.

It was Oscar, though somehow I recognized as I sobbed that the absence of hope which I associated with the loss of my cat in fact had started sooner, started with the light brown dog with the pale yellow eye lying on the street in Georgetown, breathing fast and shallow, blood on the asphalt by his mouth, the man who'd hit him baffled and ineffectual, me trying to find the owner, trying to call vets from a scuzzy student apartment, coming back down to the street to find the dog had died, the yellow eye still open, the position unchanged, the strange ethereal stillness. Started with the riots in L.A., sitting in the car in the parking lot of a marine-supply store in Annapolis listening to the news, remembering the '65 riots in Watts, an era when I believed tumult could lead to catharsis, could lead to change.

It was the world, the sense of it out there and around me, a world with Bosnias and Somalias, way too big for me to grasp.

It was all of it and none of it, as if despair were an inevitable force and my soul was grasping for explanations, as if images were waiting quietly in line to step forward and claim their share of a crying that wouldn't stop.

I don't know where I started to cry, but I ended up sitting on the teak-and-holly floorboards, wedged between the starboard bunk and the mast, my face against the mast's cool white smoothness. Image after image. Afraid because these images were always there, and I didn't understand the difference between the times that I could live with them and the times that I couldn't.

At one point Monica showed up, worried, asking if she was somehow the cause of this, and I managed to say no, I'm just like this, sometimes I have to go through this.

In the end I found my way up to the marina office, the crisis resolving in part because the office was on the verge of closing.

Skyli and Lisa had already moved *Antelope Medicine*. Skyli had come back to the clearance dock to help me if I needed it, had even insisted on a slip for *Sonnet* on the same dock as *Antelope Medicine*. Some young people in a dinghy had given her a tow to the docks and then been scolded by the port people, who preferred to do the towing themselves for a hefty price. The whole of Vilamoura was a shock after Horta, the cost of a slip, no sense of welcome. The skipper of the square-rigger said no one had told *him* not to help us move our boat, and he had a nice hard dinghy with an outboard, so we set up a tow surreptitiously.

The focus of moving the boat was good for me. We lashed the dinghy to *Sonnet*'s starboard quarter rather than towing with a bow line, a technique I'd learned on *Alaska Eagle*, more power and control. The turn into Dock S at Vilamoura was tight—constrained by shallow water, made difficult by wind—but we slid *Sonnet* in, then squared away dock lines and fenders, familiar, comforting tasks.

I made it through until evening, still fighting demons. By the time the four of us headed out to dinner I could joke about it, joke about falling apart, but it was only as we shared a meal, as Atlantic-passage anecdotes tumbled out, as I looked at the faces of Skyli and Monica and Lisa, that I realized we'd all done a pretty impressive thing.

I felt bad that I hadn't exactly made a fuss over landfall, for Monica's sake. I'd kind of screwed up on the "doing it for Monica" resolution. Maybe I'd expected too much of her; I realized how little Lisa knew about navigation, about sail trim, any of it, and it didn't make her any less proud—justifiably so—of having crossed an ocean on a small sailboat. I resolved to be more of an ear to Monica, to be receptive if she wanted to talk about this accomplishment.

Unfortunately, what she wanted to talk about when we got back to *Sonnet* was Carlos. She was sure he'd be impressed by what she'd done, asked me if I thought she should call him. When I said, "Were you planning on calling Brian?" it came out more snippy than I'd intended.

We didn't talk much more before going to bed.

In the morning, I felt like a jerk. This woman had made a lot of sacrifices on my behalf. She'd made a major double-handed ocean passage, one she'd looked forward to for months, but rather than celebrating with her I'd fallen apart the minute we hit the dock. She was elated about a love interest, and I'd gone and gotten judgmental about it.

I'd slept in the forepeak. She was gone when I got up. I left her a note before heading up to the harbor office, told her I was sorry I was being such a pain, maybe we could just go out to lunch together, do something fun.

When I got back from a round of errands my note to Monica was gone. Monica was gone again, too. I was doing great, still nearly two thousand miles from my destination, stuck in a place I didn't want to be with an engine that didn't want to work and an alienated crew.

One step at a time.

I wrestled the cover off the Westerbeke, stared at it with a mix of despair and mistrust, then hopped off the boat and walked down to *Antelope Medicine*. Lisa was in town checking on flights to the States. I asked Skyli if she'd come listen while I turned my key, see if she thought this sounded like starter motor failure. She said she was no expert, but of course she'd help if she could, and we walked together back to *Sonnet*.

She stationed herself below; I stationed myself behind the wheel. With trepidation, hoping I wasn't injuring my starter irreparably, I turned the key for just a split second. The engine didn't sound all that bad, all that unusual. Skyli made me try the key and not let go this time; four seconds, five seconds, six. The engine turned over.

I felt like an idiot. She thought it was funny. We let the engine run, to charge the batteries, and talked it through. Likely as not, what happened south of the Cape was basically the same thing that had happened on my solo passage. Monica had forgotten to turn the key back to up-right, the switch had stuck, and the starter motor had continued turning, eventually heating up and binding up, making the awful noise. This time the solenoid hadn't been damaged, maybe because it and its wire were new and strong, so the noise I'd heard when I'd tried to restart the engine was either the starter motor working itself back into position or—not entirely unlikely—a figment of my imagination.

I felt like an idiot not to have tried the engine again offshore, to have gone through that dangerous, stress-inducing engineless docking. I had a serious attitude problem toward the Westerbeke, almost expecting it to fail me. The amazing thing was, I didn't feel judged by Skyli.

And I didn't feel lectured by her, when she gave me some helpful hints. Clean the sucker; she had some good cleaner she'd contribute to the cause. Get the engine as spotless as you can, so it's easier to spot problems when they arise. She said the engine cover looked cumber-some; how'd I get it off under way to check my fluid levels? I rarely *checked* my fluid levels under way . . . ?

I'd left a note at the mechanic's shop, saying that both *Sonnet* and *Antelope Medicine* might be interested in his services; while Skyli and I were talking he arrived at *Sonnet* with a young "English-speaking" as-sistant. I shut down the Westerbeke. We all retreated to *Antelope Med-icine*, and were looking over the Perkins and plowing through language barriers when Monica showed up. I suggested we maybe put off our lunch out until tomorrow, since it was getting kind of late, and Monica said okay. I got her involved in the engine discussion, and then she and I had sandwiches together on *Sonnet*, getting along fine. After lunch I headed for the telephones by the shops-and-restaurants complex at the far end of the marina, a fifteen-minute walk from Dock S.

I'd already tried in the morning to call Steve; some of the pay phones supposedly took credit cards, but I hadn't been able to get any of them to work. It was late enough now to call California; I called Beth using my AT&T number, getting her message machine, telling her I was safely on the mainland of Europe and asking her to call Steve. Next I called my contact at Magellan, explained the problems I was having with my GPS. He wanted to run the symptoms past one of his technical types and asked that I call back in an hour.

I then managed to place a collect call to La Pajarera.

Mom answered. The condition she was in when she answered

shouldn't have surprised me—I was bound to call and find her like this sometime on this voyage—but it hit me like a physical blow. She was completely drunk, virtually incoherent.

I don't remember much of the conversation. I remember yelling, "I sailed across the fucking ocean, and this is what I find . . ."

"I know you sailed across the *fucking* ocean," she spat back. Astonishing, the way she could slur words and spit them at the same time.

It wasn't the first time we'd yelled at each other on the phone. One of us finally hung up on the other; I'm not sure which.

What was I expecting, anyway, in my quiet child's soul of souls? That she'd be sober when I called, because I needed it? That she'd quit drinking out of sheer pride in her younger daughter, when in fact when she wasn't oblivious to my adventures they gave her a good excuse to get upset, along with my sister Layne and her four and a half children and missionary husband in a tiny apartment in Amman?

Was that why I'd sailed across the fucking ocean, because I thought it would make her change? Was that all any of this amounted to, a stunt fitting neatly into the profile of an Adult Child of an Alcoholic?

The Hero. The Overachiever.

I walked awhile among the warren-like shops—more of them empty than occupied—then down the east side of the marina to the big hotel, which was hosting some kind of convention and was closed to the public. Again I was struck by how different this place was from Horta, commerce coerced to grow out of a master-planned marina, rather than a marina that had grown naturally out of a vital, waterfront town. What was I doing here, anyway?

I walked, feeling trapped and forlorn, reminding myself I'd be gone in a couple of days, this wasn't like Maryland, or Horta, the boat was basically sound, I could pretty much head back out, though heading back out took me to Gibraltar, to my parents' front yard.

There was something else going on, and I wasn't sure if it made things easier or harder: I wanted Skyli to help sail *Sonnet* to Gibraltar. Lisa was leaving for the States as soon as she could get a flight, Steven Morgan wasn't flying down from England for more than a week, and I was pretty sure she'd make the hundred-mile sail if I asked her.

If I did, would it be way too hard on Monica? Would Monica feel threatened by Skyli, who had so much more in common with me than she did? Should I not ask Skyli, for Monica's sake? Should I not only ask her but push hard for her to come? Shouldn't the three of us just be able to go sailing?

I headed back to the phones, called Magellan, learned that my unit was irreparable but that Shepherd's—the big Gibraltar chandler—could replace it. I wasn't ready to go back to the boat, so I walked to Dock H, where *Cardiff* was, to thank them for their help when we came in.

The boat was a big ketch, immaculate. A man was sitting in the cockpit, in his fifties maybe, salt-and-pepper hair, roughly attractive. A woman emerged from below when she heard us talking, attractive too, younger than him by a bit, tall and slender, her thick short hair prematurely gray. They introduced themselves as Dean and Carol.

I thanked Carol for yesterday. She said not at all. They invited me on board, offered me a glass of wine, said they'd watched me come onto the customs dock, assumed I'd gotten my engine working, as smoothly as I'd come in without sails. I told them with some embarrassment that I had in fact gotten my engine working, but not until today, the docking had been engineless.

We talked, sailors' talk. Dean told a story about nearly getting hit by a freighter, seemed almost proud of his insistence on right-of-way, how he'd maintained course and speed (he'd finally tacked; if he hadn't, they might not be sitting here), during which story Carol pretty much kept her gaze down and her mouth shut. I felt like waving at her and saying, "You're *right*. There's no such thing as right-of-way out there," but I didn't.

His interest was piqued when he heard I'd sailed alone to the Azores; he was intrigued by what makes a solo sailor tick, why people do it. We talked about destinations; they were heading into the Med and planned to winter in Spain. I brought up Skyli's saltwater-in-the-oil problem, and that piqued Dean's interest, too; he had some ideas on what might have caused it, said he'd come by in the morning and take a look.

In the evening, I mentioned to Monica the idea of Skyli sailing with us to Gibraltar. She said how great it would be. About the fifth time she said that in the course of the evening, the forced brightness, I said I'm glad you feel that way but it surprises me a little, in fact I feel a little bad suggesting it, if I were you I wouldn't be all that thrilled, and she conceded that yes, in ways it would be hard, she'd read somewhere that doing anything with three women was more difficult and complicated than doing it with two women, but in other ways it would be great.

I wanted to push her somehow, shake her, wanted to say: *Admit* it, having Skyli on board would feel threatening to you, don't lie, not to me, not to yourself. I left it as it was, not sure I was doing the right thing.

In the morning when I got up she'd left me a note, very sweet. She said she was sorry if she was being difficult, pretty much echoing my note of the morning before. She said she didn't quite know how to handle women friends, didn't know the right thing to say. She said let's have lunch today for sure. And she said, from now on, she'd rather not talk about Carlos.

I walked over to *Antelope Medicine*. Dean was in the cockpit talking with Skyli, Carol below with Lisa. I got just a glimpse of the two women below, leaning across the table from each other; Lisa was listening and Carol was speaking quietly, shaking her head. I felt a strange pang; in reality, I didn't know what to say to other women any more than Monica did.

I had no problem sliding into the conversation in the cockpit. Dean's theory was that Skyli's raw-water pump was the culprit; he figured that if the seals in the pump and behind the engine failed at the same time you could potentially get water in the crankcase. Monica showed up. Lisa and Carol emerged; Carol looked a bit like she'd been crying. Lisa and Monica made plans to go into town together later on; Lisa wanted to restock *Antelope Medicine*'s galley before she left tomorrow morning, and Monica had volunteered to provision for our mini-passage through the Strait.

I asked Skyli if she wanted to sail with Monica and me to Gibraltar, figuring this was a good time to ask since her answer would affect the provisioning plans. She smiled slightly, said she had to admit the idea had crossed her mind. Lisa was instantly excited, said how great that would be, and I couldn't quite define why I believed her when she said it in a way I hadn't believed Monica.

When lunchtime rolled around, Monica and I headed for a restaurant in the harbor complex. I wanted the meal to be comfortable, un-weighted. Monica started in again about Skyli—how good it would be to have her along—but on a slightly new tack. She said she hoped Skyli understood about *Sonnet*, that we didn't use the toilet offshore, didn't have pressure water. Said it more than once. I was intrigued by her concern, since I never gave a second thought to these details. I *liked* washing dishes with saltwater in the cockpit; the view was much nicer up there than down below. Come to think of it, I rather liked the bucket, for the same reason. Skyli had spent many a night camping in the Sierra; my guess was that she didn't feel a compelling need for flush toilets. I wasn't sure if Monica really thought *Sonnet*'s facilities would upset Skyli or if she was trying to communicate what a challenge they'd been to her.

I wasn't sure she really knew, herself.

We went to work cleaning the engine when we got back to the boat. About twenty minutes into the project I dropped a screwdriver into the bilge, then proceeded to get myself both filthy and worked up, lying on my side digging around blindly in the oily engine bilge trying to find it. Monica hovering over me didn't help. I decided I needed a break, went up on deck and onto the dock to wash my hands.

She had a habit of saying "uh-*huh*," or "I know," always in just the same tone, which bothered me more than it should have. She'd followed me as far as the cockpit. Two little local boys converged on me at the faucet, watching me from point-blank range as I washed my hands, then trailing me back to the boat. *Not* what I was in the mood for.

"You have a couple of shadows," Monica said. It was crystal-clear from her tone that she found them thoroughly cute, and imagined I did, too.

I said, very testily, "I could do without them," and she said, "I know." Said it for the umpteenth time that day.

I handed her the soap and told her I thought I'd take a five-minute walk.

I headed down the dock. Skyli was on the bow of *Antelope Medicine*, and looked up cheerfully as I approached.

"My crew is driving me crazy," I said.

Her expression changed to amused sympathy. "Poor baby," she said.

I shook my head and kept walking, stretched my legs for five minutes and then walked back.

Monica was waiting for me in *Sonnet*'s cockpit, a smile like an angel's on her face. She held up the screwdriver triumphantly.

"You *found* it," I said. "That's great."

She said, "I found it on the very first try."

She told me how she hadn't wanted to put her hand down in that dirty bilge but wanted so badly to find the screwdriver for me. She'd closed her eyes and said a little prayer. "It's like my hand was guided right to it."

I thanked her profusely, and meant it. She'd seen my foul mood, and wanted to make things right, and was incredibly pleased to have succeeded.

I was grateful, but I also saw such a potential for a pattern here, a pattern I didn't like, likely to keep repeating. I would get along with Monica, and then get exasperated, maybe lash out at her, then feel guilty for my exasperation, and the whole cycle would start again.

It might be easy to say: Just go with it. Just keep trying. Just sail with her as far as Malta. But it was so tough on a boat, a boat was such a pressure cooker. We were just too different. I couldn't see that she would change, or that I would. I couldn't believe that staying together on the boat would be a smart thing for either of us.

She left on her outing with Lisa. They came back laughing; Lisa had been giving pointers to Monica on what to feed Skyli, get carbos into her fast if she's starting to get a headache, and you'll know when she doesn't like something, she starts chewing slowly with her lip curled and her mouth open, like a five-year-old forced to eat spinach. Don't give her bananas. Whatever you do, don't give her almonds, she's hated almonds all her life.

They came back with goodies for both boats, and again I felt grateful, but still resolved.

1 Sept

Holed up in my forepeak, Monica already asleep. Incredible relief, just to have opened the possibility that it might not be best for her to sail all the way to Malta, that once we get to Gibraltar maybe we should reassess.

Said, "Monica, I'm worried about something." Heart thumping at bringing it up. Said I didn't want things to go wrong, didn't want to keep sailing together when it wasn't really right and then split up in Malta disliking each other. Told her I felt close to her, that I didn't want to push it too far and ruin things. Told her that I was worried because the week in proximity to my parents was going to be tough for me and I'm not very good at accepting support, need to be left alone, and she said maybe it would be a good time for her to take off on her own for a little, spend a few days in Gib, then take a tour of Spain, which in fact might be enough, maybe after a break from each other we could blast on through to Malta.

I don't, right now, feel very close to her. Don't like the fact that I wasn't really telling the truth, to tell her I did. Don't like it because it's what I've told her upsets me in her, that hedging of honesty. Wanting to be with people to whom I don't need to be false.

The morning went something like this: Lisa left for the States. Skyli got up early and walked Lisa to the airport bus, which only gave her a few hours alone on her own boat before moving onto mine. Monica woke up before I did, went over to *Antelope Medicine*, and told a tale of woe, dragging Skyli into *Sonnet*'s internal politics before Skyli even became an official member of the crew. I woke up. Monica returned to *Sonnet* and we shared a good-natured breakfast before she headed off to make phone calls. I stopped by *Antelope Medicine* to collect Skyli's passport for the immigration office, and mentioned to Skyli that Monica and I had had a healthy conversation last night. Skyli, grappling with the decision whether to be a confidante to Monica or shoot straight with me, decided on the latter and told me it appeared that Monica was saying one thing to me and another to her, though at this point she didn't tell me the whole of it.

2 Sept

Monica was the one who suggested it might be best if she took off a week or so once we get to Spain. I felt greatly relieved, this is all last night; she waxed on about friendships, the different ups and downs of friendships. I thought things were going fine, maybe we could make this work, and this morning she goes over to *Antelope Medicine* and tells Skyli I'm kicking her off the boat in Gibraltar, she doesn't have anywhere to go, doesn't speak any languages, doesn't know what to do.

Enough already.

The plan of "doing it for Monica" didn't work.

I was having doubts that *Sonnet* could be the Miraculous Women's Boat I'd dreamed about. I was having doubts about how smoothly this little triple-handed passage to Gibraltar would go. I found myself wishing—which I didn't do often—that women were more like guys, less emotionally convoluted.

I walked down to the harbor offices, ship's documents and three passports in hand, intending to check on the weather before checking us out of Portugal. I called the Gibraltar phone number I'd gotten from my Med book, expecting a recording such as you get with weather numbers in the States, and got instead a very nice man who told me what I wanted to know, or what I really didn't want to hear, that by tomorrow there'd be an easterly *levante* in the Strait, probably force six and probably lasting for days.

I walked outside. It was a beautiful morning, and it would be even nicer offshore than in Vilamoura marina. I started feeling stubborn. I didn't see waiting for days; there was no reason *Sonnet* couldn't make a 150-mile trek to weather. And there was no reason she couldn't make it with a three-woman crew.

I checked us out of Vilamoura, out of Portugal, and headed back to the boat. I told myself if we just got offshore, plunged ourselves into the challenge of it, into the environment all three of us loved, everything would be okay.

I would try hard to make it work. I would try hard to make Monica feel like the established crew member, the one who knew *Sonnet*, the one who could show Skyli—our guest—the ropes. We could make something of this passage; we'd all sailed a major portion of the Atlantic, and now we could share the adventure of sailing the final Atlantic miles to the entrance of the Mediterranean.

Skyli sidelined me on the dock, carrying one small sea bag, and asked if I was sure I wanted her to come along. I said I was sure. I hopped on board, asked Monica to give Skyli a tour of the boat, show her the gear, show her the safety systems, then left them to it, went below to secure things for passage-making.

By 1100 we were off the dock.

8

Three on board—there was one there were two—
bound for the Gates of Heracles.
Squeeze
between shore and shipping lanes, dawn pale blue.
How could I have doubted you,
my sweet black sloop, my poem in motion. Breeze
builds to gale force (gusting), seas
build, full keel slices through.
So what if it takes all day (in spray-fly)
to beat this bi-continent moat.
(We duck the salt-sting flung
from bow-crash, laughing.) Why
should we need heroics on an all-woman boat.
The wonder is young.

The day was hazy, the wind was light. We powered southeast out of Vilamoura, a direct course toward the Strait, cutting across the wide mouth of the Gulf of Cadiz.

We ate a pleasant lunch in the cockpit, already out of the sight of land, the Autohelm driving. I eyed the wind, ready to put up the sails and shut off the Westerbeke as soon as there was enough breeze to push us at three or four knots. Skyli watched in amusement; Monica told her I was always like this, I hated to run the engine. Skyli said she had to admit she liked powerboat rides, or that she simply liked *boat* rides, she'd rather be sailing, but she liked powering, too, a powerboat ride had its own pleasures, nothing to fuss with, the straight run, the smooth water, you tuned out the sound of the engine, or incorporated it in your brain as a part of the whole, appreciated the noise-maker for pushing you where you wanted to go.

We talked about some of her powerboat rides on research vessels. She'd been on more powerboat rides than sailboat rides, at least until buying *Antelope Medicine*. Studying reef fish in Alabama and Texas. Studying sharks in California and the Bahamas.

By afternoon we had ten to twelve knots of northwesterly wind, and we raised the main and put up the gennaker. Within an hour the boat was moving like magic, the wind just right for her, the sails just right, with three people on board for whom such simplicity smoothed out the rough spots in their souls.

Around sunset, as Monica napped, Skyli and I sat on the weather rail and talked. Talked with incredible ease. Monica was right, three people were more complicated than two; it was impossible not to pair off, at least at times, impossible right now not to feel slightly relieved that Monica was sleeping below. But I allowed myself a lack of guilt, allowed myself a pure wash of gratefulness at finding this friend.

Not too long after dark, all three of us on deck, we started seeing a light we couldn't identify. A single red light, moving strangely. Seeming oddly high off the water, close to us but not very bright—the port light of a sailboat's masthead tricolor?—then not seeming close at all, not approaching in the way we'd expect a sailboat to approach.

I liked the way the sea at night was a coded world; a light was not the object it identified. Sometimes it was easy to translate specks of brightness into a solid, logical form, to focus on range lights and red or range lights and green and visualize the hull shape of a freighter. Tonight logic and experience weren't kicking in.

And then we realized, as we watched the red light, that a ship we'd been seeing in the distance—with indecipherable lights—wasn't moving, and that the red light was some kind of aircraft, which finally approached its mother ship and landed. Mystery solved, and not solved at all. Why was it only lit red? Airplanes used nav lights like boats did, red to port and green to starboard, plus strobes, so you couldn't miss them; wouldn't this helicopter—or whatever it was—be confusing to an airplane?

Sailing along, sailing away from it. Darkness again.

The wind was temperamental as we moved into the night, died, clocked, built, backed, died.

At 0130 Skyli and I again were awake together, the Westerbeke pushing the boat. I'd roughed out a watch schedule, thinking what a luxury it could be sleepwise with three instead of two, but it was hard to convince Skyli to go below and sleep and I wasn't going to insist, I was enjoying her company.

We were sitting in the cockpit, talking. I was proud of myself for barely minding the engine; maybe Skyli's nice-engine philosophy was rubbing off. And then the engine started sounding awful. *Awful.* We looked at each other, eyebrows raised. Not the starter motor this time; it sounded like the whole engine was about to rattle itself out of existence. I bolted behind the wheel and throttled way back, which seemed to eliminate most of the noise. I reached to pull the kill switch and Skyli said wait, maybe we should take a look at the engine before we shut it down, so we put it in neutral, went below, took off the ladder, rolled back the cover, and shined in a flashlight.

A hell of a lot of movement in the shaft; had it been like that before?

We shut down the engine. A bit of a breeze had come up, just enough to sail on. We rolled out the jib. I was as amused about this as I was upset; I hadn't *really* thought the engine would behave itself, had I?

The activity had woken up Monica and she offered to come on watch. I was ready for some sleep. Skyli stayed up. At one point, after I'd slept for a while, I heard a new round of activity on deck, a pretty impressive flapping and banging, and I simply curled deeper in my comfortable bunk, figuring if they needed help to work out whatever the problem was, they'd wake me up and ask for it.

I got back up at four. The problem, it turned out, had been the shackle connecting the mainsheet to the traveler; it had worked itself loose, liberating the boom. They'd worked it out.

I sent them both to bed. Skyli resisted the bed idea but she'd hardly slept at all since we took off, so I pulled the captain thing and told her at least to try to rest. On the one hand, I understood the temptation to stay up—the slightly addictive nature of sleeplessness—and knew this was a short enough passage that we could count on a good onshore sleep in the foreseeable future. On the other hand, we didn't know what the Strait itself was going to fling at us and I didn't see any point in self-imposed sleep deprivation.

It was a peaceful, dark pre-dawn. Close-hauled now, but still on course, sailing quietly at four or five knots, nowhere on the globe I would rather be. Standing in my cockpit, arms resting on the dodger, at home. Letting the time go by. Filling time in the way I'd filled it before on night watches, other years other eras other boats, reciting poems.

3 Sept

0450 West of the Strait of Gibraltar. Darkness, stars, a streak of deep orange along the horizon ahead of me. Standing at the dodger, reciting sonnets out loud, quietly, Monica and Skyli sleeping below. Milton, Alan Stephens, words rolling rhythmically over the water, and then my own, not brilliant but mine, poems I hadn't thought about for years. The *August Moon* sonnet, the Bermuda sonnet, knowing there were others but not quite remembering, then remembering: backcountry camping, reciting it out loud, voice catching because I'd forgotten, forgotten the poem, forgotten the pressures of that trip, forgotten the vacations, Hawaii, Europe, compromising my sleep at night to wake up and walk with Dad in the morning.

Poems, the slosh of water, an all-senses wakefulness in the dawn. Sadness at things passing, but no sense of sadness in the present.

And I should scribble this before I start rebelling against it, start feeling exhausted by it: these past twelve hours have been my best, purest hours on the boat. Feeling at home in the middle of an ocean (not quite the middle anymore), feeling right, the boat feeling right to me, my boat, the boat I was meant to own. Feeling the awe, solid solid solid, and it's virtually all from having Skyli on board. Know it's got to be hard on Monica, to sense that, but it's too important to ignore.

I wanted her to come along not just because it sounded like fun but because I wanted to see if I could sail with her. Not knowing if I would feel threatened by her, not knowing if she would feel threatened by me, but none of that, at least on this side, I think on hers, too. Absolute confidence, when she's awake and I'm not, that she'll either act on a problem (which she did when the traveler came loose) or wake me for anything she can't handle (which hasn't yet happened). Someone who's giving, not just taking, who can come up with solutions, sometimes better ones than mine.

By 0730 the wind had veered, so I tacked, which woke my crew. Skyli was ready within five minutes of getting out of bed to take a daylight look at the engine; we discovered that the big 15/16" nut on the forward port motor mount had backed off a full half inch. It wasn't an easy nut to get at, and we ended up taking off the raw-water pump to get a good purchase. I couldn't help wondering if the mechanic in Cambridge who'd done the alignment—and who'd had a notable fondness for his mid-morning non-tobacco smoke—simply hadn't wanted to be bothered.

A couple of the other mounts were loose, too. We tightened it all up the best we could, then tried the engine. Some vibration, but nothing like last night. Definite movement in the prop shaft at the stuffing box; even in neutral the engine's vibration started the shaft spinning slowly, and you could watch it shift up and down, at least a quarter inch.

Dean and Carol had told us about the chat net they participated in with a few other cruising boats, every morning at nine on 8 Alpha. We listened in, and when the conversations had begun to slow down I called *Cardiff*, chatted with Carol for a bit about our progress toward the Strait, then asked if Dean was around.

Dean came on, and I told him about our engine movement, asked him what he thought. He surmised what we'd pretty much decided ourselves, that the alignment was off, that we'd probably be fine to run the engine in neutral to charge batteries but might not want to put it under much of a load.

After I signed off, Skyli challenged me good-naturedly. Why had I chatted with Carol about our location, then asked for Dean to discuss our engine problems? Granted, we both knew he was more of a mechanic than she was, but why not ask her opinion first, then let her turn me over to Dean on her own accord?

Good point, willingly taken.

The wind was still temperamental, but we managed to keep moving under sail, tacking with the shifts. By noon we were south of Cadiz, and could see the coast of Spain, brown summer hills in haze, this land I'd known for a very long time. Twenty years ago, driving with my parents to the U.S. military base at Rota, twenty miles north of here, on Cadiz

Bay. Twelve years ago, driving with Steve between my parents' house and our own little rental house in Portugal, stopping at a *tapa* bar tucked in the walls of Tarifa, a memory both clear and elusive.

Skyli was sleeping; I pointed out to Monica the round stone Moorish towers along the coast, spaced so they could be seen one from the next, for hundreds of miles.

Close-hauled and tacking, wind beginning to build, skipper insisting that everyone rest when they could. Loving my boat, loving being out here, two continents narrowing down toward our destination. Late afternoon, sixty miles to go.

Around 1930, stars out, dinner finished, we turned on the engine to charge the batteries. It ran for fifteen minutes, then started hunting, the revs going up and down. I worked the throttle, but the engine wound down and died; some sort of fuel problem.

Monica stayed on deck, washing dishes. Skyli and I rolled back the engine cover, pulled out tools, and started bleeding the fuel lines. The boat was heeled and heaving, hardly facilitating our labors. We'd been at it ten minutes or so when Monica called down.

"Lydia?" Her voice from the cockpit sounded quite calm. "Maybe you should come look at this ship."

I was tightening the bolt on the injector pump. Skyli said she'd check out the traffic. One foot on the engine block, the other on the mahogany trim by the icebox, on up.

Skyli's voice this time from the cockpit: "Lydia, *now!*"

I flung myself up after her. A medium-sized freighter, *right there*, huge red side light.

I scrambled behind the wheel, disconnected the Monitor, told Monica to stand by the jib sheet to starboard, Skyli to port; if we had to, we'd tack. I feathered the boat up into the wind as much as I could, enough that our bow was now pointing at his stern.

No one said a thing as the freighter crossed in front of us—way too close—and churned on toward Cape Trafalgar.

I steered through the far side of the wake, then reconnected the Monitor.

"How long had you been watching him?" I asked Monica.

Only now did she start sounding flustered. "Awhile."

We must have been on a textbook collision course—unchanged bearing, decreasing range—for at least five minutes. I didn't want to chew her out, especially not in front of Skyli, especially since it was pretty clear she knew she'd screwed up royally. Still, this was basic stuff, something you learned in a sailing-club course, on top of which I'd told her always, *always* to call me on deck if she wasn't sure about shipping. I guess that's what she'd done, but she could have done it sooner.

"Let's just sail," I said. "We can fuss with the engine in the morning, when we have some light."

The wind was building steadily, the infamous *levante* blowing clean through the Strait from the east. Good time to reef, before we absolutely needed to. Good time to reduce the headsail, to get squared away for a beat.

I'd learned, in the shipping lanes off Portugal, that *Sonnet* didn't much like going to weather on a triple-reefed main. I opted for the second reef for tonight, especially since we had three on board to hand steer, to feather into the wind if necessary.

I talked my crew through our roles for reefing, Skyli on the wheel, Monica in the cockpit, me at the mast. Skyli bore away onto a reach, reducing the apparent wind, bringing the boat more upright, calming things down. We were losing ground, but we had plenty of time, no one had a date in Gibraltar.

Monica eased the mainsheet. I eased the main halyard, pulling down the leading edge of the sail. Big grommet secured on its hook, halyard back up tight, grinding with one hand, tailing with the other. Cleat the halyard, start hauling in on the reefing line. Call to Monica for more slack on the mainsheet. Reefing line onto the winch on the boom, grind in the last of it. Nice and tight. Sweating a bit from the effort. Clean, though, and easy.

I moved back to the cockpit, eased the jib sheet for Monica as she hauled in the furling line. Jib rolled in all the way. Skyli steered slowly back up toward the wind as Monica brought the mainsheet in. Marvelous, this teamwork thing, when it worked the way it should.

Back forward again, to secure the loose foot of the main.

I was exceedingly pleased with that finished second reef, the flat sail, the neat tight safety line around the boom at the new clew, the loose fabric tightly rolled and neatly gasketed. Aware how long this would have taken alone.

Sonnet was moving sluggishly now, without a headsail. Wet from breaking waves. I moved the blocks for the jib sheets forward on their tracks, led the sheets inside the shrouds, and moved back to the cockpit, dragging a soggy harness tether behind me, enjoying this.

Monica and I worked together to bring out a tiny bit of jib, her grinding in the sheet, me easing out the furling line. Got it just right, the lead just right, the sail impressively flat for being furled like that.

Sonnet found her stride, newly balanced, surging up and over the waves. What a sweet boat.

Twenty-five to thirty knots apparent, still building. I didn't plan to push my boat if the weather really got nasty—we could always turn around and scoot back downwind, all the way to Cadiz if we had to—but I was excited to see how she'd do.

Seas building. Lights of Barbate de Franco.

By 0100, Monica sleeping, Skyli and I were deep in a game with the elements. If we got too close to the Spanish shore the wind died; we would tack when we felt it dropping, head back out, feeling it build. If we got too far offshore, sailed a minute too long, we were blasted, gusts to forty knots, hardly able to get through the tack back toward land.

We got into a rhythm, sailing fifteen minutes or so at a stretch, one of us catching a nap in full foul-weather gear at the chart table, the other at the wheel, steering, sniffing the wind, waiting for that moment on the into-shore tacks when the pressure began to ease off the sails, on the away-from-shore tacks when it threatened to overwhelm us. Call the napper up on deck. Wind, water, night sky, glints of light on foul-weather gear. Tack; flapping sail and snaking sheets; grind hard, grind fast. Trade roles.

From 2230 to 0600 we averaged two knots velocity-made-good, and it was amazing what a victory that felt, what fun it was, how satisfying. The wind was blasting from the east and still our little boat was moving in that direction, the pencil marks on the chart were moving east-southeast, the coast was slowly slipping behind us. Two knots VMG would have been desperately depressing on a long passage—with five hundred or eight hundred or a thousand miles to go, you can't help thinking how long it would take to reach your destination at the speed you're moving *right now*—but this was a self-contained passage, two days out wouldn't be that much bigger a deal than one day out, and with each tack we were closer.

By the light of dawn we could see another boat—we'd seen her nav lights at night—and that made it easier. We paced her for hours; different tacks, diverge, come back together, see where you stand, like a race. She was a dark-hulled cat-rigged ketch, motor sailing into the wind, making far shallower tacks than we were, slowly winning the race, but *Sonnet* was doing pretty damned well with no motor at all.

Monica came on deck, and Skyli—at my insistence—went below. Waves, wind, beating to weather in early-morning light, Monica handling sheets. The world of it. Happy on the helm of my boat, looking to windward, gauging the waves, steering over them, identifying, when I saw them, the ones I wasn't going to escape, the ones that would crash at *Sonnet*'s bow and soak me. Just before they hit I'd twist and duck, taking them on the shoulder.

That world, and another, the dry one below, the beautiful sculpted world of *Sonnet*'s interior. I could see it looking down through the square of the companionway, see both worlds at once, see wind-whipped water and mist-dimmed sky and the sun-warmed coast of Spain, then see the slender confines of my boat, varnished mahogany, teak-and-holly sole, white bulkheads, shifting oblongs of sunlight on objects that maintained their spatial relationships. I could see Skyli propped on pillows, safe behind the leeboard on the main port berth, looking up through the companionway. Every time I turned back forward after twisting away from a wave, after the duck that preceded the crash that preceded the soaking, turned back and wiped the salt from my eyes, she was laughing.

Between 0600 and 0800 we covered five miles; doing good.

Around 0930 Monica and I sailed *Sonnet* around the fortified peninsula of Tarifa and entered the narrowest part of the Strait. The cat-rigged ketch had pulled ahead, out of sight. Another boat was going the other way, staying close to shore, surging downwind on just a reefed mainsail. A mile and a half separated the rugged coast from the edge of the shipping lanes; we tacked our way east between them. When Skyli woke up and came on deck I pointed south, to the misty hills of Africa.

My turn off watch. I went below, and slept soundly in spite of the boat motion. Twelve miles more to Gibraltar.

Sleeping. The boat slowing down. Slower. Footsteps on deck, reefs out. Jib out. Better speed. Deep sleep. Boat slowing down again. Occasional sail slat; were we getting becalmed? How long had I been sleeping?

Enthusiastic rolling session, complete with banging blocks. I clambered over the leeboard and went up on deck. Less than five miles ahead, huge and hazy, was the Rock of Gibraltar.

Skyli was seething. An Algeciras ferry had just steamed past at point-blank range, leaving *Sonnet* slopping in its wake. She strongly advised we try to get the engine working, better to damage the bearings by running the engine misaligned than to get T-boned by the next ferry.

We sailed slowly to the left, out of the way of traffic. Slower, slower. After a while we were hardly moving at all. Wasn't this the boat that four hours ago had been bashing into a gale? We were now due west of Punta Europa, the southern tip of the Rock, drifting along near the west side of Algeciras Bay.

Skyli and I heaved the engine cover off and out of the way, pulled the tools out, and went to work. Monica, hand steering, started getting worried that in fact we were drifting west, inshore. She asked me to come on deck to check. I scrambled up and took a look—still seemed okay to me.

Back below to deal with Mr. Westerbeke. We went through the usual drill for air in the fuel lines, crack open the bolt at the top of the secondary fuel filter, pump with the hand-operated lifter pump until no bubbles, close, crack open the little bolt at the side of the injector pump, pump with the lifter pump until no bubbles, close, crack open an injector . . . The problem was, when we got to the hit-the-starter-switch part, the starter motor churned and churned and the engine showed no sign of starting. The same thing had happened last night; we couldn't do this many more times before killing the batteries.

Monica was on throttle-and-key-switch duty. She once again voiced concern that we were drifting in toward shore. Skyli had brought along *Antelope Medicine*'s GPS; I passed it up to Monica, told her I thought we still looked fine but she could keep an eye on our coordinates; increasing longitude would mean yes, we're drifting west.

Once more with the fuel lines, from the top. What I noticed this time was that the fuel didn't squirt very enthusiastically from the side of the injector pump; when I'd done this before, you could see the pulses clearly.

We checked the fuel tank; plenty of fuel. What next?

"Please come look again. *Please*." It wasn't a pleading "please"; it was imperative.

I scrambled up over the engine again, looked around. She was absolutely right; we *were* getting closer to the shore. Might be wise to get an anchor free.

It took me about ninety seconds. Whip out the knife, slice through the lashings on the dinghy, shove the dinghy away, slice through the anchor lashings, carry the anchor forward.

I looked up at the masthead wind indicator. Shit, why hadn't I looked up earlier? The breath of breeze was now directly behind us, rather than forward of the beam, and the sail was still strapped in tight. I trotted back to the cockpit, freed the mainsheet, shoved the boom all the way out to catch the wind. Looked over at the water. Nothing. Or wait. Movement. Slow, slow, but movement. Slowly away from the rocks.

We all stayed in the cockpit for a while, then Skyli and I retired back below. We followed the fuel lines carefully, but saw nowhere fuel was leaking out, letting air in.

We opened up the Racor filter. The filter element was black with algae, totally clogged. Culprit.

Skyli asked if I had spare elements. I said I'd only had one, and I'd changed it in Horta. She asked when I'd last checked this one. I said I hadn't checked it since I changed it.

I was given a clear, impassioned lecture: I wasn't to admit to anyone that I hadn't been checking my fuel filters. As women, we were judged enough as it was. I could say I'd run out of filters if I wanted, but not that I hadn't been checking.

We pumped some clean diesel from the tank into a jar, and dropped in the Racor element. A bit more wind. Slowly northeast across the bay as Skyli cleaned the Racor element, fold by slimy fold. Slowly toward Gibraltar. Some part of me thought to hell with the engine, let's just forget it and sail, and the greater part of me recognized that Skyli was right, so I left her to persevere.

We got becalmed again about a mile from the Rock, could see the wind line not a hundred yards off the beam, the darker water. I'd always wondered why that big paddle was on board, and now I pulled it out, and lay down on my belly on the deck at the lowest part of the sheer, from which position the paddle easily reached the water. One long stroke, another; how good this felt. Monica pitched in on the other side with an oar, and *Sonnet* glided gently toward the wind line. Another new thing learned about my boat.

Not long after that, Skyli got the Racor reassembled, and we bled the fuel lines. Nice steady pulse from the injector pump; tighten it up. Nice steady pulses from the cracked injectors as the starter motor churned; tighten them up. Not too surprisingly, the engine started. I didn't at all like the vibration when it was in gear, so we left it in neutral, with Skyli reminding me we could use it if we really needed to.

Close now, seeing the moles, checking out the chart, making our approach.

I'd sailed years on *Alaska Eagle* in a position of authority, a position of respect, always afraid of failing, always devastated when I failed, made some little mistake which probably nobody noticed. Maybe what Skyli gave me was the freedom to fail, the license to be less than perfect. Which maybe also gave me the freedom to be good at what I did.

We ghosted slowly into the narrow channel south of the airport runway, that east-west stretch of concrete built out into the water when the border was closed between Gibraltar and Spain and the Rock might as well have been an island. I was focused on sailing, obsessed with wind angles and sail trim, not sure we'd be able to slip past that docked fishing boat, sailing as close to the wind as we could.

I said, "If the wind shifts we're in trouble, there's no way she'll tack twice in this channel," mind racing, why did I have to have such a hard-tacking boat?

I added, "Let's get the fenders over the starboard side. If we have to, we can go alongside the fishing boat."

Skyli said, easily, "If we have to, we can use the engine."

Good *heavens.* I'd completely forgotten about the engine, which was presently running only because she'd insisted we could get it to run.

I popped it into gear, kept the revs low. Vibration, yes, but not bad on this flat water.

We motored slowly closer to the runway, rolled in the jib, hauled down the mainsail, and five minutes later were approaching the customs dock. It wasn't an elegant arrival but it was a first: *Sonnet* came onto the dock under power.

The Atlantic was behind us.

III

Circlesight

9

Behind the halyard clack I hear the Med
heaving. Ahead are leaves, and something white;
I guess an eggshell. Calcified and light,
it's dogshit. Kicking it I see a dead
black bug, one wing awry. The days in bed
bequeathed perception. Walking in the bight
of this marina, floppy hat and high-
topped tennies, baggy workman's jumpsuit, head
still aching, I'm no knockout but I've known
such sunset clouds at sea. I've seen them. That
was summer, that was when the evening storms
were local. This brisk autumn breeze has blown
for days. I think of a wave; crashing at
the jetty, it withdraws, and then reforms.

"Cabo Pino," 1979

5 Sept

It is extraordinary, the extent to which everything feels changed.
The awe is here, nearly a constriction in my chest, moored beneath the Rock of Gibraltar on my own boat, circling back to
origins. Transitions; that was the Atlantic, this is the Mediterranean, everything starts new.

So happy beating against the *levanter*, happy in the way I've
been on *Alaska Eagle*, in the way I was at nineteen on *Zeelandia*,
at twenty-one on *Gemisun*, learning this boat which is mine, this
wonderful, full-keel, metal-solid boat which goes to weather like
no boat I've ever sailed, her lovely hull slides up and through the

waves, lifts heels crashes I was happy, braced at the wheel, feeling the rhythm of her, trusting her, white water everywhere.

This happiness, to a great extent, is a gift from Skyli, whether she wants to recognize it or not. Gratefulness in my soul; I'm not going to be scared by this friendship, or I am and I'll tough through the scary parts. She's *there* for me, takes up the space of my lapses, and I don't feel ashamed of the lapses, I just feel completed.

Goddess, this is so fun, so marvelous. Chaotic on deck as we came onto the customs dock, uncoiled lines and scrambling crew; I would prefer to have arrived with everything pristine, and at some point I'll do it, but the wonderful thing right now is I don't care, the boat has no control by rudder when she's moving slowly angling toward the dock, and I can't straighten her back to port, so I pop her into reverse and presto, big ole stern-kick to starboard, nice smooth bow-turn to port, straighten her out in forward, learning her, it's like this wonderful game, this wonderful gift that maybe the real challenge is to accept.

At some point I'll come flawlessly onto a dock with an all-female crew, for me, for my crew, not to impress whatever idiot happens to be standing there. For my sense of completeness.

We had moved the boat, after clearing customs, to a slip in Marina Bay, hadn't even nosed our bow into the dock and tossed our bow lines ashore before *Peryton* Greg was greeting us. Sure enough: the distinctive wishbone boom, two boats down. Skyli rolled her eyes and shook her head. Not that she didn't *like* Greg—he was good-hearted to the core—but he was hard to ignore ("I *admit* it, I'm an ugly American") and she'd gotten quite a lot of him when he was two boats down in Horta.

He wondered—loudly—what the hell Skyli was doing on *Sonnet*. Did she sink *Antelope Medicine*? Drown her crew?

He suggested we all go out to eat, and we said let's do it another night, tonight was our crew dinner.

Monica and Skyli and I headed into town at sunset, around irregular ramparts, past the produce market where I'd shopped for provisions in 1973, before my first Atlantic passage. I looked off to the right, wondering if the old destroyer pens still existed. In the early seventies, when I'd done most of my sailing in these parts, visiting yachts had usually been berthed in the pens, rafted two or three deep against the high concrete walls.

Plenty of memories here. I'd sailed through the worst storm of my life in November of '82, a day out of Gibraltar on my third Atlantic passage, winds gusting over sixty knots. I'd been fathomlessly seasick, so sick and dehydrated my hands had started to cramp, finally recovering enough on the second day to stand watch, huddled in the shelter of the dodger as the autopilot drove, looking out at the huge foam-streaked seas, the horizontal-blowing spray. We toughed it out offshore until the storm abated, then limped back into Gibraltar for repairs, amazed by the damage suffered by boats in the protection of the harbor.

Monica and Skyli and I ate Indian food in a restaurant off Main Street, and slept on *Sonnet*. In the morning I walked alone across the border, into the country my mom would like me to think of as my adoptive home.

I'd first come to Spain when I was seventeen, five days before I would have given a speech as valedictorian of my high school. My parents had sold the only house I'd ever known and packed what possessions they hadn't disposed of into an eight-by-eight-foot crate to be shipped overseas. Their friends in California tended either to think they'd completely lost their minds or to admire them for their gutsiness. Not many knew that Dad's early retirement hadn't been entirely voluntary, that more and more he'd been so worried about Mom he hadn't been able to concentrate on his work. Not many knew that Mom had sworn this would be her new start, that things would change in Europe.

They had decided to buy a home in Spain before they ever set foot in the country, choosing the Costa del Sol on the basis of Mom's research. The climate of the coast was much like Southern California, real estate prices were good, and they loved to travel, saw Spain as a jumping-off place for roaming the world. They made their first trip to Andalusia in 1970, buying a piece of property in the cork-oak hills above San Pedro de Alcántara, also buying from plans, impulsively, an apartment at the under-construction marina at José Banus, as investment property. The idea was that Dad would return in '71 to oversee the building of the house, and Mom and I would follow after I graduated; Layne still had two years of college.

By the time Dad had hoped to be poring over house plans, he'd barely gotten plot plans and had discovered the hilly San Pedro plot to be more problematical than expected, so he and Mom came back and bought a nearly finished house, this time near the sea, halfway between Marbella and Fuengirola. When the three of us came over in '72 the house still wasn't finished, so we moved into the closer-to-finished apartment at Puerto José Banus. I stayed with them for a month before embarking on a bike trip through Europe; it was at Banus that I first got hooked on boats.

We took off together in mid-July—traveling for a week with my bike on the roof of their little dark-green Renault—and split up in France. I returned to Spain in time for my eighteenth birthday in late September, left again to go sailing, and kept circling back, biking and sailing and hitchhiking, finally heading west across the Atlantic toward college in the winter of '73 on *Zeelandia*. I would continue to circle back to Spain—from the States, from Portugal, from Paris, by land, sea, and air—in the years that followed.

By the time I stepped off my own boat in Marina Bay, and walked across the runway, my parents had lived more than twenty years in Spain. I flashed my passport at customs and strolled into the town of La Linea, smelling olive oil from open kitchen windows and looking with pleasure at the Spanish-language signs. I wandered a bit, asked directions, found one of the Telefónica places with six or eight booths where you pay when you're finished talking, and called.

Mom was sober. As soon as she picked up the phone I didn't even question it, and we talked easily about Layne, about social events in Spain, about the cats, about her conversations with Beth and with Brian when *Sonnet* was crossing the Atlantic. The conversation brought back all the ways she was great: witty, smart, irreverent.

I'd last been in Iberia, last been at my parents', six years ago, the summer I'd been scheduled to sail *Alaska Eagle* from Newport Beach to Hawaii, and a month after that from British Columbia back to Newport. The college cancelled the entire voyage two days before departure, because of a licensing squabble with the Coast Guard.

I'd flown impulsively to Europe to race on the California team of the *Tour de France à la Voile*, and had been in France ten days before even contacting my parents to let them know I was on their side of the Atlantic. I was afraid to call; instinct maybe, the same kind of intuition that had been such a powerful, positive force between me and my mom when I was younger.

When I'd finally called, she'd been so drunk she couldn't talk, and I'd ended up, when my coins ran out, sitting among strangers at the post office in Arcachon with my head on my arms, sobbing. But I'd gotten on a plane and headed for Málaga.

She was sober when I arrived, and far from recovered from what Dad told me had been a two-week bender. I was struck, a to-the-gut blow, by the fact that the body we'd always marveled could take so much abuse wouldn't take it forever.

She hadn't eaten in a week; Dad, ever the enabler, would put a glass of orange juice in front of her with a straw in it and she couldn't even pick up the glass, would steady the glass with a shaking hand on either side of the table and lean forward to the straw. Shaking so hard she couldn't walk, could barely dress herself; this went on for days. At one point, trying to get her onto the little fishing boat Dad had at the time— we had her sit on the dock, and put her feet on the bow, and with me on the dock and Dad on the boat we tried to maneuver her on board— she'd started feeling panicky, and her muscles had started to jump like nothing I'd ever seen, muscles with no tone, no control, like flopping fish out of water. I was terrified.

Mom and Dad were coming that year to California to visit Steve and me at Christmas. It would be only the third time they'd been in the States since they'd moved; Mom strongly resisted America, got furious when Dad inadvertently called California home instead of Spain.

Before they came, I did one of the hardest things I've ever done. I arranged an "intervention." It was difficult enough logistically, with Layne in Strasbourg at the time and Dad in Spain, neither of them quite grasping what this was all about. It was devastatingly hard emotionally. In some very deep place I didn't believe it would work; I had always been skeptical of therapy sessions and twelve-step programs, and though I'd urged Mom in every way I could to go to AA—which she'd done for two brief periods, once in the States, once in Spain—I knew how deeply she resisted it, too. I also knew she was killing herself, that I had to try whatever I could.

We scheduled the intervention—led by Carolyn, a recovering alcoholic herself and a licensed psychologist—for two weeks into their three-week trip. Dad, Steve, and I all talked to Mom: Here's what your drinking has done to me, over the years. Here's what I've seen it do to you. Layne participated in absentia, having written a heartbreaking letter, which Carolyn read.

Mom had gone into treatment mostly to get out of the room, saying she'd only go for a week, only until the day of her scheduled flight back. We all hoped she'd spend that first week in the program and then decide to stay the full month, but she'd flown back as planned, and continued to drink. She never forgave me for what she saw as a betrayal, never saw it as a desperate act of love.

You're supposed to come up with a "consequence" at an intervention. "I want you to get help, and if you don't, here's what I'll do." Neither Layne nor Dad felt comfortable stating a consequence; it might be tempting to say if they had it would have made a difference, but I don't think it's true. I'd said: "I want you to get help, and if you don't I won't be coming again to your home."

You think you've come to terms with things and then they change. I stuck with my consequence. I thought I'd come to terms—at least somewhat—with my parents living and dying in Spain, living out their tragedy, their mutual illness, mutual addiction, and then suddenly it wasn't only Mom who was ill, wasn't only Dad in the role of caretaker. The terror of it all, for years now: *What if she falls and lies in a puddle of blood the same day he takes a walk and doesn't know his way back again?*

My not visiting them in their home meant very little to her, certainly not enough to drive her to sobriety. It meant everything to him. Home was the only place he was close to being himself, close to having some grasp of his past, his surroundings.

As soon as I started planning my voyage on *Sonnet* I knew I would visit them. I knew Mom would pretend my six-year hiatus was just a result of logistics. I knew, to some extent, that I'd pretend, too. There was a chance she wouldn't drink once I got there; she had true, perverse strength, she hadn't been drunk in my presence in the six years since the intervention. On the phone, yes, but not when we'd met in Montpellier, or they'd come to Washington, or we'd met in the Alps, or they'd come to Abidjan. All good times, close, but each time my dad had slipped further away. At least he still knew who the people he cared about were. Not like his sister Leila, who'd come to me twice the last time I saw her, several years before she died, asking brightly, "And who are you?"

I knew if Mom did drink I would totally lose it.

I also knew—and this meant everything—that I'd have somewhere to go, that *Sonnet* would be there for me, a two-hour drive back to Gibraltar.

This meant everything.

So I told Mom, when we talked, that I'd take the bus or rent a car, tomorrow or the next day, depending on how long it took to get things organized with the boat. Visit for a day or two now, then sail to Fuengirola and visit again from there. She knew I'd be bringing Monica this first visit—she'd been arranging with Brian to get Monica traveler's checks through her bank in Fuengirola—and I told her I'd be bringing another friend, too. I'd had trouble talking Skyli into coming to my parents'—Skyli was uncomfortable in social situations, in spite of the fact that she always seemed at ease; one of many things I was learning about her—until I told her Mom and Dad had three cats and the odds were good she could get one of them to sleep with her. She was more of a dog person than a cat person, but she'd been in animal deprivation for a while now.

I made inroads that day on boat projects, arranged for Shepherd's Chandler to swap my GPS, researched a new starter switch and Racor filters, found a mechanic who could come tomorrow to look at the engine.

The next day Skyli and Monica and I tried to climb the Rock. I'd climbed it every time I'd come to Gibraltar, even dragged Mom and Dad up one time ages ago when we'd been here together. This time I couldn't quite remember the way up, and we got lost, and had to backtrack, and by the time we finally got it figured out my knee was killing me, so I told Monica and Skyli to go ahead without me, I'd meet them back at the boat.

In fact, it wasn't just my knee. I was once again convinced it was best for Monica and me to part ways—here, not in Malta; sooner, not later—and I needed some time alone to work it through. I'd be doing some serious bridge burning by telling her I didn't want her to sail through the Med, but it felt like the right decision.

Skyli and Monica came back from their walk, and Skyli went off to make phone calls, and I talked to Monica. I told her I'd been giving it a lot of thought, and I felt my original impulse of having her sail only the Atlantic was the right one; I didn't think she should continue on to Malta. I didn't want her to take it wrong, feel kicked off, this was simply what felt right in my whole concept of *Sonnet*.

I figured she knew this was coming, but she was devastated, started to cry, wanted to know if it was because she wasn't good enough, if it was because of the near-collision with the freighter, or the slow drift onto the rocks, and I said of course not, everyone makes mistakes, and in the latter case you were right and I was wrong, you were worried about going aground and I wasn't even paying attention. She shook her head as if she didn't believe me. I said this isn't because of anything you did, we're just parting at the point we'd originally planned.

She asked if Skyli was going to keep sailing with me and I said no, Skyli had her own boat to deal with, a husband flying down from England, her own responsibilities. I didn't know yet who would sail with me through the Med.

She kept crying. I got her a glass of juice. She asked if she could still come to Spain with me tomorrow and I said of course. She asked if there were travel agents where my parents lived and I said yes, there were plenty of travel agents, and I'd help her with her plans however I could.

When she settled down a little I headed over to the pay phones at the marina, shaken by the undercurrents of dishonesty and unkindness in what I'd just done, by my lack of generosity as a mentor and a friend. Monica was right; part of why I didn't think she was the best person to sail with me through the Med—a tricky body of water with relentless shipping and weather changes—was that she wasn't a very good sailor. She *wanted* to be a good sailor, but I didn't have it in me to help her out by letting her stay on *Sonnet*. She felt supplanted by Skyli, but I wasn't ready, for Monica's sake, to ask Skyli to go away.

I reached the pay phones, dropped in some coins, and dialed my parents' number. Mom answered, drunk. My remaining equilibrium disintegrated.

"We might have come today," I said. "What if we'd come today?"

"Won't you come today . . ." the sadness creeping into her voice now, wanting me to be there. Years of this, always the same and never able to handle it any better.

I kept walking, away from the marina, and found an unlikely little triangle-shaped park near a yard with a goat and some chickens. I pulled out my journal and started playing around with rhymed verse for the first time in years, made it into an exercise more than a creative endeavor, two self-imposed rules. First, I had to write a Shakespearean sonnet start to finish, no reworking. Second, once I'd written one word of a rhymed pair (e.g., "started"), I had to use the first partner-word that popped into my mind ("farted"? I can't use *"farted"*!).

> It looks as if you've got to pay these days
> to walk up the rock of Gibraltar laid my face
> against the cool of the mast, the granite maze
> of tunnels, windows in the stone a race
> against the hurricane season is where this started.
> Red paint splattered on a tree trunk, trash,
> I've circled back, circled around, farted
> around . . .

The result wasn't brilliant, but it was interesting, the beginning of something, a small gift from the past from my boat. I decided to try to write a sonnet or two a week, some version thereof, even if only fourteen single words.

I went back to the boat. Both Monica and Skyli were there. Monica's eyes were red but she seemed all right; she was already telling Skyli about the trip she might take back to Portugal, she'd always wanted to see Lisbon and it hadn't worked out to stop off on her way to the Azores to meet me.

Skyli had talked to her Steven, who'd be flying from England to meet her a week from today. On her way back to the boat she'd been waylaid by Greg, who'd dragged her into the bar, insisting on buying her a Coke if she didn't want a beer; when some two-sheets-to-the-wind buddy of his had confused her with Sascha, Greg had said, "You got it all *wrong*, this isn't *Sascha*, this is the skipper of the *dyke* boat, that met the *other* dyke boat in the middle of the goddamn *Atlantic*."

The mechanic had come by; he was in the middle of a job, and was putting off our appointment until tomorrow.

That evening, I made some phone calls to the States; it was starting to sink in that once Monica departed I'd be crewless for the Med. I called Anne—she'd been married two months now—but she still didn't feel she could take off. She'd told me when we'd talked in the spring that she'd be thrilled to go sailing if John could go too, but that wasn't what I wanted of *Sonnet*, and this time we didn't even mention it.

I called Elizabeth, whom I'd met when I was training with the U.S. Women's Challenge for the 1989 Whitbread; she was one of the few crew members who'd truly seemed solid to me, smart and fit and capable. She was pleased to hear from me—I was interested to learn she was no longer involved in the '93 Challenge—but she'd just begun a veterinary-assistant training program and couldn't go sailing. Strike two on the crew search.

In the morning I reserved a rental car for three days. I wanted Monica's departure from *Sonnet* to go smoothly, and she had way too much gear to haul across the border and load easily onto the local Spanish bus.

I tried to stay out of her way as she packed, working to get *Sonnet* ready to be left alone, reinforcing dock lines, adding chafing gear, securing halyards. I talked with Greg and Sascha about keeping an eye on my boat.

The mechanic was supposed to come by at one; by four he still hadn't made an appearance. I was restless, wanting to see Spain by daylight. I finally went into town to pick up the rental car, leaving a list of things for Skyli and Monica to ask the mechanic should he deign to show up.

He was there when I got back. We ran down the list, what to do about the alignment, whether or not the ignition-switch problems I'd had were likely to have damaged the starter motor, how I should go about cleaning my fuel. I gave him the combination to *Sonnet* so he could do the alignment while I was in Spain.

And then we were loading baggage into the car, and making a final check on the boat (sea cocks closed? cooking gas off? batteries off? bilge pump on?), and heading across the runway. This was the first time I'd left my boat in eight weeks.

It took more than an hour to reach the front of the long line to Spanish customs. We finally drove through La Linea, and onto the road to Málaga.

Hard to predict what would make my heart catch: the angle of a sloping hill, fence posts made from irregular branches of trees, long shadows from the sinking sun. The glint of the Med above a red-tiled roof.

By Soto Grande it was already dark, and Spain slipped past black and distant on either side of the headlights.

We drove past the bustle of Marbella, along the familiar stretch of road to Cabo Pino, and pulled into the driveway as the front door opened. Mom and Dad stepped out onto the marble entry porch, so happy to have me home. I could see the interior of the house dimly lit behind them, the Chinese rugs, the now-rusty sixties-era hanging lamps Mom had brought from California.

Papa's hair and beard were much whiter, still curly and thick. His eyebrows still dark. His shoulders so thin.

Mama was moving shakily, as she had to one degree or another for twenty years. Looking so much older than she should, twelve years younger than Dad and not seeming it. Still that easy Southern grace, welcoming Skyli and Monica, chatting, laughing, a grace that could dissipate so quickly.

The sailors tumbled in, bag and baggage.

A cat was underfoot almost immediately, looking up at us. I looked down.

"This is your Siamese?" I asked incredulously.

The Siamese cat had been a yardstick of Dad's illness, early on. For years after they'd adopted her he'd asked every phone call, every letter until he quit writing letters, "Did I tell you we have a Siamese cat?"

"This is Abbey," Dad said proudly.

I started laughing, and could hardly stop. I'd visualized this cat for years now, visualized slender limbs and straight-nosed face, an Asian elegance to complement my great-grandfather's porcelain and rugs. Instead, I was looking at the silliest Siamese cat I'd ever seen, a tiny thing, dark, swaybacked, a wide curious face—no haughtiness here—and crooked, prominent jaw.

Mom was laughing, too, but trying to be defensive. "What's wrong with her?" she said.

"Her *face*."

"She's got a *beautiful* face."

"Her *tongue's* hanging out."

"Well, it usually does."

Abbey followed us all into the kitchen, seemingly oblivious to the fact that she had ninety-five percent less body weight than anyone else in the room, standing among the moving feet and legs, looking up happily from face to face as we chatted.

The other two cats made an appearance during dinner. Sybil was the elegant one, a simple tabby but long-limbed and beautifully shaped. Percy was tiny and a little skittish, and Skyli responded to her more than to the others, said she seemed sad, but couldn't get close enough to her to pet her, except when Percy was accepting shrimp tails at the dinner table.

After eating, we worked out the sleeping arrangements. Dad had been sleeping for the last few years in the guest room with twin beds, since he snored and had nightmares that woke Mom up. Mom insisted on calling the room "Layne's room," though Layne had never spent much time in it; Dad would relinquish it to Monica while we were here, and sleep in his own twin in the master bedroom. Skyli would sleep in "Lydia's room," the guest room with the fold-out couch. I would sleep downstairs, where I usually slept at La Pajarera. A luxury for the three of us, each to have her own space.

8 Sept

Wake on my parents' couch
with an unprecedented sense of peacefulness
wander upstairs and Dad has crawled in bed with Mom
both sleeping, a quiet ease I haven't seen in years.

I'd forgotten what a beautiful place this was. I'd slept with the living-room doors open, the sound of the sea drifting up through pines. When Mom and Dad had first moved here there'd been nothing along this beach for miles in either direction, and Dad had taken long walks, seeing no one, finding "treasures" along the shore, shells and strange sculptures of driftwood, which he brought back and displayed on shelves on the covered, tiled-floor porch. They'd almost been relieved when the plans went through for the little Cabo Pino marina; something was bound to go up sooner or later and it could have been much worse than this.

The living room and dining room opened onto the porch. From there you could look through pine trunks to the water, the sea itself straight south, the marina slightly to the right, boats moving gently on Med moorings. It would have been wonderful to bring *Sonnet* here, to see her from my parents' house, but the breakwater was badly designed and the harbor entrance silted up, and *Sonnet* was too deep-drafted to come in.

The household woke up slowly; we finally sat down together for break- fast around ten. At some point my mom, who'd been talking about going to the market, surveyed the table and said, "Where do we stand on fruit?"

After the slightest of beats my dad came back with, "Stand on fruit?" Just those three words, but his tone and timing were perfect; why would we want to stand on fruit? Wouldn't it get squashed? I rolled my eyes, a habitual reaction to my dad's humor. Skyli cracked up; Dad was pleased. Later she said to me, "I love your dad: 'Stand on fruit,' " and it was liberating.

I realized, looking back, that Dad's illness had started manifesting itself as early as '86, that I'd seen the first signs when he and Mom had come to California. He'd always been eager to do jobs when he came to visit me or Layne, fixing anything that needed to be fixed, building anything that needed to be built, and Steve and I requested a simple bookshelf for our bedroom. It seemed like a perfect project for Dad, who was acting distracted, and I was looking forward to going to the lum-beryard with him, smelling the sweet smell of sawdust, looking forward to working with wood, as we'd done together so much when I was younger. He made a few primary sketches for the bookshelf, and then shook his head, said he simply couldn't focus, couldn't concentrate. I blamed it on anxiety over the upcoming intervention.

By '89, when my parents visited us in Washington, the change was radical. Dad repeated things, sometimes only minutes apart. He was obsessed with his illness. How many times in that two-week visit did he say, "Honey, I don't know if you've noticed, but I'm having trouble with my memory"?

He'd read everything he could about memory loss. He told me over and over how this might be one of several things. It might be an Alzheimer's-type condition like his sister Leila had; a terrible thought, but it might be true. Or it might be a hormone imbalance, a thyroid problem. Or it might be the result of years of stress.

He read the Sunday comics again and again. By the time he'd read one page he'd forgotten the last one, and would go back to it.

He was almost always tired that visit, and frequently depressed.

Mom and Dad had bought a ticket for Layne to come from Jordan, the only time she'd been away from her children since the birth of her first son, six years before. Layne and I spent hours with a tape recorder, talking to Dad about his past, the dry farm he was born on in Idaho, his landing in Normandy on the sixth day after D-Day, his service under Patton, the liberation of Paris, his incredible German shepherd Tommy, the early years with Mom in California. His memories were crystal-clear, and the tapes invaluable.

Mom and I took him to the military hospital at Bethesda for an assessment after Layne had flown back to Amman. At one point Mom and I were waiting outside the curtained cubicle, and the neurologist came out and said we could go back in, and she came back in herself a couple of minutes later, and said to Dad, "There were three things I asked you to remember for me. Can you tell me what they are?"

The look on Dad's face was heartbreaking. Concentration, distress, almost guilt. He shook his head. I expected, when she told him what the three things were, that he'd slap himself on the forehead and say, "How could I have forgotten?" She said, "A red car, a box, and a tree," watching him closely, and he shook his head again. Nothing. No memory. She said kindly, "It's okay, it doesn't matter."

Mom took Dad to the military base in Wiesbaden for more testing, and learned nothing.

The following winter they came to Abidjan for two weeks at Christmas. For years Dad had been saying he should write his memoirs, he'd lived such a history-spanning life, could remember the first time he'd seen an automobile. I'd found him a nice blank book and mailed it to him a year before, with "Guidelines from the Editor" encouraging him just to have fun with it, write whatever came to mind, I'd put it into the computer at some point for editing and chronology. I thought it would be a perfect project for him, since his long-term memory was still good. Or maybe because I enjoyed scribbling in blank books I assumed he would, too.

He brought the blank book to Africa, though he hadn't written a word in it since I'd sent it. I sat him down out on the screened-in porch the second day of their visit, was pleased to glance out and see him still there as I moved around the house, went out to check on him after nearly an hour and he'd written only a couple of sentences, had been sitting there agonizing, smoking cigarette after cigarette. I felt terrible, imposing a burden on him rather than a pleasure.

I thought he'd enjoy our collection of Calvin and Hobbes cartoons. He flipped through the books, but they only confused him.

He couldn't remember things one minute to the next, but if you got exasperated with him it struck some deeper chord of his consciousness, and he would feel low for hours.

He could still play backgammon. He and Mom had played for years, keeping a running score which mounted into the thousands. We played together in Africa; the moves were still second-nature to him, and the regular rattling of dice was soothing to both of us. I thought it would be fun for him to try the backgammon game we had on our computer, but he was frustrated almost to tears, time after time not understanding how to work the mouse. I finally recognized that there was no longer room in him for anything new.

I got him out into the yard; working with soil was something he'd loved for decades. We spent hours together under the mango trees, transplanting *citronnelle* from big established plants to a new row along the walkway, and it was as if nothing was wrong with him. He would dig a hole with the short-handled hoe, settle a plant I would bring him into place, tamp the soil down with strong, confident hands, measure the distance to the next plant with the hoe's handle. Sitting in the comfortable Third World squat he could maintain for ages, which left my knees screaming after thirty seconds.

By the time I saw him in Spain nearly three years later he no longer even glanced at the comics, no longer worked in the garden. The terraces below the lawn, with that once-sandy soil he'd composted over the years until its yield was prodigious, were a tangle of weeds.

He watched television. Mom had complained, when they visited us in Africa, that he did nothing at home but watch television, with the sound unbearably loud. Now he watched with the sound off completely since he really didn't follow what he was watching, sat on the end of the couch, head tipped at a slightly awkward angle, switching channels with the remote. He went to the market with Mom sometimes, had an anise at the bar while she shopped. People knew him there, chatted with him. He got up early to feed the cats, though Mom said she often wasn't sure if he'd fed them or not, he said he had, but they were hungry.

He was losing the past, as well as the present. I'd hoped he would tell Skyli and Monica the story of his survival at sea, but I didn't even ask him to try. In 1971, a year before the planned move to Spain, he'd gone to Baja California with his friend Bill Knorr to participate in a group fishing expedition, seven boats harbor-hopping their way from San Felipe to Santa Rosalia. Bill's 16-foot outboard *Lazy* turned out to be the smallest of the lot, and Bill knew virtually nothing about boating. They'd had trouble keeping up with the group, and decided to stay and day-fish out of Puertocitos while the others pushed on ahead. They set out one day with only enough food and water for lunch, had engine failure, anchored hoping to flag down a tow, and got swept out to sea by a storm.

By the time the alcoholic American camped next to them in Puertocitos realized their tent had been empty for days, and got word to the closest town with a telegraph line, and the message worked its way north and a search was organized, Dad and Bill had been adrift nearly a week, the longest anyone had survived in the Sea of Cortez in similar conditions. On day ten they were spotted by a Coast Guard amphibious plane, on the last pass of the last day of the search.

Monica, Skyli, Mom, and I went to town to pick up the traveler's checks Mom had ordered for Monica and to talk to a travel agent. Dad stayed home; Mom said he was like this a lot, he simply had no interest in getting out, and she didn't see pressing him.

In town, it took Mom an unbelievable length of time to walk the two blocks from where we parked to the bank. She'd walk a few steps, stop and breathe, walk again. It had always upset me, how little she exercised. In Africa I'd tried to get her to ride our exercise bike, explained how you had to work up a little at a time, and she'd at least pretended to take interest. She now said her doctor had told her she shouldn't get exercise, shouldn't do a lot of walking, because of her heart condition. This surprised me; I thought moderate exercise was advisable for just about any heart condition. She said it was hard to walk anyway, because of her hip. She'd had hip-replacement surgery several years ago after she broke it in a fall, and more surgery last year because the first time hadn't worked out right.

We went to the bank, to the market, and to a singularly unhelpful travel agent who gave Monica flight information for Portugal but knew nothing about buses or trains.

Back home, I got on the phone to the bus companies and the train station. Monica had decided for sure to head for Portugal, but there wasn't another bus to Lisbon for several days, and the trains took convoluted routes. I got more complete flight info than the agent had given us, but it sounded as if the flight Monica wanted on Wednesday was booked. While I was at it, I got some prices and dates for flying from Spain to Bulgaria.

It had been Monica's suggestion that I think about visiting Steve before heading through the Med. I didn't jump at the idea—I didn't want to spend the money, and I particularly didn't want to break *Sonnet's* eastward momentum—but it made sense at least to find out about flights. It would have been nice to run the idea past Steve himself, but I was having a terrible time getting through to Sofia, sitting at the upstairs phone and dialing for forty-five minutes at a stretch.

I did get through to Layne in Jordan. Mom and Dad both chatted with her for a few minutes on the downstairs extension, and then Layne and I talked for another half an hour.

I loved my sister something fierce. We'd been immensely different as children—she'd be curled with a book in her lavender bedroom, while I tore around the cul-de-sac on my bike or rode my horse in the foot-hills—and immensely close, allies against an often incomprehensible adult world. The closeness had wavered for a few years in our late teens and early twenties, when she'd found the answer in Jesus and I wasn't buying it, but it had settled back in again.

She said she was feeling fine, only seven weeks to go. I worried about her every time she had a baby. She'd gone into back labor with David—number one, born eight years ago in Germany—and I'd sensed from five thousand miles away that something was wrong, made frantic call after frantic call from California which she didn't answer because she couldn't get out of bed to reach the phone. I'd been with her when number four was born—Rachie, the second little girl—but the visit grew strained while Layne was in the hospital, since my brother-in-law Robert and I weren't getting along too well.

She told me about Mom and Dad's recent visit to Amman, how hard it had been, how much worse Dad was, how he hadn't taken a shower the first ten days he was there, and Layne and Mom finally sat him down in the bathroom with soap and a towel, and a half hour later realized he was still sitting there, no idea at all what to do.

It made me sad that Layne was so far away, that I saw her so rarely.

I proposed a game of backgammon to Dad in the afternoon, and he said he didn't remember how to play. I fought back a rush of despair and said let's at least try. When I pulled out the backgammon set he couldn't remember how to set up the pieces; even Mom couldn't remember, it had been so long since they'd played, but then between me and Mom and Monica we figured out the setup, and as soon as I got Dad going he beat the pants off me.

He was relaxed with Skyli and Monica—in Africa he'd withdrawn into silence around our friends, maybe sensing their discomfort with his disorientation—and didn't seem afraid to say things from the blue.

"I'm remembering something," he said at one point. "I'm remembering going across the street in the middle of the night, half dressed . . ."

I picked up on it immediately, said, "I bet it was when I caught the mouse"—Christmas of '72 when Layne was here—"and we went across the street to set it free," and he seemed so pleased. A mouse had been chewing their couch cushions for weeks; they'd seen it a time or two but didn't have the heart to set a mouse trap, and didn't have a cat yet, so I'd built a better mouse trap, spent all day on it, a quart-juice can, a string from the top of the door across the top of the can down a hole to a paper clip wrapped in cheese. Nibble the cheese, trip the paper clip, door drops down and stays there with a magnet. I'd slept downstairs in case I caught the mouse, caught it the first night, wakened by the clack of the little metal door closing. I woke the whole house, and we all traipsed across the street in our nightclothes.

So odd, the passing of time, the ache of loss and inheritance. This my papa, who'd kept himself and Bill Knorr alive in the Sea of Cortez by making a saltwater still out of fishing gear, an empty gas can as a boiler, an empty water bottle as a condenser, a hose from the bait tank linking them, sealed air-tight to holes in respective lids with monofilament fish line and unraveled nylon rope. Burned a mixture of gas and oil in burners made of oil cans, lit the fuel by sparking the battery when the matches ran out. This my papa, who no longer possessed that talent for problem-solving, that perfectionist willingness to lean for hours over a painstaking project, but who'd passed some part of those qualities on to me. These intertwining lives.

Just before sunset Monica and Skyli and I walked through the woods and out to the end of the breakwater. From there you could see how the press of civilization was only along the coast; the mountains rose just past the *carretera*, stark and lovely, mountains I'd ridden through on horseback that first summer my parents lived in Spain, dotted with old *fincas*, and groves of cork oaks, and sweet-smelling anise. This place on earth I'd known for so long, the dusty warm smell of it in the summertime, the clear air of the fall, views across to Africa and Gibraltar. The water crashing at the jetty.

The sun was orange, a hand's width above the horizon. Monica sat down on the marina side of the breakwater, looking at the boats. Skyli scrambled down in the rocks on the sea side, looking for sea life. I walked out to the very end, there by the mini-lighthouse, and started doing my Eight Pieces of Embroidery, facing the setting sun, repeating each stretch until it felt right to do the next.

Celebration. Celebrate the good and pure. Celebrate *Sonnet*, celebrate Steve, celebrate this spinning globe. Celebrate these friends, look for the best in each of them. Over and over, arms stretching overhead, then out and down, breathing things in.

Pull-the-string-back stretch, first to the left, then to the right, in knee-bent horse stance, a stylized archer, eyes at the front of the bow. *Focus.* On healing: healthy knee, steady heart. On family, when it was time to be a daughter. On fuel filters, when it was time to be a mechanic. Slowly, facing left. Slowly, facing right. Focus on fingers lightly pointed skyward, focus without distraction.

Circlesight, a simple stretch. Natural stance, hands on hips, twisting the upper body all the way to the right, looking over the right shoulder, then rotating slowly all the way to the left, looking over the left shoulder. I let my eyes swing smoothly at horizon height from the Cabo Pino breakwater, through all the points of the compass, to the north, the dunes and hills of Spain, Monica and Skyli on the low-sun-lit rocks behind me to the east, the heaving Mediterranean to the south, the invisible bulk of Africa in the haze, the west-setting sun, everything that lay to the west, all of my life I'd spent there, all of my life I'd spent in Europe to the north, in Africa to the south, *circlesight*, what had come before, what would come next to the east, not letting the present take on too much weight, not letting hindsight or foresight take on too much weight, weighing the whole of it, feeling the tension ease out of my shoulders.

On through the rest of the eight then, *equilibrium, power, perspective, range, release.* I hadn't done the stretches in a long time because I hadn't believed in them, hadn't believed in much of anything, but it was easy to do them now, left me feeling strong and calm.

After dinner, I wandered up to where Skyli was reading in "Layne's room," pulled an album out of the closet, and we started flipping through it. Pictures of me my first day of kindergarten. Pictures of Layne and me in costumes for ballet recitals. Pictures of our part-Manx cats, lolling around with catnip mice under the Christmas tree.

Memories of the house I grew up in on Skyview Drive, split-level, in the foothills of the San Bernardino mountains, with spectacular views—when it wasn't too smoggy—of the L.A. basin. The incredible work Dad had done over the years to turn the weedy lot into a haven. The pool and deck, the bright bougainvillea twining up to a balcony off the master bedroom, the lily ponds connected by waterfalls. Mom had spent a lot of her childhood on her grandfather's estate in Florida, and loved the lily pond there, and Dad had built her lily ponds in both houses they lived in in California.

Mom came in while Skyli and I were looking at albums, propped herself up easily on a bed, and we all looked together. Pictures of Mom in the early days in Pasadena, wearing off-the-shoulder sun dresses, tanned, her blond hair swept away from her face.

I said to Mom, "Gad, you were beautiful."

Skyli said, joking tone but I knew she meant it, "What do you mean she *was* beautiful?"

She was right to call me on it; there's no reason an older woman can't be beautiful. But in fact my mother at sixty-five, more often than not, wasn't beautiful. It wasn't that her face was lined. It was that those lines, when her face wasn't animated, drew a record of deception and denial. It was that the body that might still have had some strength had none.

Tonight she was animated. I found an old journal of Layne's from a driving trip through England, when Layne was fifteen and I was thirteen. We decided the statute of limitations on privacy ran out after twenty-five years and I read it out loud ("Lyd and I want something exciting to happen, like get stuck in the mud in the rain or go out on a rough ride in a sailboat"), starting with me and Skyli and Mom as audience, then with Monica wandering in, and Dad, and Abbey, five people—and a silly Siamese cat—sprawled on the two twin beds and laughing.

So many tremendous vacations, when I was growing up. Mom adored traveling, pored over the travel section, checked out stacks of books from the library, began planning next year's vacation as soon as we got home from this year's. We might economize the rest of the year but we always traveled. By some odd fluke of her illness Mom was a different person on vacation, she drank but rarely got drunk. Vacations were the only time our family felt whole and uncomplicated; maybe that's why both Layne and I had become such incorrigible wanderers of the world.

So much good in my family, so much right, and so much wrong. There was nothing in those photo albums to record the surreal arguments that stretched on to nowhere. Nothing to show the days Layne or I would come home from school and find Mom drunk, passed out near the steep drop-off above Loma Alta Street, passed out near the sharp-edged credenza, bleeding from a head wound.

So much good. We'd been dyed-in-the-wool Dodger fans, listened to games around the pool on summer nights. Dad helped us on science projects. Mom packed marvelous sack lunches, went all out at Christmas. We had cats. Cats, in a way, were a key to it all. My parents, through all the cruelty and tragedy of their marriage, always had cats in common. For Layne and me, cats were a constant, a predictable, infallible source of love.

The second day at my parents', things came together and somewhat fell apart. I got through to Steve. He was instantly in favor of my coming to Bulgaria. He missed me. We'd been through a lot of separations in our years together, and we'd learned that stresses began setting in after about two months apart.

He said don't worry about the money.

I missed him, I wanted to see him, I wanted to see the place I'd be living for two years, but I *was* worried about the money, and I wanted *Sonnet* to keep moving east. True, I'd talked about sailing as far as Malta and then heading for Bulgaria, but Malta was close enough to the goal that it didn't feel like so much of a capitulation.

Monica and Skyli and I went into Marbella to another travel agent, who found an empty seat on the next morning's flight to Lisbon. Monica walked out of the agency flourishing her ticket and trying to look pleased, but it was clear she was starting to unravel, and trying not to show it. She wanted to go off on this adventure, but she didn't want to leave the protective embrace of *Sonnet*, and she was jealous that Skyli would be driving with me back to the boat.

I'd encouraged her to box up some of her stuff and mail it back to the States so she wouldn't have to lug so much around. She spent hours packing and repacking, separating her possessions into take and not-take piles, trying out different-size boxes, different combinations of bags, asking my advice, showing me dresses she'd brought along and hadn't yet worn.

I conducted my search for new crew beyond her earshot. I got through to Candace, a woman I'd met in Abidjan when she'd been driving with her boyfriend from London to Capetown in their Land Rover; I figured anyone who could make it through the Sahara and Zaire could handle the Mediterranean, but she'd just started a new job.

I figured I'd put an advertisement up in Gibraltar, hope to find someone there, or maybe try to hook up with one of the British-based crewing organizations. It had occurred to Skyli that her third crew member Amy might want to sail *Sonnet* through the Med before sailing *Antelope Medicine* across the Atlantic; she'd tried several times to reach her but hadn't succeeded. She suggested I try to contact Carol on *Cardiff*, thinking Carol might want a break from Dean.

It didn't occur to either of us, early on, that Skyli herself might help sail *Sonnet* through the Med. It had never been my secret agenda for Skyli to take Monica's place; it just transpired, things just started to come clear. I'd assumed I'd be well on my way east while Skyli was spending time with her Steven, but now it looked as if I'd probably be taking time out for my Steven, too.

It wouldn't be ideal. I didn't want Skyli sacrificing her own plans for mine, and it seemed pretty unlikely—even if we took off for Greece the day after Steven Morgan headed for the States—that Skyli could make it back to *Antelope Medicine* before the start of the Columbus 500 Rally. Skyli said the Rally had been a goal, an impetus, there was no way she would have been brave enough to launch on this venture without it, but now she couldn't care less if she missed the whole thing. I said what about Lisa and Amy? She said Lisa had gotten caught up in her consulting work and wasn't joining until the Canaries anyway, and Amy was a tremendous sport, if they blew off the start of the first leg she'd probably get a kick out of it.

By the time Monica was packing for Lisbon, Skyli and I were talking seriously about her sailing with me through the Med if I did in fact go to Bulgaria. I wasn't convinced it was the right thing to do, but we were talking. We didn't mention it to Monica, which maybe wasn't right in itself.

Monica's flight was at noon. Skyli and I took her to the Málaga airport. As we saw her through the gate the friendliness between the three of us was strained, and I felt bad, and still do.

The drive down the Andalusian coast was in sunlight this time, Gib- raltar to our left, growing larger and larger, craggy and unreal-looking, its flank bearing the pale concrete scar of the water catchment.

10

Thousands of miles I sailed this vessel alone.
Tonight I'll sail fifty. Or not quite sail: the sea
sleeps, a peaceful beast; the diesel's drone
hints endlessly, a bluffer's muffled key.
Hell-bent ships, bright-lit, go churning by.
The flood-lit Rock slips aft, black sky slips in.
The coast is known by chart-line, not by eye,
and I've been known to gamble, and to win.
There's this: tonight I'll cross the outward track—
twenty years now, almost to the day—
I traced that first night's crashing, circling back
as dolphin shapes hone in and streak away.
For now, no ships, no glimmering shore, no stake.
Just stars on dark, and one straight luminous wake.

11 Sept

Monica is gone.

The engine is running, charging batteries at the dock in Gibraltar. I'm not minding the engine, trying not to mind it, want to work with it until I've got confidence in it.

Feeling sad. I wanted things for Monica, wanted to see her change. I saw her face as she stirred the Medicine Cards, excitement, expectation, saw her as a victim, in this marriage all these years (these marriages), never discovering Monica for Monica.

Feeling angry. She kept saying how fun it was as we climbed the Rock, but as soon as I was gone she started complaining about the effort, begging Skyli to go out to lunch with her, she'd pay, they'd just *tell* me they'd kept climbing. Maybe she *did* know the difference between what she wanted and what she thought someone wanted her to want.

Relief and failure, gave her nothing gave her an adventure I don't know. I wanted friendship with her, wanted it to be good for her to be on the boat, failed at all of it.

I was an absurdly optimistic late-teens-twenties, Skyli was borderline suicidal, wrapping herself in Dostoevskyan cloaks, driving way too fast. We now have the same lacks of confidence, high IQs and low self-esteem, the same recurring dreams, haven't graduated from high school, haven't graduated from college, can't find the classroom, can't find the notes for the final.

I feel like I'm getting a cold, my traditional familial-visit ill-health. Tired today, I could have curled in the grass and gone to sleep walking back from bus-schedule-checking in Spain, Spain you couldn't walk to when I first came to Gibraltar.

I want Skyli to go away so I can sleep. I don't at all want Skyli to go away.

Monica is gone. Clear and not, happy and not, *Sonnet* around me, the future ahead of me, Skyli coming back on board after her shower. It's scary, to have bared this much of myself to another human being in such a short time. Extraordinary, though, the extent to which you can bare and still have stories untold, the most crucial of stories, the most central.

14 Sept

Now Skyli is gone.

Alone on my boat, missing Skyli, missing Steve, loving them both.

The boat moves slightly on the water. The sheet Lisa wrote my Medicine Cards on is folded between the pages of *Animal Dreams*. My animal within is the contrary Antelope. I need to remind myself into action, into creation; animals and books and friends may help.

I need in my life to accept the gift of an African deity even if in my intellect I don't believe it.

Sitting on my boat in Gibraltar, my boat I sailed from Chesapeake Bay, reading a book placed in the American Southwest, making plans to visit Bulgaria. Calmness in me; calmness and a sore throat.

16 Sept

Torn between families; less time with Steve would mean more time with my parents, more time with my parents when I come back would put strain on Skyli's schedule if Skyli ends up sailing with me. I don't want Skyli's desire to sail with me to interfere with her commitment to Steven Morgan, or to Lisa and Amy. On the other hand, can't make people's choices for them (or can I?).

17 Sept

This is *tough*, leaving my boat. I sit on the plane, feeling like I'm deserting her.

Want to get a shitload of things done in Sofia, house in shape, pound out some article ideas. Want to make some money next year; good chance I'll make not a dime this year, the biggest spending year of my life.

Airplanes are wonderful, everywhere and nowhere somehow, the roar, the impersonal food, the transition from one place to another.

A dream of Skyli's: She took *Sonnet* out alone, and it was only after she was out there, sailing around, that the full impact hit her of what she'd done. She was mortified, saw me running down a breakwater, she was sure I was furious, then overwhelmingly relieved, realizing no, I wasn't furious after all, I was pleased she was out there, I was happily snapping pictures of the boat.

And it's starting to come clear to me, my discomfort at her potentially sailing through the Med with me, though there's no one in the world I'd rather have do it. The pattern in her of doing things for friends beyond the call of duty, taking them into her home, giving them cars, all of it. I want to be a different kind of friend to her, a friend of a different era. I want both of us to be healthier for knowing each other.

It was Steve, in the end, who'd figured out the cheapest way for me to get to Bulgaria, learned about a promotional flight from London through a contact at Balkan Air. It seemed silly to fly due north to get to Eastern Europe, especially since I'd have to spend the night in England before flying on to Sofia. But combined with a good round-trip fare to London from Gibraltar, it was cheaper by several hundred dollars than going through Madrid.

I'd spent six days in Gib working on endless boat projects which now were dropping away to the south. Tomorrow I'd be flying east, rather than sailing. And tonight I wasn't sure where I'd be sleeping.

I'd tried from Gibraltar to get hold of my friend Mary in Sussex. I hadn't succeeded even in getting a ring, and suspected there'd been a change in area code. We'd known each other since 1974, when we worked a Caribbean charter season together on the 52-foot catamaran *Margay* after my first Atlantic passage, Mary as stewardess, me as cook. She'd been twenty-six at the time, I'd been nineteen. We'd seen each other six or eight times in the subsequent years; she and Peter had visited Steve and me in Portugal, and in Paris, and in Abidjan, and we stayed with them whenever we passed through England. Mary was a terrible letter writer, so I often went a couple of years without hearing from her.

We were exceedingly different, and got along exceedingly well, with a solid knowledge of each other going back nearly two decades. I had several other long-time long-distance friends like that, but somehow I felt I'd never had friends the way I imagined other women having friends, someone you talk to frequently, meet for lunch. For years, I'd felt uncomfortable with most women, a slight sense that I was play-acting, that I'd be found out, that the woman would suddenly narrow one eye and say to me, "You don't *really* know how to do this, do you?"

Maybe it was from growing up with an alcoholic mom, not sure whether you could risk bringing home a friend. Maybe it was because my best friend in grade school in fact looked down on me, and had a mother who looked down on my parents for not having college educations, on my mother for drinking, a realization I came to only slowly, over years. Maybe it was because the first time I found a soul mate, the summer between eleventh and twelfth grades, I proceeded to lose her; the letter writing we'd done for a couple of years tapered off, and then I didn't believe I'd deserved her in the first place. How could I have deserved her if I could remember the street she lived on but not the town, and not her last name, though her image had hovered near me for more than twenty years, Kim of Tryon Road?

Maybe it was because of Kim that I didn't let Deborah go by. Deborah and I met in Côte d'Ivoire. We were both living there but traveling a lot, and close to moving back to the States. I read through the novel she was working on; I loved both the novel and the creative act of editing. We fit time in together the few days we overlapped in Abidjan, and she came down from northern California when I was recovering from knee surgery in southern California. We wrote letters; we used the phone system.

Maybe it was because of Deborah that I didn't let Skyli go by.

A dream of mine: We were on this exceptionally nice yacht, like *Alaska Eagle* but more of a home, lots of flat black and polished stainless steel, high-tech gear and warm varnish. The boat belonged to Skyli's father—a completely different father than her real one—and she and I were sailing it in the mountains, steering between pine trees on a narrow trail between one lake and another.

Passing over Portsmouth, I can see rivers and yachts.

I arrived at Gatwick airport at three, checked a telephone directory, and discovered that yes, codes for West Sussex now had a new digit. I tried Mary's number and got a ring but no one answered.

I bought myself a British sailing magazine and called a crewing organization out of the classifieds. I was given the names and numbers of several women who might want to crew through the Med, but I wasn't quite ready to start courting strangers.

Still no answer at Pockford House. I had plenty of time to get into London and find a hotel if that's what it came to, so I settled down with a book. An hour later I tried Mary again, without success, then found Peter's Mazda dealership in the yellow pages. He didn't sound all that surprised to hear from me; this wasn't the first time I'd appeared from the blue.

It turned out they'd moved over the border to Hampshire. He gave me their new home number but said he was pretty sure Mary wasn't there, she'd said she was going shopping and wouldn't be back until five. I had trouble imagining where Mary would be shopping until five; she'd always avoided shopping like the plague. He told me he could use an excuse to get away early from work and to call him back if I didn't get through to Mary. I tried Mary—no one home—then called Peter back. Fifteen minutes later he scooped me up at the airport.

Peter was twenty years older than Mary, now in his late sixties, showing his age but still wiry and strong. My emotions about him were very mixed. He could be extremely gracious, but had an insidious way of undermining Mary which drove me nuts.

We headed west toward Hampshire. We talked about his business, which wasn't doing well, and the British economy in general, which he saw as abysmal. He told me about their new home, certainly not on the scale of Pockford House or even Gratwicks, but it had potential. Peter took pleasure in buying old estates and restoring them, but I was surprised to hear they'd moved, since Mary had sworn she was never leaving Pockford House.

As we pulled into the gravel yard Mary burst out of the old two-story stone house. "L.B.! I don't believe it!"

She was wearing a dress; I was amazed.

I said, "Mary, you look great."

She said, "I *feel* great," and then more quietly, linking her arm through mine as we walked toward the house, "I have *so* much to tell you."

I instantly suspected she was having an affair.

We were greeted at the door by Rupert, the marvelous black Lab I'd known since he was a pup, now losing his eyesight and moving slowly. Inside, furniture was stacked everywhere, covered with sheets and construction dust. So far, the only fully restored portion of the property was the stables.

Peter gave me a tour of the grounds while Mary changed her clothes and put some potatoes on to boil. Then Mary and I went out to meet and feed the horses, and she told me in brief and with great animation about her lover (I thought, what's *with* these women, Monica and now Mary, what's with my friends?), how this man meant everything to her. Leaving Pockford House had been devastating, she'd loved the place so much, but in a strange way it was the right thing to have happened, it allowed her an emotional distance from Peter. She'd tell me more, tell me all about it, after dinner.

As we walked back to the house she said wasn't it near here that I'd stayed with that sailing friend of mine, when I'd come over in '79? Wasn't it Midhurst? And what was his name?

His name was Tim, and yes it was Midhurst. She thought I should look him up, pulled out the phone book as soon as we got inside, and I was relieved when we didn't find a listing.

She finished making dinner for Peter and me and herself and the live-in carpenter; the four of us ate at a table off the half-remodeled kitchen. The carpenter retired, Mary and Peter and I talked for a while, then Peter retired and Mary opened a second bottle of wine.

I was uncomfortable at first, convinced Peter could listen through the ceiling if he really wanted to. I was restless, knowing I should probably be contacting crew possibilities. But then the silence continued from upstairs, and the hour became too late for calling strangers, and we just talked.

She didn't think Peter knew about the affair but he sensed some loss, and she felt that he finally appreciated her, finally loved her, finally recognized the ways he'd been cruel to her, but it was too late. She would stay with him, keep cooking his meals and running his house, sleep with him from time to time, but only because it didn't make sense to leave.

She said that as difficult as Peter was, until now she'd been faithful, fifteen years. She knew that might surprise me, considering how she'd behaved in the Caribbean, but that was a different world, something about sailing, something about the sea air, boats and movement and adventure. Plus she'd been young, the islands had been her life's big fling.

In the Caribbean, I remembered well, she'd had overlapping intrigues with at least four men, her companion depending on the island, or what yacht ended up in the same anchorage as *Margay*. I'd been younger by a long shot than she was, naïve and sexually tentative, and she'd thoroughly amazed me.

But I felt a little sting of revelation as she talked, seeing myself as a pot to a kettle to Monica. Mary was right, there *was* something about sailing, something about the air. If in '73–'74 I'd been tentative—the Atlantic crossing on *Zeelandia*, and then the season on *Margay* in the Caribbean—by six years later, coming back across the Atlantic on *Au-*

gust Moon, I'd been much less so. Steve still in the States, our relationship so new, aching for him and missing him, and at the same time caught into the swirl of more than one attraction.

I listened to Mary talk about her world, this man in her life. We went to bed late, and in the morning she put me on a train to Heathrow. By two I was on a plane again, bound for Bulgaria. By seven the plane was slanting in darkness toward the Sofia airport.

18 Sept

Looking down as we come in toward the runway, this new world to me, black of night (THUNK! not so smooth a landing), why is it so many of the lights seem to be blinking? Are they candles? I sense mountains, see lights on top of them, this place is unlike any I've been to, lived in. Very few lights for the number of buildings, people who have lived through things I've never known, virtually unlit runway, planes hunkered along it in the dark, excited and scared, maybe not ready for this, maybe haven't made any attempt to get ready.

Plane slowing to a stop.

Bulgaria. Bulgaria, for heaven's sake.

I grabbed my luggage from the overhead, shuffled forward in the press of passengers and down the ramp. A hundred-yard shuttle ride across the runway to the glass doors leading into passport control, where another planeload was already elbowing forward. A stout imposing woman handing out immigration forms; why couldn't they have given these to us on the plane?

As I emerged from passport control Steve was there, wearing his embassy I.D., the only nonpassenger in the luggage-claim area. We showed black diplomatic passports to the customs people, made our way through the crowd in the waiting room, turned down the offers of taxi drivers (*zhivéim tuk, imame kolá*; we live here, we have a car), emerged into the coolish night and crossed—talking as we walked—to the big dusty Volvo station wagon I partly owned and had never seen. Steve left it dirty, without hubcaps, so it wouldn't stand out too much.

Ten minutes later he pulled into the parking lot of the middle of three identical concrete monstrosities built to house foreigners during the Communist era. We'd heard stories about life in these *Diplomaticheski* apartment blocks before "the changes," how you'd come home and find cigarette butts in your sinks, that sort of thing, just letting you know they were there.

A male concierge greeted us in the foyer, obviously fond of Steve, curious and welcoming toward me. A grumbling Russian elevator took us up sixteen floors.

Butch was waiting right inside the door, ready to be picked up by Steve, whom he adored with an intensity more dog-like than cat-like. Steve had deeply distrusted cats when we first met; it was ironic that our surviving cat was more his than mine.

We wandered through the apartment, Butch draped on Steve's left arm like a leopard on a branch. Boxes were stacked nearly to the ceiling in the huge living room; Steve had unpacked some clothes and kitchen things and the computer but that was about all.

There were flowers for me on the dining-room table from Dora, the woman Steve had hired to come in two hours weekdays to clean the house. He told me how excited she was about meeting me, how disappointed she'd been that I was flying in on a Friday night, three days she'd have to wait before we met.

Northeast-facing windows in the kitchen, for morning light. Two decent-sized bedrooms down a hallway to the left of the entry. A big master bathroom, ugly but functional. The load I hadn't known I was carrying around came off; we could make this place work.

We settled in the living room and talked, eating ice cream Steve had found yesterday in a little privately owned store down the street, the fruits of a fledgling market economy. Butch leaped in two bounds to the top of the box pile and watched us.

Steve told me about Jim Silva, the U.S. Army attaché, and his wife, Eileen, who'd done some sailing. He'd told them I might need some help bringing the boat through the Med; if I wanted, we could get together next week to discuss it.

Steve was excited about taking me to Greece, to Porto Carras, the little marina on the west coast of Sithonia, the middle finger of the three-fingered Halkidiki peninsula. For a long time we'd assumed we'd keep *Sonnet* in Thessaloniki for the winter, the closest port to Sofia; we'd discovered Carras pretty much simultaneously, me by reading my

Greek Waters Pilot, Steve when he took a trip down with his friend Tom. Steve said it would be well worth the extra hour-and-a-half drive to keep the boat at Carras, the area was spectacularly beautiful.

He was taking next Friday off, and could leave work Thursday a little early, so we'd have a full three days in Greece. Dora would stay in the apartment with Butch.

We talked about my voyage, about Steve's work, about my parents. It now felt so right to have made this trip, to talk without the constraints of long distance, to watch the expressions of his face as he talked. Two months apart, not seeing each other. Fifteen years of knowing his face, his body, of loving the way his words wove sentences. Longer than that really; there were the months in college before I even knew his name, when I'd already fallen for him hard.

There'd been a period, after we'd connected, that I doubted our relationship could ever really work, my initial infatuation had been so powerful. A doubt maybe still intact in '79 when I went off ahead of him to Europe.

What we had now behind us was time. Enduring pleasure in each other's company, pride in each other's accomplishments, always the ability to talk. We were often enough a challenge to each other, and had differences which sometimes felt terrifying, but it struck me that first night in Sofia that I wasn't with Steve because he offered me financial security, which was much of why Monica was with Brian, or because it didn't make sense to leave, which was Mary's line about Peter. I was with him because I continued to love him—loved his mind, his spirit; loved his body, the broad straight shoulders and elegant limbs, his face, the chiseled features—and because our relationship continued to feel right.

In the morning I tackled boxes, and Steve worked on his new novel, which took his field-biologist protagonist to a West African rain forest. His first book had been published in February, with good reviews; since arriving in Sofia, he'd been writing two hours week nights—after ten hours as a diplomat—and three or four hours on weekend mornings.

In the afternoon we drove around downtown Sofia, bought produce for pennies a kilo at an open market by the ruins of a Roman wall, checked out the antique sellers around Nevski cathedral, which looked more like a mosque than a church, its bulging domes and half-domes capped by glittering gold.

Sunday we went hiking in the foothills of Mount Vitosha, with views—through dark conifers and stands of white-barked beeches—down to Sofia and across the valley to the dim silhouettes of the Balkan range. The city was ringed by mountains, which was part of what made it so miserable in winter, an inversion layer holding down the smog.

Monday morning I met Dora. She had a lovely, gentle face, dark eyes and out-of-a-bottle blond hair, and stood about five foot two. She touched my cheek as she babbled in Bulgarian, and I nodded, pretending I understood. I had some catching up to do on my language skills.

Steve headed for the embassy, Dora did dishes and laundry, and I unpacked books.

21 Sept

Lizard, Possum, Hawk, what a life I have. I look out the window at run-down Ladas trundling down the streets, amazed to be in Bulgaria.

Tuesday I took a cab downtown at seven o'clock and met Steve and the Silvas at the embassy. Jim and Eileen had been to a reception of some sort and were dressed up, Jim in uniform, Eileen in black pants and a silk blouse, with a comfortable leather jacket thrown on top. They were both strikingly attractive. Eileen had fair skin and short black hair, dark eyes, a marvelous smile. Younger than I'd expected—late twenties, maybe early thirties.

Steve led us through winding dark Sofia streets to a tiny restaurant with three inside tables and two outside tables and the street in front being torn up loudly by a bulldozer. Jim gave Steve a hard time about his famous "Italian restaurant" until he got a good look at the antipasti. The place had an Italian cook; food like this was virtually unheard of in Sofia.

The people inside were chain-smoking, so we took an outside table in spite of the noise. When the bulldozer driver shut off his machine Steve called him over and bought him a beer, asked him if he was getting paid overtime to work at night—turns out he was working on a broken waterline—and what he thought about the changes in the country. The man shook his head, prices were going up, there were more things available than six months ago but no one could afford to buy them.

When we finally got to talking about sailing Jim admitted he wasn't very enthusiastic about Eileen taking off, they had three little girls, he didn't relish handling the household alone. I said there were a couple of possibilities, Eileen could come to Spain and sail the whole way, which would probably be a three-week commitment—Jim rolled his eyes—or she could meet me somewhere like Malta, sail just the last of it.

Eileen told me about her round-trip voyage to Hawaii and back to California in her college days, pointing out that she wasn't very knowledgeable, she really liked sailing, but she'd pretty much just done what the skipper told her. As we walked back to the embassy we dropped behind the men, and she told me she'd like to talk some more, maybe she could come over tomorrow.

We talked the next afternoon among the box clutter. She told me she wasn't sure she was qualified to do a double-handed passage, as much as she'd like the adventure. I told her the boat was set up for me to sail alone, I didn't need someone with a comprehensive knowledge of sailing, in fact what was most important to me was finding someone I could get along with.

I felt comfortable with her. She seemed tough, game, and smart. We pulled out an atlas. I asked how long she thought she could be away and she said two weeks easily, Jim made a lot of noise but he'd be fine without her, especially since their Bulgarian baby-sitter would be doing most of the work. I told her two weeks would be plenty to sail from Malta, would even give us time to see some Greek islands.

By the time she left I was feeling both excited and relieved. I could still sail with Skyli, but if Skyli sailed only to Malta she might even make it back to *Antelope Medicine* in time for the start of the Columbus 500 Rally. I was excited about sailing with someone from the embassy, someone with whom I would have a special bond back in Sofia. Also, this was exactly what I'd often envisioned of *Sonnet*, for a number of women to sail on her. It now looked like three different women—very different—would sail on three different legs.

I returned to my unpacking job with a burst of enthusiasm.

Thursday afternoon I loaded the car, scooped Steve up at the embassy at four o'clock, and we headed south toward Greece.

We passed through a few large Bulgarian towns, but often it felt as if we were driving through the Europe of an earlier era. Men in blue work smocks, women in bright head scarves, cutting hay to put away for winter, working small plots of land by hand. Goats, milk cows, haystacks, horse carts, donkey carts with wooden wheels like the wheels of covered wagons. Fields of corn, fields of sunflowers, fruit trees, towns tucked into the folds of the hills, tobacco strung in great dark clumps to dry.

The land itself was beautiful, wooded hills, twisting roads through steep gorges. Over that inherent beauty, over the human struggle to make good in imposed simplicity, was a layer of ugliness, not always there, but often enough. Ugly heroic monuments, massive on-ramps of an abandoned road project, rickety ore buckets trundling overhead toward a hulking factory, a concrete ramp for changing engine oil, the soil beneath it black and saturated.

We arrived at the border just after sunset, then crossed into Greece, a place with restaurants lit by cheerful signs, and well-maintained cars on well-maintained roads. We talked about how a quirk of fate—and the fact that Winston Churchill was very fond of Greece—had landed Bulgaria in one sphere of influence after World War II and Greece in another.

We dropped down out of the mountains into olive groves and fruit orchards. The air itself was more welcoming in Greece, humid from the sea, a hint of the warmth of Africa.

We spent the first night in Thessaloniki—the bright bustle of the city almost shocking after Sofia—and the next two nights on the Halkidiki, at a whitewashed hotel at the top of the bay between the peninsulas of Cassandra and Sithonia.

Steve worked a couple of hours in the morning at the laptop. We swam in the salty Aegean. We took an afternoon walk on the beach one day, past bee boxes and goat pens set among pines on another. We ate marvelous Greek food, grilled fish, yogurt-cucumber salad, roasted eggplant, fresh fruit purchased at produce stands along the highway.

On Saturday we drove down the west coast of Sithonia toward Porto Carras. The land became more dramatic, more extreme, gnarled olive trees interspersed with pine, dark rocks encircling aqua-watered coves. I fell for the peninsula that very first time we drove it, almost dizzy, a visceral response.

The complex at Carras was nothing to rave about—two big blocky resort hotels and the marina encircled by a smaller hotel and a cluster of bars and shops—but the hills around it were rich with the scent of pine, and the sight of sailboat masts, as always, gave me a little buzz.

Steve settled down at one of the bars for a beer and I walked the entire marina. So many times, when traveling in Europe, I'd honed in on marinas, walked with pleasure along quays and docks, looking at boats. But it was strange this time, very different. Did *Sonnet* fit here? Did I? Maybe it's just a tendency I have, when I've been high for a while, to get low, but at Porto Carras a moodiness set in that was nearly debilitating. I sat alone for a while trying to shake it and finally gave up.

It was a long drive home the following day, much of the Bulgarian portion in darkness, which was tough, no white center line, no shoulder to speak of, unlit tractors and donkey carts looming suddenly out of the night.

Driving and thinking. I had bought *Sonnet* in a search for balance, but in some deep place I ached for the balance Steve and I had had before, the equality and simplicity we'd had for years, when both of us worked, both of us brought in money, both of us did housework, both of us wrote fiction and failed to publish it. The years when our flexible schedules allowed us to take off with regularity on spontaneous adventures.

We'd wanted a different kind of experience, wanted to live in new places and not just visit them, to live overseas and get paid for it. Steve had reminded me over and over, these past four years, that this was a shared decision, a shared adventure, that the salary was ours, not his. But there was no way I could feel personal pride in a well-written political cable, no way I could look at a Meritorious Honor Award and feel it was partly mine, and I struggled ridiculously with the mundane, not wanting to spend hours ironing Steve's dress shirts, not wanting to be sole cleaner of dishes and toilets and floors, not comfortable having someone do these things for us. I hoped it would be easier with Dora than it had been in Africa; with Dora the tone was more maternal affection than subservience.

So much. So much more than that.

In the morning Steve dropped me at the airport and headed for a nine o'clock meeting at the embassy. He was never a hundred percent

functional until his second cup of coffee anyway, so he didn't realize
how low I was feeling; it's not like we parted hard.

28 Sept

Sharing my Chee-tos with a scruffy black-and-white Bulgarian
cat. So many cats in the world, begging at restaurants, begging in
airport waiting rooms, ugly, skitty, unloved.

So torn up at leaving *Sonnet*, and now I'm ambivalent at going
back. Wanted to create my own place within Steve's world of diplomacy, and now I don't know if I can reconcile the two, if
Steve and *Sonnet* can easily coexist.

Unsettling dreams last night, one with high-powered types
wanting to talk about his novel, another with me petting Oscar,
thinking at least I still have Oscar, then the dreamer somehow
realizing I didn't.

Plane for London boarding.

Driving back in the dark through Bulgaria from Greece I had a
moment of utter clarity, at how hard life is in this country, how
hugely lucky I am. Feeling spoiled and also feeling blessed.

The world is too fucking big. Will *Sonnet* continue to be a
place where the world becomes smaller?

I slept on the plane to London, wandered around Heathrow for the
couple hours before my connection, back on a plane and heading south.

In the air again, flying from London toward Gibraltar, and suddenly I feel settled. Flying toward *Sonnet* I can feel the reality of
her, the solidity. Ready to do some work, replace the starter
switch, change the oil, finish off the traveler project. It was good
to get a glimpse into the future, deal with some of the push-pull
now instead of later.

Writing sonnets as exercise, not poems. Wonder if I could
write a poem.

Waves of strength, waves of weariness. Seeking equilibrium.

I had flown into Málaga a number of times, but never into Gibraltar.
The day was crystal clear, breathtaking, the world laid out below me

like a chart, the coast of Spain, the glittering strip of water between Europe and Africa, the Bay of Algeciras, the Rock's slender peninsula. I was glued to the window as we angled toward the Gibraltar runway, looking down with Hawk Medicine, watching for my boat. My life felt patterned by concentric and overlapping circles.

I walked across the runway and down to the marina. Greg and Sascha were sitting with a group of people at an outside table at the bar, and waved me over. They'd been married last week here in Gibraltar and were sorry I'd missed it; they'd been planning this for a while, mostly so Sascha could get a green card when they returned to the States.

Greg told me Skyli and her husband were here, they'd slept last night on *Sonnet*, and I was pleased. Skyli had told me she and Steven would probably rent a car in Portugal for a shopping trip to Gibraltar, and I'd told her they should for sure stay on *Sonnet*.

There was a note from Skyli on *Sonnet*'s chart table—welcoming me home, telling me they'd already imposed on my hospitality and would see me later in the day—but no other sign of their existence. When they came by a few hours later I found out they'd tried to find a hotel in both Spain and Gibraltar and had failed, had slept on *Sonnet* only with great reluctance. I wanted Skyli to sleep on my boat with ease and familiarity, not fear of imposition, but I was happy to see her.

And I was intrigued to meet Steven Morgan, as she no doubt would be to meet Steven Voien; we knew a lot about each other without knowing each other's mates. Her Steven was slight, and soft-spoken, and had a smart, cynical humor, and I liked him.

I told them I'd found a woman in Sofia who could do the Malta-to-Greece portion of *Sonnet*'s Mediterranean passage, which meant Skyli could get back earlier to *Antelope Medicine*, assuming she did still want to sail with me. I told her I could also put some notices up to find someone here, wanting to give her an out if she needed it, if she was having doubts about giving my boat priority over hers. She later told me she'd almost decided not to sail with me when I mentioned the notices, saw it as an indication that I didn't want her along. Steven Morgan had settled her down, saying she wants you along, you should go.

We worked out the details. He was flying out Saturday the third. She would make her way to my parents' right after he left, arriving probably on the fourth.

We went out to dinner that night with Greg and Sascha. Sky-li and Steven slept again on *Sonnet*, and took off in their recalcitrant rental car in the morning.

29 Sept

The extent to which I feel grounded again. Boat errands in Gibraltar, running into fellow boaters. Folks out for a *paseo* across the border in Spain, the s-dropped Andalusian Spanish *bueno dia que tal*.

I talked to my parents, told them I'd be sailing *Sonnet* singlehanded to Fuengirola, probably leaving Gibraltar tomorrow afternoon and arriving in Fuengirola marina by early Friday morning. Mom said her cardiologist was in the office on Friday, she could make an appointment if I still wanted to meet him, and I said I definitely did.

It was nine-thirty Thursday night before I finally got away from Gibraltar. Greg and Sascha cast off my bow lines. I backed *Sonnet* out of her slip and powered in darkness out of the inner harbor. To some extent I regretted that I'd be doing this passage at night, that I wouldn't be seeing the coastline of Spain from the deck of my own boat, or the Rock in daylight. At the same time it felt exactly right, not only because I liked nighttime on boats—the mystery of it, the oddness—but because the first time I'd ever been off the dock on a sailboat had been at night, and had been in these very waters.

In June of '72, when my parents and I had first moved into the apartment at Puerto José Banus, I'd met John, who had bought his little 33-foot double-ender *Caprille* a couple months earlier, and was working hard to get her ready to go sailing. I gave him my labor for free—sanding, varnishing, running errands, handing him tools when he was wedged in the engine space—because I loved being on the boat, and loved John's stories about sailing. *Caprille*'s mast wasn't stepped, and her engine wasn't running, so I never saw her off the dock, but I knew every inch of her.

In July I took off on my bike trip through Europe, after saying goodbye to John, who expected to be on his way to the Balearics within a few weeks. When I got back in late September he still hadn't left; his crew had fallen through, and he said this is great, now *you* can crew for me. I was thrilled.

My dad went ballistic. What would the neighbors say if his eighteen-year-old daughter took off on a boat with an unmarried forty-year-old man? John said no problem, we'll just take your dad along.

The crew, in the end, consisted of me, my dad, John, and a hitch-hiking mathematician named Jay. The day things at last came to-gether—what was the *date?*—we planned to leave at noon, and finally took off well after dark. John waited until we'd cleared the breakwater to gather us below for a cheerful lecture on safety procedures. *Caprille* wallowed beam-to the seas; I started throwing up about five minutes later, and threw up virtually the entire way to Málaga. Even so, by the end of that night I was hooked for good on sailing.

It had been early October. Could I figure out the date exactly, through a letter to my sister maybe, or that funny map I'd made my parents, "The Travels of Lydia"?

Tonight, sailing *Sonnet* from Gibraltar to Fuengirola, I would cross *Caprille*'s outward track from José Banus to Málaga. Twenty years later, maybe to the day.

2300 My own world. Loom of the south end of the Rock, black against the sky; loom of the part farther north, spot-lit. Enjoying the toys, radar, lights for the instruments, tricolor. Still a twinge at not sailing away from the Rock in daylight, not having walked up it, not having walked around it. It's okay; leavings can be hard, the one from Fuengirola is likely to be even harder.

By 0230 the Rock was twenty miles off my stern, mainland Spain was ten miles off my port beam—the coast dipped north in a long gentle bay between Gibraltar and Fuengirola—and I could just see the Cala Burras light flashing every ten seconds off my bow, flashing from the lighthouse I passed whenever I drove between my parents' house and town.

No wind. The Westerbeke was running. The autopilot was driving. I would sleep for ten minutes in the cockpit, stand and look around for traffic, nap again, pass fishing boats sometimes, take a GPS fix every forty minutes or so and plot it at the chart table below, amazed by my steady, effortless progress.

It was extraordinary, that night alone in Spain on *Sonnet*, as I powered along an invisible coastline I'd known for years, known in a different lifetime. Nothing touched the hull of my boat but water, nothing but water connected her to the globe, and I felt whole and alive in the solitude, at home. All the peaceful and powerful moments of the solo passage to the Azores were reaffirmed, all the terrifying or frustrating moments were justified; I knew this boat, felt the length of her, felt the soul of her, because I'd put those miles in and taken them with me.

A hint of a breeze came up in the early hours of morning. I knew how much work it would be, later on, to flake the mainsail alone if I raised it now, so I rolled out the jib and turned off the engine and *Sonnet* slid along easily at more than four knots with just a headsail, sailing impressively close to the wind for no mainsail, the water rushing quietly against the hull in the still-flat sea.

My course took me somewhat offshore, and then I tacked, sailing back in toward the spot-lit Fuengirola castle. I picked out the blinking red and green lights of the entrance to the marina, and made my approach as the wind dropped.

I'd made good time; no rush to get in. I sailed until the wind died completely and light crept into the sky, then rolled in the jib and drifted as I did my chores, coiled sheets, prepped dock lines. Such a wonderful sense of completion, rightness; doing this for me, even changing into black sweatpants rather than faded jeans because I liked the sense of myself in black on my black boat, knowing there'd be no one awake in Fuengirola at 6:30 a.m. to be impressed.

It was a pale, lovely morning as I powered slowly into the harbor toward the reception dock, then coasted, shifting into reverse to slow the boat down, then back into neutral, bringing her nicely alongside, stepping off, bow line in one hand, stern line in the other, happy as hell, loving the perfection of it, my senses intense from sleeplessness.

By the time I had my dock lines secured, the harbor policeman made his appearance. He was intrigued by this female solo sailor. We chatted a bit; I filled out forms and declarations. He told me the marina office wouldn't be open until ten to assign me a slip.

I did a thorough tidy-up below, wanting the boat to be beautiful for my parents. At nine I walked up to a phone and called them to let them know I was in. Mom had made a doctor's appointment for eleven-thirty; I told them I'd call back as soon as I knew where the boat would be, but maybe they should go ahead and get ready to come to town.

At ten I registered at the marina and was assigned the usual Med-mooring type slip. I had no gangplank for *Sonnet*—I brought her bow-first into slips, then scrambled over the bow pulpit onto the dock—so I explained my dilemma to the harbormaster and was given permission to spend my first morning at the end of Dock 4 so my elderly parents could get easily on and off the boat.

I called again, told Mom I'd be waiting for them in the parking lot, moved *Sonnet* two docks over, and headed down to meet them.

It was after ten-thirty by the time they pulled in, less than an hour before we had to be at the doctor's. Mom needed to stop every two or three minutes to catch her breath as we walked to the boat; Dad held her arm as we walked, but it was clear he needed to walk slowly, too. I remembered the times, on trips, when Dad and I would leave Mom and Layne and go off on some errand; he'd always been so proud of his long, striding walk, and proud of how well I kept up with him.

It took us nearly fifteen minutes just to get to the boat, and then Mom balked, afraid of stepping down onto the deck. I got a big bucket for her to use as an intermediary step, showed her how to grab the shrouds for support, and with me and Dad helping she made it on board.

I wanted them to like *Sonnet*, but I wasn't crushed when Dad mostly smiled quietly, and Mom said, "If I knew anything about boats, I'd know if this was a nice one." I got them settled in the main cabin, pulled out the chart of the Atlantic, showed them my daily position fixes. I would have liked to spend hours there, just having them in this world that was mine, with the morning sun shining in on the warm mahogany. But we had to get to the doctor's.

It took a long time for Mom to get off the boat, and by the time we got to the car it was twenty-five after eleven. Mom told Dad he should drive, since we were running late; he could drop us at the doctor's and park the car. He said okay, as long as she directed him where he was supposed to be driving.

I wondered if asking Dad to park and then wait for us was a good idea. Maybe he still knew Fuengirola, as he still knew their house. Maybe they did this frequently, he parked the car so she wouldn't have to walk so far.

She told him, as we drove, that he could park and then join us in a bar called Copa Cabana, it was kitty-corner from the clinic entrance.

We stopped near the doctor's. I said to Dad, "So you'll meet us in the Copa Cabana Bar?" and he nodded, without any sign of having heard this before. I ripped a piece of paper from the notebook I'd brought along, scribbled the name of the bar on it, and gave it to him. Mom told him he could probably find a parking place right up the street; if not there, in Pueblo Lopez.

Mom and I got out. I watched as the little green car pulled slowly away from the curb, watched it head around the traffic circle and into an unknown void.

The light changed. We crossed the street and walked the block to the building the clinic was in, took the elevator up.

As we sat in the waiting room—pleasant cane furniture, dated magazines in an assortment of languages, virtually all the waiting patients elderly—I had Mom give me a rundown of her heart condition, when the racing had started, when she'd first seen the doctor, whether she felt the medication she was taking was effective. We talked a bit about the clinic; Mom and Dad had Spanish health insurance through a group policy with the American Club, and a lot of people on their plan came here. There were a number of specialists—like the cardiologist we were visiting today—who only came a couple of times a month; her other doctor, Dr. Perez, was here all the time.

I said, "What do you go to him for?"

She paused a split second, then said easily, "The same thing."

It was a while before we were called into Dr. Faiyad's office. He told me the various medications Mom was taking; I jotted down the names and dosages. He was extremely nice. I asked about exercise.

He said, "Your mother must walk. I have told her this. She must walk two times a day, in the morning and in the evening. It is very important. Medicine can do a great deal for our bodies, but a great deal we must do for ourselves."

"On the flat, though," she said agreeably. "You told me I shouldn't walk hills."

"On the flat is better."

There wasn't much point in confronting her with the exercise question in front of the doctor. I asked about diet. He said she should avoid salt, avoid fats. That she should eat plenty of fresh fruits and vegetables.

"Your mother is very good about this. She eats very well."

Right, I thought. When she eats at all.

They smiled at each other amiably, Mom nodding. Shaking slightly, as she'd shaken to a greater or lesser degree for years, week to week, depending on how much she'd been drinking.

"And of course she shouldn't drink any alcohol. None at all. Because of her cirrhosis."

I was aware of a hum in the back of my sleep-deprived brain. I turned to her. She'd told me nothing about a liver problem.

She lifted a hand just slightly, dismissively, and said, "It's a different doctor."

I looked back at Dr. Faiyad, disbelieving.

He said, "My colleague Dr. Perez is monitoring her cirrhosis."

The tension in the room was practically audible. The doctor, attempting to mediate, said, "But your mother is very good. She isn't drinking alcohol."

My own hands were shaking. "If she's been telling you that," I said, my voice too loud, "she's been lying."

Mom was still trying to maintain control of the room. She'd always been good at control. She said, "Maybe the occasional glass of white wine."

She probably thought it would pacify both of us. She was wrong. The doctor's demeanor changed; he leaned forward slightly at his desk and read her the riot act. Told her that her liver was not like other people's livers. That she couldn't drink a drop of alcohol. Not a drop. A single drop, to her, was like poison. I don't remember her response.

I don't remember leaving his office, or going through the reception area, or out to the elevators. I remember saying to her in the elevator, nearly in tears, "I'm not trying to persecute you, Mama. I'm not trying to humiliate you. It's just that I love you and I'm scared."

She didn't respond to that; she never had, to the likes of it.

Out of the elevator. Into the street. Across to the bar.

Dad wasn't there.

I hadn't slept the previous night more than ten minutes at a time, probably hadn't slept more than a few hours total, and I was suddenly intensely aware of it. Dad was not at the Copa Cabana Bar. Not at a table, not at the bar itself, not in the *servicio*. How could we possibly have done what we'd done, sent him off alone with the car, with instructions there was no way in the world he'd remember?

We asked the woman behind the bar if an elderly man had been in and she said no, not that she remembered. I left Mom there and walked quickly up to where she'd told Dad to park. There were plenty of parking places, but no little light-green Renault.

I went back, asked Mom if there was a café they went to these days more than others, and she said yes, a new one down on the main street, so we asked the Copa Cabana bartender to tell the elderly *norteamericano* in the blue shirt to stay if he came, and made our way slowly down to the new café, but Dad wasn't there.

Mom was exhausted, hardly able to walk. I got her back to Copa Cabana and headed back out alone through the streets of Fuengirola. I went to every place that had ever been familiar to Dad, La Cepa bar, Las Ramblas, Julian's Book Store, though I really felt no conviction he'd gravitate to a familiar place from the past.

I stopped at a pay phone and called the house, thinking he might have found his way home, but he didn't answer. I circled back to Mom, hoping he would be there with her, but she was alone. I was afraid she might have had a drink while I was walking but she hadn't; she was upset but holding together, shakily sipping straight Coke.

I went back out, crisscrossing the streets of Fuengirola, searching for the lined face, thick salt-and-pepper hair, trimmed beard. Searching for the little light-green car. Stopping at every phone booth I found and calling the house, never an answer.

Walking, trying to put myself into his mind, to know where he would have gone, and knowing I couldn't. More and more, as I walked, it was as if my spirit were in two places. Here, in the midst of the latest chapter of a very long story, worried and unsure. And still offshore, still in the movement of the water, still on my boat. Because of the second, I was able to handle the first.

For two hours I walked, tried calling the house, circled back to Mom at the bar. Her composure was starting to unravel. It would make sense for her to take a cab home, and for me to keep searching, but Dad had the keys to the house along with the car keys; if she went home she wouldn't be able to get into the house to answer the phone.

We finally decided to take a cab together to the house. She was pretty sure the kitchen door was unlocked; I could shinny over the wall to the laundry porch and let her in. She could stay home, in case he called or someone called about him, and I could come back to town to keep looking.

In the cab I told her that if Dad was at the house, we shouldn't lay into him. He wasn't going to remember where he'd been, he wasn't going to remember that we'd told him to meet us in a bar. Laying into him would make him feel awful; the feeling would stay with him, though he wouldn't know why.

No light-green car in the driveway. An empty garage. I climbed over the wall to the unlocked kitchen door.

We called their friend Renee, who spoke fluent Spanish. She bent my ear about getting some sort of identification necklace for Dad. She also had phone numbers for the local hospitals.

I called the hospitals. I called the police, gave a description of Dad, of the car. As I talked to the police, Mom put a hand across her face, shaking hard.

Nothing.

I was getting ready to go back into town when he walked in. Nearly four o'clock; four and a half hours since we watched him drive away in the car.

He looked exhausted, but not upset. Mom, her voice harsh and trembly, started in, "You were supposed to meet us . . . ." but I shushed her.

I told him, trying to keep the tone relaxed, that we'd been back for a while now. Asked if he'd been driving around, or if he'd parked somewhere. He half smiled and shrugged. He didn't know where he'd been. No one would ever know.

Later on, I went out to the car. Mom had told me she thought the tank had been three-quarters full this morning. It now was at half a tank, which meant Dad had done some substantial driving, unless Mom was wrong. The contents of the glove box were spread out on the passenger seat, as if he'd been seeking clues. Insurance papers, owner's manual, list of Renault dealers, a couple of old receipts. The scrap of paper on which I'd written "Copa Cabana" lay there on the seat with the rest of it, looking strange and alien, even to me. If I'd added, "Meet Mom and Lydia here, 1 October, 11:45," he might have made some sense of it (did his watch have a date function?). As it was, it was senseless, words of code.

That night the *poniente* started in, wind from the west, wind for blowing *Sonnet* across the Med.

I spent a goodly amount of time the next few days sitting on the top step of the stairs which led from my parents' house down to the woods. Looking at the weedy terraces, which had once been lush with produce. Looking at the pile of purchased firewood, when for more than fifteen years my dad had prided himself on chopping every stick of firewood they burned. He'd culled deadwood from the pine trees, hauled home trees ripped out to build new houses, combed the beach. Always so proud of his muscles, always insisting, whenever we saw each other, that I admire his biceps, punch his hard belly, to see how strong he was from chopping wood.

I remembered the first few years, remembered Andrés, the elderly Spaniard who lived down the road, who liked my dad so much, brought him pepper and eggplant seeds for his garden, insisted we come to his house to pick figs for drying, and to draw water from his well, since his was so much sweeter than the water from the water tower. Hearing him still, speaking clear, formal, exaggerated Spanish to be sure I'd understand, "Usted puede venir a *verme* cuando *quie*ra." Andrés, who never quite assimilated the changes sweeping through Andalusia, who was growing old as the onslaught of tourists and expatriates hit, who was struck and killed by a car on the *carretera* right in front of the house he'd lived in since before the road was even paved.

Saddened by all of this, and somehow making peace with it.

I took walks with my parents, insisted on twenty minutes minimum a day, though Mom balked, and insisted equally that we find absolutely flat places to walk, which was virtually impossible.

I drove daily down to the marina to work on my boat.

2 Oct

The boat is such a miracle. I drive to the marina, work on *Sonnet*, away into my own world and then come back to the house, able to handle being here like never before. It's like Annapolis, driving out, working, driving back, except that it's twenty minutes instead of an hour, and the drive is through a Spain I still love, love again, and I'm doing things because I want to, because I enjoy it, not because there's a deadline bearing down on me.

The last time I was here it felt so overbuilt, but it's grown in ways that are good for my parents, the shopping area close to them, the divided highway rather than the dangerous two-way *carretera*, the pleasant, landscaped roundabouts. Still Spain just past the borders of civilization, still the air, the hills.

Dad doesn't remember Andrés at all. "I guess I've lost that one."

Falling asleep as I write and so much to write still.

Warm. The eiderdown radiating my body warmth back to me.

Looked back today, as I left the marina, with such a tremendous sense of pride. She's so *gorgeous*. None of the tug of the Swan left; none. What seems clear to me is that the Swan was right in the era I was trying to break out of, right in the OCC era, the *Alaska Eagle* and *Saudade* eras. I love those boats, always will, and in more than one way they gave me *Sonnet*. But *Sonnet* is right not only in that era but in the earlier one, the one that started here, classic boats, Beaufort scale and brightwork.

I got through to Steve with surprising ease on Saturday, and learned that Eileen would be arriving in Malta a week from Tuesday. Skyli was due on Sunday; if we took off on Monday we'd have just over a week to sail nine hundred miles, a bit of a push. Mom and Dad were scheduled to take a trip on Monday to Seville to see the World's Fair before it closed. They'd hoped I might be able to go with them, I could bring Skyli along too, but I told them it was time for me to get *Sonnet* back out to sea.

On Sunday morning Dad woke me before dawn, half-collapsed in the dark on the floor next to where I was sleeping. At first he wouldn't say what it was, only that something was wrong, and I struggled hard from the depths of dreams to make sense of it. He then said his left arm felt numb, and I was terrified he'd had a heart attack, asked if there was pain and he said there wasn't. Mom heard us talking and came downstairs, told me this numbness thing had happened before. Not that she wasn't concerned, just that she didn't think it was serious.

So odd, so surreal, grappling with both of them. What can you do? How much can you do, short of moving in, orchestrating their lives altogether?

Papa unable to articulate what was wrong, sitting on the couch, shaking his head sharply as if to clear it, squeezing his eyes shut, blinking, looking from one place to another as if the world were shifting in front of him. "This is crazy," he'd say. "What do you mean?" I'd say, but he couldn't tell me more. "Just that," he said once, "it's crazy."

Talking to him patiently, same thing over and over, I think you slept on your arm wrong is why it's numb, it's happened to you before and the doctor says it's a pinched nerve in the neck, I can feel the muscles around your neck so much tighter on the left side than the right. Do I believe that explanation? Rubbing his neck for him, his arm. Finally agreeing with Mom to wait until morning to find a doctor—why, she said, do these things always happen on Sunday—and getting Dad upstairs and back into bed.

Who would you call to help you, I asked Mom, if something really serious happened, if he fell down the stairs? There are any number of people I could call, she said. Not wanting to be orchestrated.

Dawn outside on the water as I write, a westerly wind.

Telling him over and over that the numbness had happened before, and him saying, "But has the mind thing happened before?" Me saying, "What do you mean by the mind thing, can you describe for me what you're feeling?" And him shaking his head, saying, "I don't know."

He was worrying he'd had a stroke. Over and over I'd tell him he didn't have other symptoms of a stroke (according to the ancient World Book; no medical guide in the house of any kind), that his heart was steady as a teenager's, sixty beats a minute, just what all of us would want, that his eyes were clear, pupils equal, that his speech was clear, unslurred. He'd say that makes me feel better, then start worrying again, having forgotten.

Did he have a little stroke? I asked Mom if she'd asked in Wiesbaden about this numbness in the arm and she said she was sure she had, she asked about everything. Asked her if for sure the numbness predated Wiesbaden and she said yes. Asked her if they'd definitely determined he hadn't had previous strokes, by CAT scan or whatever and she said yes, definitely.

What do you do?

Westerly wind, for blowing us to Malta.

Aching. A version of the ache I've felt every time I split with them. Last night, before all this happened, I felt some version of anger, wanting my real father back, not the one sitting listless in front of the television. And then, going upstairs away from him to brush my teeth, I felt guilty, not really tired, we should stay up and play backgammon, backcountry camping in a different incarnation.

I don't know if staying a bit longer would make any difference. Know that leaving is going to be hard in a way it's never been hard before.

This ache in my chest.

In the morning we got on the phone and found out that the medical clinic I'd been to with Mom had an emergency doctor on duty, so we took Dad in. The doctor was patient and gentle and not entirely convincing in his diagnosis.

He took Dad's blood pressure, which was fine. He asked Dad to stand with his eyes closed. Dad closed his eyes, arms slightly out for balance, swaying jerkily, then opened his eyes and grasped for the edge of the desk.

The disequilibrium, the doctor said, might be from the wax in Dad's ears. He cleaned out his ears.

The numbness of the arm, he said, might be from the way Dad watched television. He suggested Dad sit on a chair, rather than on the couch, so he could watch straight on.

That was it.

We headed home. I'd left a note at the house for Skyli in case she showed up while we were gone, and she called not long after we got back. She'd taken a bus from Portugal to Fuengirola, and had found Sonnet in the marina, so I went back into town to pick her up.

By afternoon Dad seemed okay, though tired. He seemed to have forgotten the events of the morning. Mom had said there was no way they should go tomorrow to Seville, she'd have to call Renee and cancel, but by afternoon there didn't seem much reason not to go, it'd be a shame to pass up this final chance to see the World's Fair; they could take the day easy. So we made our plans. I would take them to the chartered bus early in the morning, a few miles from the house at Miraflores, and keep the car to do final errands with Skyli, and leave it in the parking lot at the Fuengirola marina, where the bus could drop them off.

We'd made reservations the day before for paella for four at a restaurant Mom had heard wasn't bad. That first year in Spain, when we were living in the Banus apartment before I took off to go biking, we'd discovered—word of mouth—a place for paella down a dirt road to the west of the port. It was owned by a fisherman and his wife; you couldn't make reservations since they didn't have a phone, and you never quite knew when the place would be open since the wife didn't cook when the fisherman hadn't caught fish, but the paella was extraordinary—the saffrony rice, heavy with olive oil, browning and sticking just slightly to the bottom of the pan—and we'd tried for twenty years to find anything close to it.

The paella that final night with my parents was fine but nothing earth-shattering.

In the morning we got up, once again, before dawn, and I drove Mom and Dad to Miraflores. The bus, it turned out, stopped on the south side of the *carretera*, not the north as we'd expected, so I walked with them in the pre-dawn dark across the pedestrian overpass, Dad supporting Mom, each of them supporting the other, not even clear any longer who was the more frail. I hugged them both goodbye, watched as they got on the bus, watched the bus as it drove away, watched until it rounded a curve and was gone.

It was the last time I saw my father.

Back to the house. Packing. Up to the supermarket with Skyli to provision, neither of us in the mood for it.

Into Fuengirola, to the boat. Store the provisions. No diesel at the docks; we tracked it down at a service station and ferried it in the car in borrowed jerry cans.

Day slipping past. Wind still blowing from the west.

The sun was low when I finally moved the little light-green Renault to the agreed-upon parking place, dreading the moment, dreading the loss I knew I'd feel, the loss I always felt.

I locked the car up, eyes stinging, and walked quickly back to the boat.

11

"I mean it, man," she wrote in the log.
"Sometimes freighters really PISS ME OFF."
Busy place, I admit it; doffed
my cool, too, that first nasty slog
of an easterly, will like a log,
yelling, "This is BULLSHIT" from the trough
of short steep waves, reefing. Scoff-
laws, both of us. Shorelines in fog.
This my friend from mid-Atlantic, born whole,
some cross between Athena and Aphrodite,
saw my soul and wrote on it.
Saw luminescence stream down the deck, roll
back to sea, questioned life and light.
I told her to shut up and write a sonnet.

It was nearly sunset by the time we cleared the breakwater and headed out into the Med. We'd reefed to the second reef before leaving the dock, and *Sonnet* took off with the wind and the sunset behind her, moving again, heading east.

Tonight, for the second time in a week, I would cross the line I'd traced on little *Caprille* in October of '72. What a lifetime ago. What different people we were now, me and my dad.

It struck me—as I watched darkness fall on this world which felt so familiar and right—that my first time offshore on a sailboat was the first time my dad had known he was losing his little girl. Harder on him even than the day in France he'd lifted my bicycle off the top of the car and watched his seventeen-year-old ride off in one direction before driving in the other; if it hadn't been for Mom, lobbying on my behalf, he would have followed me for at least the first few miles, just in case.

On *Caprille*, when I'd been desperately seasick, Dad had tried to comfort me as you'd comfort a ten-year-old with the flu—a hand on the forehead, an arm around the shoulders—which was the last thing in the world I wanted. I shrugged off his touch, but when John the owner took me to stand at the shrouds, told me to *feel* the boat move, watch the sea, watch the stars, I listened to him as if he was some kind of god.

They say that in the Mediterranean there's either too much wind or not enough, and when there's too much it's right on the nose. Twenty years back, on *Caprille*, it had taken us nine hours, powering into a nasty easterly *levante*, to cover the thirty miles from Puerto Banus to Málaga. Tonight, as if for a birthday present, the *poniente* was behind us, and Skyli and I were well past Málaga by dawn, two women sailing swiftly on a sleek black boat.

By 0700 we'd shaken the reefs out of the main. By 0800 we were powering, by 1000 we were dodging freighters by radar in the fog, by 1300 the skies were clear and we were broad reaching at nearly six knots under gennaker.

The wind stayed behind us through that second night. The moon was lighting our world for us, two days before full. I hand steered under gennaker for hours, the cockpit lit brightly by moonlight, feeling in near-mystical harmony with the rhythms of the boat.

The next day the wind died for a while, then went northeast. At noon we were close-hauled, but still pretty much on course for Malta. We'd planned to have a crossing-the-Greenwich-Meridian party, the way people have crossing-the-equator parties, but somehow we forgot to keep an eye on the instruments and *Sonnet* slipped quietly into the Eastern Hemisphere.

7 Oct

1305 Sailing close-hauled in not quite the right direction, surprisingly happy, cooking, watch set for every five minutes to go out and look for ships, Skyli trying to sleep, sky overcast, world a bit cooler.

Two days, it seemed, was the grace period; by late that afternoon the Med began living up to its reputation.

1610 It's gloomy out, twenty-five knots apparent and a hell of a long way to go. The boat is soaked, but even as I write I feel a bit better, she's a great boat, does what's asked of her.

Skyli isn't getting a whole lot of sleep, suppose I should leave her alone on it, remember how much trouble I had sleeping when Monica was on board.

Ships like crazy out here; this isn't a passage for singlehanding. How many times already have we altered course for ships?

Relax the brow. We're sailing mostly in the right direction, this isn't much of a beat compared to the Strait of Gibraltar. No reefs yet, doing fine.

Sadness keeps creeping back at me, thinking about my dad, as this my *Sonnet* sails along close-hauled through the Med. I'm going to go places with this boat, do things with her, live a portion of my life on her. You only go around once, for Chrissake. Only once.

A place to think, a place to write.

I comforted him in the middle of the night, a reversal of roles, comforted him like you'd comfort a child, though you don't assure a child that you don't think he's had a stroke.

The wind continued to build, and so did short nasty seas. At just after midnight we reefed to the second reef, Skyli at the wheel, me fighting for handholds and footholds at the mast and boom, my stomach a long way from happy. When the reef line was finally tight, the sail no longer a flapping demon of Dacron, I leaned against the dinghy a moment to regain my humor and took a wave right in the face, right down the front of my foul-weather gear. The final straw. I made my way with admirable deliberation to the cockpit, and then to the leeward rail. I suppose I should have been pleased—considering my historical tendency to sea-sickness—that I'd made it over three thousand miles before losing my cookies over the rail of my own boat, but "pleased" wasn't a word that occurred to me at the time.

At 0200 I wrote in the log: "Tacked, retacked, sailed in circles, wind up and down, waves up, Monitor recalcitrant." Above the entry Skyli added an addendum: "Who's driving this taco wagon?"

At 0300 the weather was miserable and I started worrying about the rig. We couldn't get the leech cord tight enough on the jib, and its fluttering was shaking the entire mast, so we rolled the sail in, had a terrible time doing it, the furling gear balking, the sail whipping, the rig shuddering. We'd planned to roll back out just a bit of sail but decided to leave it as it was.

It wasn't a pleasant night. Or a pleasant morning. At 0815 Monaco Radio predicted winds associated with this low to increase to forty-five knots, northwesterly. Our wind was still northeast, and seemed to be dying, not building, but we left in the reefs.

For four hours in the early afternoon we motor-sailed into short northeast seas, gaining some sea room on Africa. The wind shifted to the southwest and kept dropping, so we finally shook out the reefs and rolled out the jib, after releading the line for the furling gear, hoping to avoid the problems we'd had last night if we had to bring the headsail back in in a hurry. It was a rough ride, seas from everywhere, but at least we were moving without having to listen to the engine.

Skyli was more or less sleeping at 1600 when the wind shifted yet again, into the northwest, and picked up. Northwest was where the forty-five knots were supposed to come from, so I quickly rolled in the jib, and reefed all the way down to the third reef—easier to reef on starboard tack than port—and gybed, then rolled back out a tiny scrap of headsail. The wind held steady, then dropped back down to under fifteen knots.

At 1730 Skyli wrote in the log: "Triple reefed main, small headsail; waiting to get blasted?"

The wind kept dropping. *Sonnet* slogged along in the waves. I felt frustrated, going so slowly, holding the boat back; should we shake it all out again?

We shook it all out.

At 2000 I wrote: "The feared NWly has gone W almost nil and the fuel lines need bleeding. Are we having fun yet? (Actually, it's turned into a lovely cloudless moonlit night.)"

Waves but no wind. We decided to wait until daylight to bleed the fuel lines and start the engine. Somehow, at this point, another few uncomfortable hours didn't seem that big a deal.

Skyli, 0100: "Only a geek would be having fun under these conditions. Call me 'Geek.' "

At eight we bled the fuel lines and turned on the engine. By nine the wind had come up sweetly from the south, the sea had lain down, the engine was off, and we were reaching easily. I felt a lightheaded clarity: These things do pass.

9 Oct

1220   Man but this is nice. We had a meal of sorts for the first time in days, did some tidying and dish washing (some of it forced by the disastrous spilling of the first lunch attempt, pasta Parmigiana everywhere), the boat broad reaches placidly with the coast of Africa hazy to the south and east.

1334   The sound of the boat moving through the water, hour after hour of this, mile after mile, just feels so right.

Skyli isn't doing so well right now. You steer at night and a wave breaks and the bioluminescence rushes across the decks and it's extraordinary but *then* what. Now what. Filled with self-doubts as no one I know. Let her talk; what can *I* say, with as much as I have of the same running around in my system.

I no longer think I should go looking for tough challenges as a sailor. I feel victorious at the end of them but this in fact is what I love, what renews me. Seasick for the first time the night before last, I'm just not a good upwind sailor even on this good upwind boat. I don't think racing the Two-Star should be on my list of serious goals.

Love my boat. Did not love her yesterday, wanting her set up better, cleaner reefing, an inner forestay so I can hank on smaller jibs. Irritated and unhappy, wind and rumors of wind, but we came through it, and sail now straight toward Malta.

We had birds, that passage through the Med. Two fluffy yellow ones who landed on the control lines of the Monitor and were carried forward and back with its helm adjustments, sitting there side by side, a few centimeters this way, a few that way. A bigger one, who angled in and landed on my head in a rain squall, then moved down to deck level and hung out between my shiny black sea boots until the rain stopped.

Another bird had found its way below and settled on Skyli's pillow before we even noticed it (we were chatting—Skyli near the mast, me at the chart table—when her gaze shifted and she asked, conversationally, "How long has *he* been here?"); it proceeded to hop around the main cabin a bit, then fly to the forepeak and hop around there, then fly calmly the length of the boat and back out the companionway, opting to make the exploratory circuit under the dodger by foot rather than wing, so close to my camera lens I couldn't even focus.

Skyli told me that a huge percentage of birds did not survive migrations. We were much closer to Africa than Europe when our voyagers stopped to rest; maybe it would make the difference.

10 Oct

I've come a hell of a long way, I still have a hell of a long way to go. 3,500 miles or so from the Chesapeake, 1,300 still to Greece.

I'm feeling slightly dizzy, not strong. A long push; my body needs nights of normal sleep now. Sense of pride to have done this, sense of readiness for the next stage.

A long way still, but all the major pushes are over, all the long layovers. A couple of days in Malta, some good nights' sleep, and then on in.

Six months I've owned this boat now, thirty-something days on board offshore. Transitions; wanting to subscribe to *Wooden Boat* magazine, accepting the image of myself as owner of a classic boat, a hundred percent.

Dizzy-headed. Such a huge world. I can't solve these problems, can't make sense of them, can't come up with any real excuse for sailing boats across oceans, but do it.

A dream, when it was so rough, hard to sleep for being flung around in the bunk. Dad was in the dream, so unsteady and disoriented, and I was telling him it's not just your age, it's not that there's anything wrong with you, I feel it too, walking unsteadily in the dream as the boat lurched in reality, disoriented, reaching to grab dream handholds.

Weighing so heavy on me. There's never been an era of my life that the lives of my parents didn't weigh heavy on me.

Thinking of families. Thinking of

I don't know how that was going to end; broken off by potential rain. We could have been so much farther along, these hours, if we'd had the gennaker up. It matters and doesn't. Doesn't matter, neither of us is particularly strong or motivated right now; does matter, not all that much work and I'd like to be farther along. Five in the morning and dizzy-headed. On a bit longer, then Skyli's turn. Her turn, my turn, to Malta, 400 miles yet, a long way.

We're not going fast; at least we're going the right direction. Extraordinary amount of shipping in this part of the world. Main shipping lane Suez–Gibraltar, but I don't see going way north to get away from it.

2210 Flashes of lightning over Africa, the moon breaking through clouds sometimes, lighting the sails, lighting the white deck, straight-edged shadows, moon colors. Even with the moon behind clouds it's bright enough to write by.

Boat broad reaches, rolls, I write standing on the engine cover, elbows on the blue cushions of the cockpit, braced against the roll, *Sonnet* sailing lightly through the Mediterranean night.

I love this body of water. I've sailed on it a lot, but never crossed it, days on end. Thinking today how there's definitely something that draws human beings to sea, this isn't a totally unnatural addiction. How the earliest recorded accounts of people at sea are from here, this stretch of water. Five hundred years ain't nothin', man, this whole big deal of the quincentenary is nothing.

Is it time to sleep yet?

Skyli had brought along *Antelope Medicine*'s GPS, so we'd have a backup if my new one packed it in. She'd brought her hand-held VHF. She hadn't brought her own foul-weather gear, since it was bulky and I'd told her I had a spare set on board. I felt pretty bad when it turned out my old stuff leaked like a sieve.

She'd brought her own names. My Monitor became Max, my GPS became Guru. At one point I read her a Talk of the Town piece from a back issue of *The New Yorker* about a dog named Louis—"our main dog Louis"; she thought that line was great—who bungles his way through obedience training, and she proceeded to name *Sonnet*'s canvas bucket Louis. The bucket had a rope attached; we used it for getting seawater for dish washing.

"Okay, Louis," Skyli would say to the bucket, holding it easily, looking straight at it and talking to it clearly the way you talk to a dog, "I want you to go get some water, and bring it back." Then she'd toss the bucket over the side.

As far as her own name, she still had the old one, and hated it, and was escalating the name hunt. She proposed calling herself Alyosha Tess, or just Tess, after her dog who'd died. I told her Tess was too literary, thinking Tess Gallagher, thinking Tess of the d'Urbervilles. She proposed I not tell Eileen her name when we all met up in Malta, she could shake Eileen's hand and say, "What do I *look* like my name should be?" but I'd already told Eileen her name in Bulgaria.

11 Oct

0600   Sonnet at dawn: Hand steering in a squall, darkness and the rush, no horizon in the direction of the squall, a ship lost in it, light beginning, the shape of the deck, dawn-blue glow to it, beginning to perceive the undulating undersides of clouds. Africa an invisible presence in the ominous opaque gray to the south, this boat was born of that continent and I won't pretend to make sense of it. Lightning, at first just bursts of light, then the intense snaking thread of a lightning bolt. A break in the clouds, three geometric luminous patches ahead for me to steer toward, a path of reflected light on the deep blue-gray of pre-day water.

So then I go forward, lie right at the bow, lean out to watch the bow cutting through the water, the reflection of foam in the glassy black surface.

0700   I look up, after writing out Stephens's "Death of a Buffalo" in the log, and Skyli sits behind the wheel, face to the orange glow of sunrise, looks at me and says, "I *like* this little sailboat ride you've brought me on."

The passage through the Med isn't a passage I tend to think of chronologically. Even the logbook—or at least some crucial pages of it—isn't chronological.

The book itself was new. I was tired of the printed log I'd used for the first two legs, with its peremptory column headings. I'd found some books I liked in Gibraltar, with marbled covers, three of them, perfect for engine log, radio log, and ship's log. The latter, the largest, was actually an address book, but I figured I could cut off the letter tabs if I ever felt like bothering; it wouldn't be the first time.

The letter tabs, as it turned out, were central. In the middle of Skyli's and my first night offshore, when I was on watch and she was sleeping, I wrote "See p. N" in the comments column. On page N, I wrote: "THE CAPTAIN PROPOSES a communal nonnet (example to left, though that one borders on making sense), two lines at a time. (Crew's first two lines will determine Italian vs. Shakespearean nonnet.)"

On the left-hand page I transcribed a nonsense sonnet I'd written years before. On the right I wrote two lines.

Skyli came on watch; I went below. I came on watch; Skyli went below. I turned to page N. Below my two lines of verse she'd written two of her own. A b b a; Italian. I picked up the pencil.

By the next watch change she'd let the poem lapse into anapest. I figured if you can have a non-pentameter sonnet you can have a non-iambic nonnet, so I ran with it.

Watch by watch, the nonnet worked its way down the page. We certainly got the nonsense part right (" . . . water-striped silver washing the dune / with more violets than violence . . ."), and I liked the strange way it looked when it was done, the recognizable shape of a sonnet, patterned by alternating handwriting. Two hundred miles from Spain (or two hundred and two hundred and twenty, respectively), we graded our creation. I gave it a "nngnh." She gave it a C+.

By the time we were north of Tunisia we were working on a Shakespearean sonnet on page S, with discussions on how to go about it on page C (for "collaboration," or "cheating"). We didn't talk about the poems face-to-face, though they were an integral part of our passage.

Also in the logbook, also never discussed, was page P (for "purple prose"), a.k.a. the Bill page, to which Skyli made frequent additions. She'd met Bill Butler the day I left Horta; he'd given her a copy of *Our Last Chance*, the book about his and his wife's long drift in their life raft, and Skyli and Steven had read it together, fascinated at how badly it was written.

The first P-page entry was a parody, entitled "Bill's *penultimate* paragraph" (" 'Tears streaked down our face as we watched the sharks swim back and forth, back and forth, circling the raft, bent on destroying us instantly, a slow and brutal death . . . ' "). Other meditations followed ("Help me! I'm trying to communicate a serious rather profound thought but Bill Butler is trying to channel through me . . . I fight . . . he's guiding my hand . . . 'The single most invaluable item I sincerely recommend not having are flares, and my reasoning is mathematical.' AAAAHHH!"). Her final comment, written sideways on the page for lack of space but all in caps, was this: "THERE IS ONE INDELIBLE FACT: BILL BUTLER HAS WRITTEN A BOOK, AND I HAVEN'T." Beside the proclamation was a quarter-inch-high stick figure of Bill, with a balloon above his head: "So shut up you little twat of one mind bent on my ridicule."

1323   Max steers the gennaker. To starboard is the extraordinary, sculpted little Ile de la Galite. The wind blows from Africa. I sit in the cockpit, barelegged in turtleneck as the sun comes and goes, teal green hat, Hobie sunglasses, thinking of this sonnet we've started, the possible ways the format could go, thinking of the format of screenplays, peeling vegetables, onion and garlic, sailing.

1720   By sunset the sky is almost entirely clear, the sun sinks down below a final band of haze and the moon is already soaring fifteen degrees above the eastern horizon. Moon's declination N11, sun's S7, moonrise around five, sunset around 5:30, moonset 6:45 in the morning, sunrise at six, we have the moon for longer than the sun is gone, how often does that happen? Up before sunset, still up after sunrise, this is one full moon.

12 Oct

0024   I was looking forward to hearing these Presidential election debates. Now, tuned to the VOA on the SSB, I feel like I'm listening to a dog-and-pony show, and I can't quite integrate that complex world of politics and political debates with this simple world of a two-women sloop crossing a historic stretch of water.

All three of them sound like fools to me, sound like human beings with far too many failings to lead a country like America. Again, the clarity: that this world of *Sonnet* makes sense, this is the right thing for this human being to have done.

Hate the sound of Bush's voice, disappointed to realize I don't like the sound of Clinton's, either (some Arab female vocalist seems to be making inroads here), sounds like a well-trained schoolboy, enunciating just a bit too clearly. Surprised that Perot strikes me as gutsy rather than ludicrous. Do I have the guts to have my own opinion on anything? There's no cohesion to this entry—listen, pause, write, listen, pause—but I'm now getting intrigued by the debate, moving from one mood, one mode to another, way too tired I suppose to be rational, gennaker up all day, happier rigging barber-hauler blocks than sleeping. Bush talks of Tiananmen Square, sanctions on China, Foreign Policy seems important to me, I'm tired, I can't understand this very well at all, the reception's degenerating.

"I've felt a little sadness creeping in all afternoon," Skyli says. "We can handle it. We're queens of sadness." Can I handle it? Can I handle her sadness as well as my own?

Clarity comes from fatigue, but so maybe does lack of judgment, cutting the entrance to Tunis a bit too close. We're running out of wind; this is one reality. And the engine seems to be overheating.

Bush is saying something about fathers, families, and I can't quite hear what. Am I all right? Have I written anything on this page at all? Do I have the discipline to write anything worthwhile? Drug-related crime now; the issues crackle out, there aren't answers to any of them.

("I do think there's some fairly good news out there." Cocaine use down, so on, who's he kidding?)

There aren't answers to the continent massively to the south of me, or the continent to the north of me, *Sonnet* sailing among freighters in between, this is a powerful body of water, even out of the sight of land you can feel the magnetism of land masses. Reception's getting worse and worse.

Clinton: "I've held crack babies in my arms . . ." Odd intrusion, these male voices, these world issues, entering this female boat.

Racism now: "Why is this still happening to America, and what would you do to end it?" *Sonnet* between Black Africa and Old World Europe, the New World crackling over radio waves. The New World that wiped out its natives. Skyli on board instead of on *Antelope Medicine*, Columbus 500 Rallyers rallying in Spain. *Sonnet*, giving me distance from things that baffle me so massively. Is there a theme here, on the justifiability of escape?

AIDS. So many issues, of such weight and importance, individual issues which for many people outweigh the rest. Flash of despair, for those people.

Flash of sympathy for politicians, trying to juggle it all. A certain amazement, that anyone would try.

Too tired; this isn't good. Wanting to fly the gennaker, did it today, didn't yesterday.

Fifteen minutes more of this (aren't we done yet?), how many hundreds of hours have they spent in preparation? That world's a complex place, more complex than this one.

Can any of this do any good? Was just saying to Skyli (". . . health care costs . . .") that it's not just the U.S. economy that's stumbling, look at Europe, Americans don't seem to recognize how global it is (". . . health care reform . . ."), blame our politicians. I dunno, maybe some of it can do some good, other countries have better solutions for health care.

Odd, though; there isn't any conversation going. And there's virtually no possibility (". . . the woman whose husband lost his job after twenty-seven years . . .") of conversation between these men; linked more closely just now than maybe any others in the States ("Let me tell you a little bit about what it's like to be President . . . foreign affairs . . . democratic country . . . Middle East, we had to stand up against a tyrant . . . nuclear war . . . we need to do better on education . . . strength of the American family . . . trust . . . I ask for your support for four more years . . ." sounds like he's running for class president . . .) and they'll never just talk.

Enough already.

0300   All the freighters, all the worries of shipping lanes, and suddenly the sea is empty. Worries of average speed, and suddenly I'm planning to drift all night rather than try to figure out this most recent engine problem by flashlight.

0704   " 'Dear Diary,' " Skyli says as I reach for my journal. She's getting ready to go to bed, mostly because I sent her there ("I'm mad 'cause *I'm* always the guy that has to go to sleep," she said earlier, still in the cockpit). " 'My crew is very pissy today.' " Keeps prepping her bed. " 'I'm stuck with a very pissy crew woman.' " Growly cartoon voice.

I come up to a lovely dawn and she's sitting tense in the cockpit. " 'I'm *mad*,' " she growls. "That's what my dog would say, if my dog could talk." Tense is not quite the right word, or maybe it is, tension to the face, the muscles; tension and resignation: "It's been the most beautiful night, and I'm sad. I'm mad because I'm sad." She's joking about it, and not joking at all. "I don't quite know what to say to that," I say, joking tone, too, but I don't.

I tell her, more serious, that I don't know if she experienced anything along these lines on her Atlantic passage, but something I've learned about myself is that I get moody when I sail. Crawl into my bunk and cry, am almost used to it now, some level knows it will pass. She says, "You're lucky you can cry." I say, "I cry ridiculously easily."

Finally ready for bed she says, "Okay, I'll tell you why I'm sad. Yesterday was a good eating day on *Sonnet* but what about *today?* It's like Christmas. You look forward to it, and then it's over. What good is *that?*"

She told me at one point she isn't moody, but she's worse than I am. Gets low, gets despairing, then regrets getting despairing, regrets that she might be pulling me down too. Works her way back to the premise that the only important thing in life is having fun, but can never believe it.

1305   Get up, look around, open up the book casually, not sure if there'll be any response in this behind-the-scenes conversation of ours, this quiet experiment of collaboration, and she's scribbled this line as a potential part of our sonnet, part of the section on freighters, ". . . deny those sullen forms their prey with elegant evasion," and I almost start to cry (well, okay, I cry easily), the sense of this boat out here, the sense of her capturing it with words, the sense I get of potential creativity, of human intelligence. These are the things that are important to me.

And then everything deflates in me. I've spent hours and hours trying to write sonnets, and I've never written a decent one.

One step at a time, one foot in front of another. Striving for completion.

1433 Up on the bow, *Sonnet* sailing along at three or four knots, she'd be sailing faster under gennaker but in fact there's no point in sailing faster and arriving in the dark.

Another bout, and I have no idea how to handle it, I've got the same disease but she's got it worse. That none of this means anything, that she has no idea what her place is in the world, no talent that can be of use to anyone. She wants to write about her passage with *Antelope Medicine*; I tell her just to do it, just to write, but I have no idea if she has any talent, I know I have some grain of talent and I'm terrified myself of doing it and failing. Finally fling the logbook at her and tell her to write a sonnet, take that line she woke to at age fourteen and write.

Skyli did write a sonnet, after a bit of bitching ("Did *Monica* have to write sonnets?"), wrote it while I slept. I'd finally written down the first line for her, to jump-start her, the one she'd heard in her head as a kid without knowing what it meant, wrote it on page H (for "Heavens"), "Sound asleep in the heavens, wide awake / on the bow."

She didn't use the "assigned" first line, and she didn't write in the log. She left the sheet of notebook paper folded in the logbook, and instructed me to throw it overboard as soon as I'd read it, which I didn't do. At the next watch change, when I told her I liked what she'd written, and she saw me actually fingering the paper she'd written it on, she got *mad*.

And then *I* got mad. I got mad at her for not trusting herself. I got mad at her for wanting to be a writer but never keeping the things she wrote. She'd told me already that she'd spent the better part of her bus ride back to Portugal writing about our passage through the Strait of Gibraltar, and then had consigned what she'd written to a Vilamoura trash bin. I would like to have seen those banished sheets of paper.

I got mad at her in part because I was mad at myself for having thrown things out, over the years. I told her that nothing makes sense, life doesn't make sense, but somehow I'd ended up with a boat named *Sonnet*, one of life's little curve balls, and she wouldn't have written a sonnet if I didn't have a boat with that name, and I wasn't going to throw the sonnet out.

I slipped the poem in my *Be Your Own Diesel Mechanic* book, and let her stew about it.

13 Oct

0200   Nighttime, full moon, fishing boats.

Morning: Rain, dim views of Sicily.

It was Tuesday. Eileen was due to arrive today in Valletta. *Sonnet* was still sixty miles northwest of Gozo, the smaller, more northerly of the two main Maltese Islands. I pored over the chart, figuring out ETAs, worrying about Eileen having to wait for us; she'd said she'd get a hotel if we hadn't arrived yet, and I supposed one night in a hotel wasn't the end of the world, but I hated the idea of continuing a precedent.

0811   Skyli's getting grouchy about landfall, the way I have in the past, no desire at all for a passage to end.

*   Quote: "I hate Maltese people. In fact, I've never met one I liked."*

The wind had clocked steadily from the reaching westerlies of yesterday, and by midmorning we were close-hauled on starboard tack in an east-southeasterly wind. Our progress slowed as the wind built; by mid-afternoon I was intently reworking my ETA.

By 1600 the wind had backed again to the northeast. Gozo was still invisible twenty miles off, and we weren't quite fetching its northern coast on port tack.

At 1700 Skyli wrote in the log: "The last Mediterranean sunset?"

If Poseidon had been weighing whether or not to let us slip easily into Valletta, this may have tipped the scales against us; Malta—the crossroads between the western and eastern Med—wasn't a destination to be taken lightly.

By 2000 the wind was blowing at over twenty knots, and we'd reefed *Sonnet* to the second reef. The night was dark but oddly luminous, the moon obscured by clouds. It was Skyli who proposed the obvious: go down the west side of the islands, not the east. It was the longer route—Valletta was a third of the way up Malta's eastern shore—but the right one. If we went down the east, the entire length of the islands would be a nasty lee shore.

The wind clocked again, blowing straight from the east, and continued to build. We squared away the claw-to-weather sails we'd used in the Strait of Gibraltar, second reef flat as a board, a mostly rolled-in headsail sheeted inside the shrouds. We could just pick out the light of Gordon lighthouse on Gozo's northwest coast, flashing faintly every seven seconds off the port bow.

Life's more complex, intractable concerns—world injustice, personal despair—tend to evaporate on a small boat in a gale. So do worries about onward crew members, about a pattern of keeping them waiting.

I remember at one point staring at the mainsail, wondering if I should retie the reinforcement line at the clew and realizing no, the wind has reached that point where you don't want to move around on deck more than you have to, you should clear your mind Zen-like of worry. The crucial thing was this: we trusted the boat, and we trusted each other.

Starboard tack for an hour, hand steering to keep the mainsail just on the edge of luffing; heave through a tack; port tack for an hour; three miles closer to the island at the end of two hours, trying to claw our way close enough to get into the lee and find some respite from the wind. It felt, for a while there, like we'd live the rest of our lives in range of the Gordon lighthouse.

Around 0400 the lightning started, sheet lightning illuminating colonies of cloud, distantly in the west and north, flash after flash. It was only now that it struck me how big the gale was, how big the globe, how much bigger it all was than we were, two human beings on one tiny boat, flicked into an immensity of moon-dim water and howling wind.

The light show moved into its second act, too awe-inspiring to be frightening. From a central void—a black-hole patch—filament-thin lightning would race away in five or six directions, opening the sky like cracks in glass. Overhead, then astern; we watched in disbelief, heads swiveling in different directions for the next flickering explosion. Skyli captured it when she said, "It's primordial."

It was oddly silent at this stage, no noticeable thunder, though given the noise level on board it's hard to say for sure. When the lightning bolts started slamming—thick as pillars—straight into the sea, the thunder was deafening. At one point Skyli saw mist rise up where lightning hit water.

Never had I been happier to own an aluminum boat, an entire hull as ground connection. Never had I been happier my aluminum boat had a wooden deck.

We stayed well away from metal. We'd turned off all the electronics. We let Max steer; when we tacked I steered by sail ties looped through the spokes of the wheel. I have no idea why we didn't get hit—our mast was the only high point for miles—but we didn't.

There was so much lightning, in so many forms, in so many parts of the sky, that it was hard to know if the eerie glow was coming from electricity or the cloud-shrouded moon. But then the pale light intensified slightly, and we realized it was coming from the dawn.

The show lasted nearly three hours. Next came the onslaught of rain, with no slackening of wind. The quantity of water hurtling from the sky was unbelievable; I was worried about losing the mainsail, not from wind but from the weight of rainwater in the folds of the reefs.

It didn't make sense for either of us to get undressed and go below where it was dry. Something might break, demanding both of us; we stayed in the cockpit, harnessed in.

I remember Skyli heaving herself straight from time to time, letting the water run down and out the leg openings of her borrowed foul-weather gear; the waterproofing was shot everywhere except the reinforcement patches at the butt and back of the legs, which were doing a better job keeping water in than keeping it out.

I remember patting my own jacket, noticing some moisture at the neck, and saying, dead serious, "You know, Henry Lloyd doesn't keep you *completely* dry," and her bursting out laughing.

I remember long stretches, sitting hunched next to each other against the downpour, denizens of that violence of motion, that cacophony of noise, braced against the crash and howl in a surreal, companionable contentment.

I remember one wave that smashed into us, breaking entirely over us, filling the cockpit, swirling; someone spirited here from suburbia would think these were two women in extremis. We looked at each other calmly and agreed that the temperature of the crashing waves was quite a bit warmer than the temperature of the torrential rain.

By midmorning we were ten miles from the west coast of the island, close enough to raise Radio Valletta on the VHF. I asked if we could come into Marsaxlokk harbor rather than around to the capital, since the weather was so bad. I was told the weather was no problem, come around and on in.

No problem for *you*, maybe.

At last the rain slacked off, and the low coast of Malta, pale and rocky, materialized to the east. Around noon, after fourteen hours of blasting easterlies, the wind died. With deep feelings of relief we shook out the reefs. Twenty minutes later the wind blasted us from the northwest. This meant a good fast reach around the south coast. It also would mean—insult to injury—a final beat against the wind up to Valletta.

On the reach, we took turns sleeping. We sailed within half a mile of Filfla Island, shaving the edge of an area marked "entry prohibited" on the chart, not in the mood to cover distance we didn't need to. A much tighter reach after Marsaxlokk, along the craggy southeast coast.

By 1630 we were rounding the last corner and heading again into thirty knots of wind. The waves didn't know what to do with themselves after that long night of easterlies, the wind now northwest. Less than four miles to go, but nasty ones. We turned on the engine, in spite of the overheating problems, and motor sailed at low rpm's against the wind.

At 1730, our ninth day at sea, we were finally approaching our destination. Silhouetted spires of Valletta hunkered against an impressive, post-storm sunset sky. The engine protested; the boat lurched violently on confused seas. We were starting to feel just a tiny bit deprived, of sleep, of comfort, of something to eat besides peanuts. My non-meat-eating crew, with her quirky aversions, decided veal almondine sounded just right, with banana flambé for dessert.

Radio Valletta instructed us into Grand Harbor for customs, the southern portion of the city's double bay. Floodlights lit acres of ancient fortifications, mirroring the fading orange of sunset clouds.

Skyli was steering. My navigation, as we closed on land, appeared to be drawing our still-heaving vessel straight into flood-lit stone, and Skyli made decidedly doubtful noises. I checked the radar one more time and announced rather squeaky-voiced that yes, you will leave the round tower to starboard.

At that moment, looking like something out of *Star Wars*, the impossibly huge bow of a freighter emerged from the illuminated walls of Fort St. Elmo. It was all out of whack with space and time, dwarfing the fortifications. We seemed to have confirmed the entrance to Valletta harbor.

The freighter pivoted slow and steady out of the narrow gap: green light, white lights, red light big and bright in the deepening twilight. We sidled close to the round tower, passing port-to-port; a pilot boat bobbed cheerfully between us.

The stillness inside the breakwater was stunning after the violence outside. The silence was deafening. *Sonnet*, her engine a steady hum, seemed pulled along the straight smooth track of a Disneyland ride. To starboard stretched the flood-lit fortress walls. To port, every few hundred yards, were "creeks" with massive ships nestled deep inside them. The entire town was built of warm-toned limestone; it looked unreal, like a backdrop. And then, from a tower above us, came the hollow clanging of bells.

On in we powered, a mile and a half, deeper into the harbor of Valletta. Not wanting it to end, this difficult and harmonious voyage together. We pulled down sails, prepped dock lines, watched cars zip along the highway, toy cars on the massive ramparts.

By 1800 we had found our way to the customs building, sidled up against the cumbersome wall, and stepped ashore.

12

And if I were like lightning
I wouldn't need no sneakers
I'd come and go whenever I would please
And I'd scare 'em by the shade tree
And I'd scare 'em by the light pole
But I would not scare my pony on my boat out on the sea
LYLE LOVETT, "If I Had a Boat"

Clearing formalities in Valletta was close to surreal. Nighttime. A stairway up the side of a limestone building. Notices printed in a language with way too many x's and tt's. Antiquated typewriters, a shelf with a shrine to a plastic Mary, lit by a single Christmas-tree light. A round man whose function I never determined, appearing at the edges of rooms from time to time, singing snatches of arias. Land legs: I came close, more than once, to being thrown from my chair when it lurched on a ten-foot wave.

This, I was told, was the Port Authority. Tomorrow I must go to another office in Marsamxett harbor, the next bay up, then a third, in Ta' Xbiex.

I filled out forms, passed around my documentation papers, moved from office to office, then was released, told to return to my boat, to take her around to Marsamxett to anchor for the night. I said I'd prefer not to anchor, asked if there was anywhere I could spend the night alongside. I was told, pleasantly enough, that I would anchor; tomorrow the Yacht Center would assign me a berth.

I was tired. Very tired. You can push yourself past limits when the weather demands, when the boat needs you, but if you slow down it's hard to get the momentum back.

We got *Sonnet* away from the wall, motored back down past the creeks and the ramparts, back out past the round tower, back into the surge, and slipped west into the harbor of Marsamxett. We powered slowly, looking for a place to go alongside in this strangely lit world, seeing nowhere. Fine; we would anchor.

The logical anchor for a dubious night was the 44-pound Bruce, which was firmly lashed below deck under a mountain of anchor line and chain. Skyli powered in circles while I struggled by flashlight to liberate the Bruce, wrestle it out of the chain locker, and lug it up the companionway and to the bow, nearly in tears from fatigue.

Anchor down. Something to eat. Worried about Eileen; I'd thought we'd at least to be able to make contact tonight, even if she'd already paid for another night in her hotel.

Sleep.

In the morning I got on the VHF, talked to the Yacht Center, and was told to come ashore for further immigration paperwork and a berth assignment. I asked if there was any way I could be assigned the berth by radio, and then come ashore after we were moored. My dinghy was rather hard to free and then restow, and I preferred not to launch it.

The Maltese, in my limited but increasing experience, possessed an intriguingly good-natured imperiousness. The Yacht Center man said, in the same agreeable tone I'd heard from every Maltese official I'd spoken to, "It isn't a matter of *preferring* to launch your dinghy. You will launch your dinghy and come ashore."

So I launched my dinghy, went ashore, found my way to the proper past-its-prime high-ceiling building, and filled out more forms. From there I was sent to the Yacht Center, a smaller building close to the main road, where little dated cars zipped along the left-hand side, British-style. I was assigned a berth, and told that a woman had been waiting for me. She'd been asking since Tuesday if *Sonnet* had arrived, had seen the boat anchored this morning, had waited here for quite a while, and just left.

I wrote a note to Eileen, told her I was sorry I'd missed her, that I'd try to check back every hour on the hour until we connected.

Back to the boat. Skyli and I tried to get the anchor up, and failed, and I missed my first chance to connect with Eileen. It was starting to look like a good idea to move the boat with three on board rather than two, so I went ashore on the hour and found Eileen reading by the Yacht Center. I was glad to see her; she seemed easy enough with the waiting she'd done, and game for whatever was next on the agenda.

We rowed back out. The three of us tried to get the anchor up, and failed. Hauled the anchor line in to the vertical and cleated it, full power forward, full power astern, absolutely no way that sucker was coming up.

Skyli wanted to dive on the anchor, said we could probably rent diving gear ashore. Last night, she'd mentioned that a little sore throat had been escalating for days, she hadn't wanted to mention it in the storm. I wasn't going to let her dive.

Eileen and I rowed back ashore, to try to locate some divers. Skyli's voice implored us across the water that all we needed to locate was a tank and regulator. We'd barely tied up the dinghy when a small open truck rumbled by, loaded with diving gear; we flagged it down and made a quick deal. Two divers started pulling their wet suits back on as Eileen trotted into town to change money to pay them; the divers hopped in the water and I rowed *Couplet* alongside them out to the boat.

Skyli was agitated and demoralized at our women's boat getting into this mess and then bringing in men to rescue us. I told her not to be ridiculous, shit happens, anyone could have dropped an anchor where we dropped ours, we'd done what we could to get it up and we were lucky to have stumbled on the divers.

The anchor, it turned out, was thoroughly fouled on an underwater cable. The men freed it in about five seconds.

And then they were swimming back toward shore, and I was rowing back toward shore to meet Eileen and settle up with them, and Skyli was powering *Sonnet* around the harbor until Eileen and I got back out. I'd taken my camera along in the dinghy, was shooting pictures of the boat against a backdrop of fortifications in warm afternoon light, and it struck me: Skyli is singlehanding *Sonnet*, and I'm taking pictures, as in her dream.

So I don't know. Maybe *Sonnet*, when she arrived in Valletta, was too filled with me and Skyli for Eileen to slip in easily. Maybe if the boat had already been in the berth when Eileen first came on board, and we'd all sat around and chatted for an hour or two rather than launching into frenetic activity—dealing with divers, dropping the anchor off the stern as we nosed bow-first into the quay, rigging the dinghy on a pulley system to get us ashore since we couldn't nose in quite close enough for direct disembarkation—it all would have worked out better. Maybe if I'd given Eileen the bow-to-stern tour, as I'd so firmly intended—given it to her all at once, taking three hours if necessary, rather than showing her things in ten-minute increments between other distractions, which is how it worked out—things would have been better.

Or maybe I'm overestimating how badly it went, early on. We all got along well in Valletta; the glitches were in fact pretty minor, things like the bank incident, the second day. Skyli and I for months now had been agreeably disagreeing as to who had the bigger biceps, both of us amazed at how strong we'd become simply working on boats. I don't quite remember how we started arm-wrestling in the bank lobby, but when we ended up nearly knocking a table over, Eileen stepped away from us, hands in the air, saying, "I'm not getting involved in this," looking as if she'd been coerced into babysitting a couple of ten-year-olds, a perhaps understandable reaction. The arm-wrestling competition was a draw.

It was also unfortunate that both Skyli and I had trouble remembering Eileen's name. We caught ourselves nearly calling her Irene, or Elaine, arriving at the point in a sentence where we should have uttered her name and coming instead to an involuntary pause, which couldn't have felt very welcoming. We finally came up with a sailing image as a memory crutch, a woman on a heeling boat. Think: I *lean*.

Maybe it would have worked out better if Skyli had left from Malta rather than sailing on to Greece. I certainly gave some thought to crew dynamics when Skyli was debating whether or not to stay on, reminding myself that three on board hadn't worked so great before, recognizing that Eileen and I would have a better shot at closeness if it were only the two of us. I wanted Skyli to leave, for those reasons. I wanted her to leave because it seemed the right thing to do, in terms of her commitment to Amy, to *Antelope Medicine*. I wanted her to leave because I thought we both might be ready for a break from the intensity of our friendship. At the same time, I didn't want her to leave at all.

16 Oct

Skyli is so fucking complicated, so hard on herself. She completely wears me out, and at the same time (or maybe not at the same time) I'm so utterly at ease with her, the sense of completeness, sailing with her.

Little love-hate relationship, while we're at it, with Malta. *Being* here is just so difficult, customs, immigration, more customs, Yacht Center, hung-up anchor, berth, can't pay for the berth 'cause no one's there, can't pay for the berth 'cause they don't have the receipt book, getting chewed out nonetheless for not paying for the berth.

And yet the *place*: old, warm-toned limestone buildings, rounded corner façades, acres of sprouting TV antennas.

We were three days total in Malta, ticking items off the list, dealing with officials, getting the malfunctioning Autohelm repaired, hand-repairing sails, provisioning, trundling jerry jugs of diesel back and forth from the service station in a wheelbarrow. Skyli wanted to do everything she could to help *Sonnet* on her way, even if she wasn't coming along.

As far as getting herself back to Portugal, there weren't easy answers. We found out it might be cheaper for her to fly from Athens than from Malta. She rationalized that it'd only take about five days to sail to Greece, how much difference could *that* make, since *Antelope Medicine* had already missed the start of the Rally? Wasn't it likely Amy would enjoy a day or two on the boat alone?

I was doing my own rationalizing. Eileen seemed far more grounded and straightforward than Monica, surely she and Skyli and I would get along fine. A triple-handed passage would be seamanlike, allowing all of us more sleep as far as Athens, after which Eileen and I could develop our friendship while we harbor-hopped the rest of the way to the Halkidiki.

Skyli found a patient travel agent close to the boat, who did everything she could to wrangle the cheapest possible fare. We sat in the little office while the agent clacked intently at her keyboard. On a piece of scrap paper Skyli wrote "Fly to Portugal," and under it "Sail to Greece," and drew a box around each. She pointed for me to the top box and said, "This is what I *should* do." She then pointed to the other, "And this is what I *want* to do."

Back and forth, no easy answers. She finally made her choice: she would fly back to Portugal.

The travel agent wrote up the ticket. Skyli said, "For once I made a mature decision." I headed back across town to pay for another day's berth fees—tomorrow was Sunday, Skyli didn't fly out until Monday, and I wanted her to have a place to stay—and Skyli went to scoop Eileen off the boat to do some final provisioning before the stores closed.

I definitely felt a degree of relief when Skyli decided on Portugal. By the time I got back to *Sonnet* the relief was gone, replaced by a kind of panic. I'd found a friend, and now I was losing her.

When I heard Skyli and Eileen on the quay, pulling the dinghy their way to load in bags of groceries, I headed to the bow and said to Skyli, "Are we doing the right thing?"

A week or so into our passage through the Med I'd given Skyli my backup Timex Ironman, which I'd bought in the States mainly for the singlehanded passage. She'd been wearing it for several days, since her own watch ceased to function, and the night I said "I want you to take my watch" she thought I meant I wanted her to take my three hours on deck; she'd been agreeable but a little surprised, since I was always trying to get her to sleep more.

She looked across at me from the quay of Malta. We looked down at our watches. It was five minutes to four, and the travel agency closed at four.

I pulled the dinghy back my way, tumbled in, and hand-over-handed myself to shore. Skyli trotted and I did as best a hobbling jog as my knee would allow. The woman in the travel agency didn't seem all that surprised, after all her work, that we'd ask her to tear up the ticket and the credit card receipt.

Eileen didn't know what to make of us.

We left that same day, just after sunset. I would rather have taken off well before dark, for Eileen's sake, and at first it looked as if we'd be able to finish the last of the chores before the sun was gone, but last-minute boat chores always take longer than you think. As the daylight slipped away I asked Eileen how she felt, if she'd rather wait until morning, and she said she thought she'd be fine leaving at night. I asked if she wanted any seasick medication, I could offer scopolamine patches or Kwells, and she said she'd never been seasick.

Some sailors say you should never begin a passage after three in the afternoon; that late, you might as well wait until morning. I tend to figure you'll be sleep-deprived by the end of the passage anyway, so if the boat's completely ready you might as well put the night miles behind you. Besides, I'm not wild about mornings.

I was proud of our all-women crew as *Sonnet* vacated her berth in Valletta. A big old wooden schooner had come in next to us. Backing out and getting our stern anchor up without snagging our rigging on theirs was a little tricky, but Eileen and Skyli and I had talked it through and we worked together well. One of the charter crew helped with our lines; the guests lined the rail of the schooner for some evening entertainment.

Outside, it was somewhat lumpy but not bad, nothing compared to the day Skyli and I had come in. I felt a quiet elation. This was the last offshore push.

We'd been clear of the breakwater for about forty-five minutes when I noticed Eileen was getting very quiet. Fifteen minutes after that, she said, with utter candor, "I'm feeling really groty." Five minutes after that, she was throwing up.

In my experience, there are three groups of people, seasickwise. The ones, like me, who definitely get sick, but unpredictably, and tend to get over it. The ones who get sick and don't get over it, end up hanging over the rail indefinitely if conditions are rough; on *Alaska Eagle*, with crews of twelve, we tended to have one of that no-cure category every trip or so, and I always felt bad for them. The lucky ones never get sick at all.

I'd never seen anyone go from one group to another, and it surprised me when Eileen got sick; she'd made both the passage from California to Hawaii—which tends to be uncomfortable the first couple of days— and the passage from Hawaii back—which tends to be miserable for the first week—and never been seasick. I felt terrible that I hadn't insisted she take some sort of seasick medication, or opted to wait until morning before taking off.

She was miserably sick, dry heaves after the first hour, and Skyli and I put half a scopolamine patch behind her ear. For a while we kept her in the cockpit for the fresh air, harnessed in two directions, but I started getting worried at how weak she was, so we moved her below with a bucket.

The southerly wind moderated by midnight, veering slowly. At 0100 we shook out the reefs, and I hoped Eileen would start feeling better.

In the morning she was still violently ill, so we put on the other half patch. We kept giving her water, or diluted Gatorade, and she kept throwing it up.

The wind settled out at around fifteen knots from the north-northwest. The day was hazy, stretching on. Skyli and I made dinner on the camping stove in the cockpit so Eileen wouldn't have to smell the cooking food.

18 Oct

2030   Deep sense of happiness last night heading out of Malta, pride in my boat, my accomplishment. Loving every inch of her, the peeling paint of the cockpit, the three-strand halyards, all those things that used to bug me.

Tonight I feel discouraged, wanting to be there, wanting it all to be over. Feel awful about Eileen. Feel angry with the things that don't work, the overheating, vibrating engine, the Autohelm that's so hard to put on, the flashlight you have to jiggle to get to work. Feel tired, tired, just wanting to sleep, counting the minutes to the end of the watch.

Dreamed my last off-watch about Oscar. Wonder why it's still hitting me so hard, if it's something to do with my parents, the reminder of mortality.

By 2200 the wind had dropped to under ten knots. I was sleeping below; Skyli wrote in the log, "Slow, quiet, dark, lovely."

At 2300 she wrote, "Thoughts start to turn to Westerbeke."

We stood three-hour watches through the night, keeping an eye on Eileen, changing her bucket when necessary, dealing with a dying, clocking wind and an overheating engine. 1300 rpm's kept the temperature at 180°, at least for a while. For a while I steered close-hauled by hand. In the morning I cleaned the raw-water filter—and the bilge while I was at it—but the engine still overheated.

19 Oct

1245   This is not a happy ship. Forty hours out and Eileen is still seasick. Skyli, denying for days there's much of anything wrong with her, can hardly swallow, and has broken down and started taking antibiotics. Eileen keeps asking how long it will take us to get there, how long at *this* speed, this course?

Sonnet and I are doing okay, getting toward the end of the line.

Another long slow day, close-hauled, long tacks, barely seventy miles in twenty-four hours.

By late afternoon Eileen was starting to feel better. She ate a bit of dinner. I asked if she wanted to take a night watch, figuring she'd be glad finally to be participating as crew, and she said sure. I only learned later that my willingness to trust her alone in the cockpit was part of what caused her to distrust my judgment.

I knew she wasn't having a whole lot of fun. I'd kind of gotten the impression that she wasn't very impressed with my boat, but I didn't realize that what I saw as cosmetic evidence of a long hard admirable haul she perceived as a lack of seaworthiness. It wasn't much of a jump from doubting the vessel's seaworthiness to doubting the skipper's seamanship.

The first night she took a watch, I blew it good. We were sailing along okay at not much over four knots with Max at the helm. I'd charged the batteries after dinner; the engine ran coolly in neutral but the noise had driven me nuts as usual so I'd only charged for an hour. When Eileen came on deck for her watch I told her since there was good visibility and no sign of another boat we could sail without the running lights. Any sign of shipping, flip the lights back on.

She was totally scandalized, though she didn't utter a word to me, saved it instead for Skyli, saying, "Wait till Jim hears about this."

A confession. It wasn't the first time *Sonnet* had sailed without running lights. I rationalized my lapses on the grounds that more boats did this than admitted it, race boats as well as cruising boats; weight was crucial on race boats, and fuel was weight, and running lights took lots of amperage. A crew member of a big downwind sled on a Hawaii race told me a story about sailing under spinnaker at white-knuckle speed in the blackness of night and hearing an odd sudden *whoosh*. The trimmer blurted *What the fuck was that*, and rushed below and flipped on the running lights, just as another set of running lights was flipped on, too. They watched a bit stunned as the other sled receded at fifteen knots on the opposite gybe.

Sonnet was never without lights—if nothing more than my brave little 6-volt strobe—when I was alone. With two crew or more, she was never without lights if no one was on deck, never without lights if another ship was in sight, even the dimmest of lights on the horizon. But yes, she had sailed without running lights.

I talked about this with Skyli, about power amperage, engine hours, mental engine tolerance hours, traffic patterns, the likelihood of another guy out there doing the same thing, and she said, "Is that really it?"

She was right. Maybe that wasn't all of it. Maybe part of it was how the boat became its own world, a dark shape slipping through the night.

Another confession. I did it on *Alaska Eagle*. A Coast Guard–licensed Sail Training Vessel, yet. In 1991, on the final night of a passage from California to the Marquesas, Gil and Joe and I—on the 2 to 5 a.m. dogwatch—turned off all the lights. Turned off the running lights, and the compass light, and the instrument lights, and all the dim red night-vision lights below. The radar, and the GPS, even the pale green solenoid light for gas in the galley, *everything*, so the 65-footer cut like a phantom through the moonlit night. Nine people asleep below, lost in wave-tossed dreams, not knowing. Three awake on deck, steering under sail by the track of moonlight on the water. Just that, and the vastness of the Pacific. It was my final night offshore on the *Eagle*—thousands and thousands of miles over the course of nine years, an enormous part of my life—and I carry it with me. It wasn't *right*, but it was the type of thing that Skyli could understand and Eileen couldn't.

The wind the next day continued light and on the nose, our progress uninspiring. We switched in the morning to the big genoa, but it was so stretched out it didn't do very well sailing close to the wind and we switched back to the smaller one around sunset.

Eileen tended to chat easily with Skyli when they overlapped in the cockpit; I could hear them joking and laughing. When Eileen and I overlapped, her tone would switch to an awkward civility, and frequently enough she'd slip below to her bunk.

20 Oct

People are so much on a boat, and I get so wrapped up in it.
Hate this, that if I know what Eileen's thinking it's because she told Skyli and Skyli told me.

Turn off the flashlight, surrounded in a flash by darkness and stars. Black sea black sky, black boat sailing.

I go through my usual drill, running over and over in my head what I could say to Eileen at this point to make things right, then give up. Maybe I'm gaining more confidence in myself, allowing myself to be flawed.

Maybe it can work, maybe it can't, Eileen's the wife of a military man, respectful of rules, and I'm in many ways a rule breaker. Wife of a computer whiz in the Atlantic, wife and mom in the Med, not enough in common on so small a platform, I don't know.

The only leg that truly felt right, simple in the way I want of sailing, was the leg with Skyli. Why haven't I written more Skyli? That we love this for the same reasons. That we complement each other. That we each now feel less alone.

The wind built toward daybreak. Skyli and I reefed; the wind dropped again. At 0900 we set our watches ahead to Greek time, still close-hauled in a southeast breeze.

21 Oct

I steer for quite a while from the leeward rail, watching the trim of the headsail, dipping my foot into the blue Ionian.

It comes together slowly, this picture, not yet completed. But a voyage, the longest voyage I've ever made on a sailboat; what a wonderful thing.

Who I am, what I am. Not too many pages left in this journal. Not too many days left of this voyage. More than three months since I left the dock at Cambridge and powered into the thundersquall night.

This my sonnet. This my boat.

"Tell them about Butch!" Skyli calls out when the dolphins come. "They love pet stories!" But then she dreads her night watches, all the craziness coming down on her, all the cruelty of the world. Feeling no place in it.

A dream she had last night: She was on *Antelope Medicine*, or wasn't, was in the water, floating on her back looking at the boat which looked beautiful, the blue of the water looked beautiful. She was in the water because the man on board—her thesis adviser—had pushed her in. Floating there thinking it wasn't a bad way to go, wondering if she should just swallow water and be done with it. And then the man started shooting at her with the flare gun, not to finish her off but to teach her a lesson, shooting off to the side, only he didn't know the gun didn't always shoot straight and he was likely to hit her. And I was out there on a little sailboat, potential salvation, potential hope, and she kept motioning me over but somehow the me of the dream didn't understand what was going on, and kept tacking around beyond her, and never approached.

At 2000 Skyli wrote in the log, "Peloponnisos ho," dim lights to the north-northeast.

By dawn we were rounding the north end of Kíthira, birthplace of Aphrodite, born of the foam of the sea. I stood on the seat behind the wheel, balancing there as *Sonnet* powered grouchily between the island and the Peloponnisos, exhausted and calmly awed. From here my course would be more north than east; the push toward the sunrise was over.

Skyli, 0800: "We got Greece, man."

The wind went west, then south. We rounded Cape Malea at six knots under sail. The morning moved on, the wind came and went; for a while we would sail, and then the wind would die and we'd fire up the reluctant engine. Always, though, an intense awareness of place, the blue Aegean, the dim rocky shore.

At one point, abeam of Parapola Island, when the wind was light and shifty and Max wasn't doing too well, I suggested Eileen steer by hand for a while, thinking she'd enjoy being at the helm on this magic day in Attica. She took the wheel, but I heard her mutter, "This is so stupid."

I was taken aback. *What* was stupid, that I'd trust her to steer under sail? What could go wrong, a back-winded jib maybe, something we could straighten out in about two minutes?

The incident brought home a reality I'd been trying hard to ignore: Eileen would not be delivering *Sonnet* the rest of the way to the Halkidiki. I'd been harboring the fantasy that a subtle change would come to pass, she'd get her sea legs fully, get excited about Greece, decide to keep sailing with me after Skyli got off—even though she'd been hinting for days that she'd better get home to her kids—but it wasn't going to happen. I realized, with a small shock of sadness, that Eileen and I might have ended up buddies if we'd simply met at a cocktail party in Sofia;

on *Sonnet*, each of us who we were, we hadn't had a chance. I told myself that if what Eileen wanted was to return to her family, her world, my task was to let her go graciously.

I studied my *Greek Waters Pilot* for the best port of entry. I was hoping for somewhere that gave Skyli and Eileen access to the airport, but kept *Sonnet* more or less on her course toward the Halkidiki. There was Lavrion, southeast of Athens; according to my book, buses ran daily from there to the capital, but I wondered how easy it would be to find out about flights.

I finally realized the only logical solution was to go straight to Marina Zea, in Piraeus, the port of Athens. It would mean a fifty-mile detour for *Sonnet*, and by all accounts the marina was a pretty unpleasant place, but Piraeus was a bustling suburb—plenty of travel agents—and closer to the airport than Athens itself.

I flipped farther ahead in the *Pilot*, wondering how I planned to manage the final two hundred miles from Zea to Porto Carras. Singlehanding would be tricky; there was way too much traffic in the Greek archipelago for me to run safely day and night, but sailing days and stopping nights sounded awfully hard. Maybe I could rig the Bruce anchor at the stern to make singlehanded Med-mooring workable. Maybe I could stop only at islands where it was safe to anchor out, not even go ashore, just sleep and keep moving.

What I really wanted was for Steve to help me sail *Sonnet* the rest of the way to Carras; maybe he could get the time off.

By sunset we were off the island of Hydra. Fifty more miles; by dawn we should be in port.

22 Oct

2140 Moonless full-star night, all those characters from Greek myths up there as we power across the Saronic Gulf from Hydra to Piraeus. Study in points of light on dark, ship lights, land lights, airplanes, lighthouses, dark masses of land. Stars, darkness, shooting stars. The distant, extraordinary loom of the city.

At 2300 Skyli wrote in the log, "Motoring @ 1100 rpm's; getting a little lift from the mainsail. Magic night— Thanks, my captain."

I went below sometime after midnight, away from the dark and lights of deck, the spatial puzzle of busy waterway at night, and found

Skyli—at that point still unwillingly Bridget—leaning intently over the chart, a lovely British Admiralty thing engraved in 1863. It took me a minute to realize she wasn't trying to figure out landmarks or lights.

"I've got a couple of possibilities on names here," she said, running a finger along the coastline.

One was Zea, the marina we were heading for, only she'd had a bird named Zea once and wasn't sure she wanted to name herself after a dead bird. The other was the Peloponnesian cape off the north end of Hydra: Cape Skyli.

At 0115 she wrote, "We got Athens, man."

We kept on our northerly course, past the island of Aegina, sometimes sailing, sometimes powering. The closer we got to the mainland shore, the more clearly we could see the anchored ships, scores of them, brightly lit against the dark night, or pinpointed in green against the dark screen of the radar. We tracked ferries by radar, tracked them by eye from the cockpit as they made their way in and out of Piraeus.

An hour before dawn the slenderest orange crescent of a moon rose above the orange-patterned lights of the suburbs of Athens.

We picked out the entrance lights for Zea. I'd hardly slept, and wasn't tired. We figured there wouldn't be anyone in the marina office at 6 a.m. anyway, so we throttled back a half mile offshore and took our time, lowered the mainsail, flaked it neatly, coiled the sheets, even put on the mainsail cover. A banana-shaped hydrofoil zipped past us in the dark, its yellow strobe flashing. A tiny fishing boat puttered past us powered by a one-stroke engine; dim running lights bobbed in the chop, and the solo fisherman stood at the stern to steer.

Around six-thirty we motored slowly inside the breakwater. It was just beginning to get light. The boats in the dense inner harbor, piers radiating like a star, appeared to be mostly Greek. The smaller foreign-flag boats seemed to be rafted along the seawall; the bigger, snazzier ones were across the way, closer to the swing of things, with bow anchors out and sterns to the quay.

We kept an eye open for a reception dock, or a harbor official, anyone who could tell us where we belonged. Finally someone motioned us back out to the seawall.

We motored slowly along, checking things out. A lot of spots were already two boats deep, or too tight to slip into. I finally chose a likely parking place toward the open end of the marina, alongside a white-hulled sailboat. We put out fenders and readied dock lines, starboard-side-to, talking it through.

A Beneteau, it looked like. We approached slowly at a shallow angle, straightened up in reverse, and came alongside gently. Eileen and Skyli stepped off *Sonnet*'s beam onto the beam of the other boat; Eileen moved forward with a bow line and Skyli moved aft with a stern line and they tied us off smoothly.

A man came up the companionway of the Beneteau, sleep-groggy but bustling to help, in his late fifties maybe, with a reddish face and mussed thinning hair. He looked from one to the other of us, perplexed, and finally said, "Are your man crew sleeping?"

Skyli and Eileen laughed, stepping back onto *Sonnet*.

"No man crew," I said. "What you see is what you got."

At 0655 Skyli wrote in the log, "Engine off; alongside—somewhere in Greece."

We made ourselves an unorthodox breakfast, packaged brownies cooked on a skillet like pancakes, all feeling sweet-toothed after the long night. For virtually the first time since we'd pulled out of the slip in Valletta it felt like we were a team. Better now than never.

I headed ashore at eight with my yacht documents and all our passports, hoping I could get *Sonnet* cleared into Greece and liberate my crew early enough for them to make flight plans.

The paperwork took hours. Along with the usual customs and immigration, *Sonnet* had to be issued a "transit log" for Greece. I started at an office in Zea, then was sent across town to several more offices at the main Piraeus port. The complexity of it all was mind-boggling, almost made Malta look simple, gear lists and crew lists and customs declarations, fill out this form in this building, pay for that form at that building, go to a kiosk on the corner to buy stamps to put on a third.

I went back to Zea and scooped up Skyli and Eileen around noon. Eileen was traveling with only a diplomatic passport, and the required Greek visa had expired, and I needed her to go with me to the immigration office to straighten it out.

Skyli asked me—as the three of us walked across town—what I thought of the name she'd found herself last night. Apparently I wasn't the first one she'd asked; Eileen rolled her eyes as if she couldn't believe the subject of self-induced name changing was coming up again. It took me a minute to realize how serious the question was, and another two seconds to realize how much I liked the name. I never again called Skyli anything but Skyli.

We ducked into a travel agency to check out flight schedules for both of them. When Eileen requested the earliest possible flight to Sofia, and looked almost fierce when there wasn't one before seven in the morning, I was surprised at how crushed I felt. She laid down her credit card with conviction. Skyli kept working on a ticket to Portugal and Eileen and I headed over to the immigration office in the cruise ship terminal.

We walked the first bit in silence, and then I got my nerve up and told Eileen I was sorry the adventure hadn't been more fun for her, needing desperately to get some of this out in the open before she was gone. She was evasive, said sure it'd been fun, she enjoyed the sailing part, she just figured it was time to get home, her kids weren't getting their riding lessons, Jim was no doubt getting tired of being an only parent. This was a very different story from what I'd heard in Sofia, when she'd said she could be gone two weeks easily, but I tried to go with it.

We worked out the passport problem—she was issued a two-day transit visa—and rejoined Skyli, who'd wrangled a special fare for seamen's wives by claiming her husband was on a merchant ship in Faro, ill and in need of wifely ministrations. Her flight, routed through Frankfurt, left tomorrow morning at nine.

We found an OTE telephone place and Eileen and I both tried to get through to Bulgaria. There were a couple of different numbers for the embassy, so Eileen tried one and I tried another, over and over, fifteen minutes straight, and neither of us was able to get through. She then started trying her home number, and managed after a while to get a ring.

I could hear her through the wall of our connecting booths as she talked to her three daughters, one after the other, oldest to youngest. Her voice, her syntax, was slightly different but equally natural for each of them, and I could sense the excitement in the kids through Eileen's voice, sense the love zipping back and forth along the Sofia-to-Piraeus phone lines. To the oldest girl she explained what time her plane would be arriving tomorrow, said you need to pass this on to Daddy, write it down so you're sure you don't forget. To the middle she explained that yes she was in Greece now, she'd arrived on the sailboat and would be flying on a plane up to Sofia; to the youngest she mostly just said that yes she was coming home, she'd see all of them tomorrow, she could hardly wait.

By evening both Eileen and Skyli were packed. Eileen was thinking about sleeping at the airport to be sure she didn't miss her flight, but we finally talked her into sleeping on the boat, we'd been told that taxis were easy to find at the Zea ferry landing, we'd set backup alarms if she wanted, to be sure she got up.

We went out to dinner, my treat, wandered the streets of Piraeus near the marina and found a small restaurant with rough wooden tables and stunning food. Skyli had been getting a headache—I'd come to recognize what she looked like when one was coming on, the way her right eyelid drooped slightly—but it improved as she ate, and she became progressively more animated under the influence of the kind of food she approved of, lots of garlic and onion and eggplant, tiny fiery peppers and salty white feta cheese. Eileen became progressively more silent, almost sullen; on the way home she walked ahead of us, searching store windows for presents for her kids.

I heard her leave well before dawn and lay awake in my bunk, feeling torn, oddly abandoned, feeling that old sense of failure. I wished— deeply—that things could have worked out better, that a second crew member wasn't leaving my boat under less than ideal conditions, but I wasn't sure I could have behaved differently with Eileen. I wasn't sure I could have behaved differently with Monica; I wasn't sure Monica could have behaved differently with me.

I heard the putter of a fishing boat, crawled out from under the covers, and stood on the edge of my bunk to watch it pass, head and shoulders out of the forward hatch. *Sonnet* rocked slightly as the wake of the fishing boat reached us.

Maybe I should try to shake the sense of guilt, that I hadn't been able to create the Miraculous Women's Boat I'd imagined. Maybe I should recognize that you can't predict. You can create, but you can't know exactly how the creation will turn out. I'd wanted to be friends with Monica, with Eileen, but you can't just will a friendship into existence. Or maybe some people can, maybe I was just too difficult, inaccessible, inflexible.

There ought to be more than one word for this. The difference between a friend, someone with whom you can be friendly, and someone who can understand your soul.

And then, in the cool morning air of Piraeus, I started thinking not about what I'd lost but what I'd found. At the very conception of this journey I'd longed for a sailing soul mate; if I'd learned along the way how difficult and unlikely it was to find her, it only made Skyli all the more a miracle.

One out of three ain't bad.

I crawled back in my bunk, went back to sleep for a while, got up when Skyli got up, said I'd go with her out to the airport. She protested; I said don't be ridiculous.

As we ferried her luggage across Man Crew's boat to the seawall she told me the sailing had been fun but I'd failed her dismally on the haircutting front—I'd told her at some point that I cut Steve's hair, and she'd been bugging me ever since to cut hers; I'd always said no, because I didn't have decent scissors and was terrified of screwing it up—so I told her I'd cut her hair at the airport, but only if I could do it my way, I wasn't going to shave her head, leaving an embossed anchor like she'd begged of Sascha. Her hair looked good this length, just needed some shaping, shorter at the sides. She agreed begrudgingly, so I went back and grabbed my dull paper-cutting scissors from the chart table.

We found a cab easily at the Dolphin Boat landing, rode the twenty minutes to the airport, checked her in, then went outside to try to find a halfway private spot for a haircut. No such spot available; the only place with decent light and no wind was right outside the main terminal entrance, so that's where we set up the barbershop, to the great amusement of everyone coming in and out.

24 Oct

Sent Skyli on through the passport control, noticed a final stray strand at the very last moment ("Get it!" she said. "Go on, get it quick!" and I pulled out the scissors as a new horde of boarders approached which would have slowed her down, quick snip and she was off, both of us laughing), then wandered around the airport a bit, pleased to be there, pleased to be in Greece, bought myself a kiwi tart (have I eaten *any* bad food in this country?), ate it by a sunny plant-filled window then went in to call Steve when I was sure he'd be at the embassy, attempt after attempt after attempt (as usual), hearing announcements a time or two, paging such and such a passenger to board for Frankfurt so I knew she hadn't left, got through to Steve, *excited* about him coming, he's virtually sure he can get the time off, back outside and hearing a plane and rushing out from under the eaves to see it, calling goodbye out loud as the plane climbed up over the Aegean, waving, acting silly, not caring if I looked a bit odd to passersby, "Good-by-ee!," a child's singsong, waving as the plane climbed and disappeared into clouds, "Goodbye, Skyli!" the new name sounding just right.

There at the airport of Athens, homeland—more or less—of Odysseus, I felt my life circling around me, felt the people I cared about circling toward and away from me, and I was happy.

IV

Couplet

13

The sea's off somewhere, doing nothing. Listen.
An expelled breath. And faint, faint, faint
(or are you hearing things?), the sandpipers'
heart-broken cries.

ELIZABETH BISHOP
"Twelfth Morning; or What You Will"

24 Oct

Don't always write at times like this, when happiness swells, but
should. Gorgeous blue sea to the left of this bus from the airport
back to Piraeus. Deep blue out a ways, paler green-blue close to
the beach, wind, whitecaps, up ahead the massive anchored ships
I saw two nights ago by radar.

Greece. How many times have I thought of Greece, of reaching this destination?

Two hills of Piraeus, blocky apartments sprawl but I don't
mind. Loved the sense of history, of place, sailing up the Peloponnisos.

Excited at the prospect of sharing the boat with Steve. Deep
sense of happiness every time I think of Skyli. A slight edge of
worry, that this elation will end, which it will, but thankful
while it's here, accept love where you find it, accept happiness
where you find it.

Steve had never sailed our boat. In fact, he'd only *seen* her a half
dozen times. In the three and a half months we'd owned her before I
left America I almost always drove out to work on her alone, the first

two months to Annapolis, the last month and a half to Cambridge, where I usually stayed for several days at a time. During that period, Steve hardly even saw *me*.

Still, he'd done his share of sailing. The first four years we were together he hadn't known a thing about boats, but we bought a Lido 14 dinghy when we moved back to California from Paris, and he learned to sail on Newport Bay. When I started teaching he came out with my classes. We took charter boats to Catalina Island. He came along on a couple of short *Alaska Eagle* cruises, took an ocean-sailing class with my boss Brad, did some racing, and in '87 Brad set him up to help deliver a race boat back from Hawaii after the Transpac.

Steve and his three shipmates had a tremendous time on the Pacific crossing, in spite of nearly running out of both food and fuel, and the reality that fast downwind boats are miserably uncomfortable on the mostly upwind trek back to California. He later delivered the same boat back from Cabo San Lucas, with a less harmonious crew, and probably would have been happy to cut short his offshore career after that first long passage. He was glad that he'd done it. Once. He liked being around boats, he liked sailing, but he didn't like being out there days on end. He liked hot showers, exercise, intellectual stimulation, and decent sleep.

At one point I couldn't have imagined having a mate who wasn't a serious sailor, but I'd come to recognize—and recognized now more than ever—how right Steve was for me, even in the realm of sailing. He knew both me and my sport well enough to understand my passion, and to support me, but my accomplishments were very much my own.

And somehow, in the weeks—and miles—since our visit to Porto Carras, the fear that *Sonnet* couldn't fit into both of our lives had faded. Steve did respond to sailboats, and this one particularly. I had made my long voyage, met my big challenge, and right now maybe we wanted the same thing of our boat, in the same place. I could sense the pine-and-olive tranquillity of Sithonia two hundred miles to the north, as well as the more stressful reality of Sofia. Steve and I felt different pressures from diplomacy, but we both felt them; *Sonnet*, moored at Carras, could be our floating home-away-from-home when we needed to look at the sea.

I launched into cleaning as soon as I got back from the airport, operating on the assumption that Steve would in fact be joining me, that making the boat welcoming was more important than working out singlehanded anchoring techniques. Around noon my next-door neighbor and his wife clambered back onto the Beneteau after a provisioning run.

The wife smiled tentatively and disappeared below, and Man Crew paused to chat, asking where my crew had gone. His boat was a retired charter boat, his wife wasn't all that wild about sailing, he actually hadn't done all that much sailing himself, mostly day sailing in Sweden.

They were planning on leaving first thing in the morning for a trip down to Aegina with some friends. He'd planned to request we switch places today so they wouldn't have to bother me in the morning and now he was nonplussed, how could he ask me to move my boat when I didn't even have Women Crew to help me? I told him I could probably manage to get her off and back onto the seawall alone.

I got things organized on deck and returned to my cleaning. When Man Crew tapped on my hull to let me know he was ready, I started up the Westerbeke, received my lines from Man Crew & Crew, powered away from the Beneteau, then puttered in circles as the Swedes fussed around on deck.

A slight breeze stirred from the west, but I decided I'd come starboard-side-to onto the seawall anyway—figuring I could counteract the breeze on my stern with reverse gear from the engine—because I knew how *Sonnet*'s stern tended to kick to starboard.

The Beneteau pulled off the seawall, barely squeaking around the big old fishing boat ahead of her on the wall. There was only one boat both ahead and behind the vacated parking place—in plenty of other places, boats were rafted two deep—but both boats were fat ones, and the space in between suddenly didn't look all that much longer than *Sonnet*. This wouldn't be as easy as it had been yesterday morning, coming alongside Man Crew's boat.

I draped the ends of both bow line and stern line at the beam so I could grab them easily as I hopped off, made my approach slowly, barely fast enough for steerage, coasting in neutral, cut in as closely as I could to the boat astern, closed on the wall.

Wheel hard to port. A shot of reverse. A bigger shot of reverse, engine protesting, fenders squeaking on the seawall. Momentum pretty much stopped, or at least I thought so. Throttle back, jerk the gearshift into neutral, stumble to the beam, hop off, heart thumping, dock lines in hand.

The boat was still coasting forward gently toward the gnarly-looking bowsprit of the fishing boat. I whipped some turns around a bollard with the bow line to hold her, which started to spring the stern out. Stood on the end of the bow line, hauled back in on the stern line with all I had, knees shaky. Finally stopped her, safely if not entirely elegantly. Deep breath.

I centered *Sonnet* in the space as my heart rate returned to normal, thinking the whole thing through, whether it would have gone more smoothly in the opposite direction, a different set of obstacles. So much always to learn.

I secured my lines, added a spring line, then took the Swedes' lines as they came back alongside.

Man Crew crossed back and forth over *Sonnet's* deck a number of times during the afternoon, always apologetic, always wanting to chat. He was curious about what gear I had on board, intrigued by my GPS and single-sideband. He gave me a pamphlet on sailing in Greece which I'd already picked up at the Zea tourist office. He offered me a tour of the Beneteau and I put him off.

A Brit on a run-down powerboat two boats away wandered over at one point to warn me about the surge, how bad it could get when the fishing boats and ferries went in and out in the dark of morning, moving way too fast once they exited the inner marina. He told me to set up plenty of fenders, plenty of spring lines. He was more than a little drunk, late afternoon. I nodded at his invitation to come visit his boat some-time, with no intention of taking him up on it.

I spent the day alone on *Sonnet*.

In the early evening I headed down to the tourist office, where there were phones for long-distance calls. Hung out for half an hour trying to get through to Steve, flipping through Greek travel brochures between attempts. Dial, no go, wait, dial again before he finally picked up. Second time hearing his voice in one day; how amazing.

He'd talked to my mom just an hour ago; she'd called to see if he'd heard from me. Apparently Dad was fine, no recurrence of the episode we'd been through the morning before I left. I asked Steve if it sounded as if Mom had been drinking when she called, and he said no, he didn't think so, and there it was, that flicker of hope in me, thinking maybe the doctor's lecture had gotten through to her. Maybe she hadn't been drunk since I sailed away on *Sonnet*, maybe she was finally scared.

How many times in the past thirty years had I thought the same thing, maybe *this* will be the crisis that leads to change?

Steve had spoken to the other two officers in the Political Section. Both would be in Sofia the next couple of weeks, so he should be able to take Wednesday through Friday, and then Monday, which combined with the weekend would give him six days, five nights on the boat. Today was Saturday; he wouldn't be able to confirm the leave days with his boss or research flight schedules until Monday, but we should tentatively count on him arriving in Athens Wednesday afternoon.

Three and a half days to putter on my boat.

Sunday morning the wind was blowing hard. Man Crew with his wife and two friends nosed tentatively out of the harbor and were back within an hour. The wind kept building, as did the surge. I set up a spider's web of lines and fenders and chafing gear to keep *Sonnet* safe.

25 Oct

Blowing to thirty-five knots inside Marina Zea, planned to go into Athens today but I'm happy to stay on the boat, monitor things, clean, rest, read, research Greek islands. Could go to Limnos for a long weekend out of Porto Carras. Lesbos with a bit more time than that. What fun.

Not minding the wind the way I minded it in Horta, long long ago.

I read through the pages on the Cyclades in my *Greek Waters Pilot*—a bit too much of a detour—and the Sporades, planning the best route for my cruise with Steve, wishing we had more time. I jotted alternatives in the logbook, juggling distances and daylight, berthing facilities and sightseeing potential. It looked as if we'd have to do at least one overnight sail, which wouldn't have been my preference.

By Monday the wind had moderated.

26 Oct

Dreamed about Mom last night, or both my parents. Dad was completely healthy, striding ahead as the three of us walked. Mom was moving more slowly but looked marvelous, I was telling her what great shape she was in, saying maybe you look so much better because you're standing up straight. She was wearing a blue skirt and a long-sleeved tight-fitting top, like a leotard, and her face was unlined and lovely.

I decided to put Athens off another day, get things done on *Sonnet*, do some provisioning, buy charts. A big American boat came in, bound eventually for Israel, and they lent me their hose, helped me pry off the heavy metal cover to the pay-by-the-cubic-meter water outlet. I pulled out all my floorboards, flooded fresh water below, the first time I'd done this since the Azores. It felt wonderful, purifying.

I checked the impeller on the raw-water pump, and opted against checking the heat exchanger. The engine managed fine at low rpm's; it would get me to Carras.

For all the cautionary tales I'd heard about Marina Zea, for all the complaints from the sailors around me, I found myself liking it. The surge was excessive, the water was scuzzy, and we few low-budget visiting firemen were banished out to the breakwater, but I liked the bustle and life.

Yesterday evening I'd stood in *Sonnet*'s darkened interior, shamelessly watching through the porthole as a young Greek couple leaned side by side against their car, his right hand holding her left, his left arm around her waist, standing as if posed by a photographer, chatting and laughing—she seemed to laugh at everything he said—until he started nuzzling her neck, at which point she would become very still, smiling slightly, gazing into the distance until he ceased and desisted, and she would slowly reanimate, and the laughing and chatting would start again.

Families strolled along the seawall. Motorbikes roared by. Greek music spilled from boom boxes and slowly cruising cars. The noise didn't ease off until 2 or 3 a.m.; not long after that, in the quiet, the fishing boats started going out. I'd gotten out of my bunk again this morning to watch them leave in the still dawn, little open boats with solo fishermen, larger ones with winches for nets, the marvelous colors of gunnels and hulls, aqua, bright red, luminous white, heading out of the harbor against a backdrop of hilly Piraeus.

In the afternoon I headed across town to an Admiralty chart vendor, only to find the place sold out of charts of the Sporades and Halkidiki. Another vendor, down by the commercial harbor, was sold out as well.

The man at the second store—looking apologetic—told me that I might have to buy Greek charts, he could give me directions on where to find them. Why hadn't anyone mentioned this before?

I found the third vendor. The Greek charts were cheaper than the Admiralty charts by a long shot, and beautiful. I knew Cyrillic from studying Bulgarian, and the Greek alphabet was similar enough to Cyrillic that place names floated on blue water and beige land in dim familiarity. Combined with my *Pilot*—which had line-drawn charts and all the English words I needed—these were perfect.

I headed back toward the boat, passing a bakery where a man was pulling big pans of baklava from the oven. I left-faced in the door, and two minutes later walked up the sidewalk eating the rich, flaky pastry, still warm, so good it nearly brought tears to my eyes.

One last stop at the tourist office, to use the phone. Still a bit early to be sure Steve was home, so I tried Spain first.

It was a short call to my parents, and the chairs at the tourist office were comfortable, and after I hung up I sat for a good fifteen minutes, feeling, ever so slightly, the movement of *Sonnet* on the water. There'd been a time when I would have heard the touch of alcohol in Mom's voice and said nothing—years of that, when none of us ever said a thing—followed by the era of saying something and getting into a fight with her, or saying nothing and feeling guilty for not confronting her. This time the panic had risen in me—think what you're *doing*, Mama, the stakes have changed—but also the recognition that nothing I said in the next few minutes would keep her from taking the next drink. So I told her calls were expensive from Greece, that we should maybe keep it short, I'd call again next week from Bulgaria.

She'd put Dad on the downstairs phone, instead of sending him upstairs to the extension, to keep it short. I told him I loved him, said how good it had been to spend time with him.

He said, "It sure was."

I wasn't certain he actually remembered my being there. His soul remembered, if his memory didn't. Some part of him remembered.

I could visualize the house so clearly, visualize Dad setting the phone down, walking back into the living room, sitting back down on the couch in front of the television. The house, their home. A vessel to carry them forward.

No room in my dad for change. Aching to believe there was room in my mom; knowing, if there wasn't, the consequences could be devastating for both of them; thinking of my dad alone.

Anguish and love.

I finally stood up, told the woman at the desk I wanted to make another call, and got through to Steve. Talking to him helped; what would I have done, these past fifteen years, without Steve?

He wouldn't be arriving in Athens until 7:30 Wednesday night. He needed to attend a Wednesday morning meeting, would drive from Sofia to Thessaloniki in the afternoon and fly out at six.

He was looking forward to sailing with me on *Sonnet*.

The next day I walked across town to the metro station, took the train to Monastiraki, and wandered through the streets of the Plaka, referring to my tourist map, buying two earrings—a tiny white moon and a tiny black star, inlaid on silver—from a West African street vendor. I stumbled upon the Tower of Winds, which pleased my sailor's soul, more than two thousand years old and perfectly oriented to the points of the compass.

I found my way to the Acropolis, walked for nearly two hours among the ruins.

27 Oct

I can't even believe I didn't bring the camera; instinct said I should, but I didn't want the weight. Sit now with the most extraordinary light on the Acropolis, want a photo, and won't have one. Sun lowering below clouds over Piraeus, dark clouds still behind the ruins.

Pleased to be in Athens as I was first wandering around, the narrow streets, the unexpected patches of antiquity. And then in the Acropolis a sudden sense of sadness, unable to handle the weight of history, the various eras, various wars leading to destruction of temples on this hill. Herded us out fifteen minutes ago and a number of us sit on this rocky knoll to the west, and the Acropolis rests there incredibly still, the stones incredibly still, incredibly old, and I sense both the stillness and the cataclysms, a lightning bolt on gunpowder, building up, tearing down. The astonishing density of this town, stretching away to all the surrounding hills, flat surfaces, stark angles, houses, balconies, concrete lit by sunset light, the occasional change of shape of a darker, red-domed orthodox church, or the ancient columns of a temple. Weight of history, weight of change, the rise and fall of religions, the driving force of hate. Ex-Yugoslavia to the north of here, signs everywhere saying *Macedonia: Greek for 2,000 years.*

Both awe at the history and distress at the cluttered present, history in the making.

From the Parthenon you can see the neighborhood of Piraeus where Marina Zea is. *Sonnet* is there, *Sonnet* who has made so much sense to me these past few days, filled me with so much pleasure. Let her be a refuge, Lizard, a source of power, Horse and Hawk. Let her be a place where I can fight this sadness. Let me accept her as such, without question.

Cool now, the sun touching clouds which touch the hilltop. Orange light on the foot-polished surface of this stone.

I've been to Athens. I'd never been to Athens, before now. I wouldn't have known it was so hilly. I wouldn't have known that from the hills you can see the sea.

From sea we should be able to see the Parthenon.

Waiting for the sunset light to fade; fading quickly.

I think I need a good Greek salad and a beer.

Lights coming on in the city, touches among them of neon blue and red.

I plunged back into the lights of modern Greece, feeling more grounded, but lonely. Knowing that Steve would be here tomorrow, that this long voyage—this self-imposed matelessness—was over. Aware of the essence of him, the fact that he could absorb the world, present and past, in ways I couldn't. Aware of the ways his temperament balanced mine, the ways that I needed him.

I ate in the heart of the Plaka with all the tourists, ate a good Greek salad and some fried eggplant, a cold glass of beer. Watched the flow of humanity, took the metro back to Piraeus and walked back to the boat.

The next day I went into overdrive with my housekeeping. I wiped down every square inch of varnished and painted interior wood. I scrubbed the Formica of the galley and chart table, never having known it could be so white. For months I'd never done more than wipe off the stove, and now I wanted it perfect, took it apart, cleaned all the parts in the cockpit, polished the stainless steel behind and beneath it.

At one point, needing a breather, I sat at the chart table and picked up my journal, feeling the heft of it. Four white sheets remaining of an eighty-sheet book, the others filled, line after line of words.

I squared things away with the harbor officials, so *Sonnet* could leave in the morning. In the evening I took the bus to the airport, got there early, and strolled around, people-watching, until Steve's flight came in. He looked wonderful coming through the gate, his blond hair still summer-sun-bleached and a bit long for diplomacy, wearing Levi's and a black henley, his purple-lined gray jacket slung over the black duffel bag.

It felt good to hold him.

I asked if he'd checked any luggage, and he grinned, told me he'd packed everything into the one medium-sized bag, admitting it was very un-Steve like. I always bugged him when we traveled about how many clothes he took, though I also tended to borrow T-shirts or socks after about the third day.

In the taxi we talked about our cruise plans. I figured the best would be a day-and-night sail to Skyros, spend a day and night there, then a day sail to either Skopelos or Alonnisos and another day sail to Carras. It would have been great to have some time together in Athens—Steve loved Greece, had devoured Greek myths as a kid, spent more time in Greece than anywhere else on his first backpack-and-hitchhike trip through Europe in 1973—but we decided, with our time constraints, we should get a good night's sleep and blast right out in the morning.

We taxied to the boat to drop off his things, then walked back into town for dinner. I wanted to take him to the same place I'd taken Skyli and Eileen, but somehow I couldn't find it, and we wandered a long time to find a place and it wasn't as good.

I told him I'd have a surprise for him tomorrow as we powered out of the marina—convinced we'd have a clear view of the Parthenon—but wouldn't tell him what it was.

By eleven we'd settled into our berths, on our boat. I lay awake for a while as Steve's breathing across the cabin became regular in sleep, then drifted off.

14

It may not be the most common perception
of love: Being elsewhere through
such crucial times. Bucking bad reception,
tough connections. Not common, but true.
We catch up on stories. You're sure no male
Penelope, waiting (I shan't compare thee); by day
you've been in the volatile Balkans, by night on the trail
of leopards. I talk of Sonnet's way.
We round Sounion, weather a mini-storm,
learn each other anew on a narrow berth.
I know this boat, her myriad lines, sleek form;
you may not know her quirks, but knew her worth.
The finest gifts at times come wrapped in black.
I'm trying here to offer something back.

The wake motion from fishing boats heading out of Zea woke us at seven o'clock. I'd talked to Man Crew yesterday, saying *Sonnet* would be leaving, asking if he wanted to switch places again, and he said no, he would move for us in the morning when we were ready to leave. By the time Steve and I ate breakfast, alerted Man Crew, got both boats off the dock, and cleared the breakwater, it was eight-thirty.

A nasty hazy smog hung over Athens, obscuring all but a few dim hills. I'd looked forward to handing Steve the binoculars, then pointing with a flourish to the north. I'd looked forward to seeing the Parthenon myself from *Sonnet*'s deck, imagined it in morning light. About all I could do now was tell Steve what the surprise would have been, if the weather had been clear enough.

The wind was from the south and virtually nonexistent, so we powered.

29 Oct

Exceedingly happy to have Steve on board, to have him like the
boat, which looks lovely below. Not real lovely on deck, but I
almost don't mind the peeling varnish, will start from scratch.

This is so entirely my world, has been for six months; he is so
immensely of my life, has been for fifteen years, and there's a
kind of completion, to having him on board.

The wind came and went; the engine was off and on as we sought
enough wind to sail on. I made lunch and served it in the cockpit,
priding myself on my domesticity.

We stuck close enough to land to see the temple to Poseidon at Cape
Sounion, which made up a bit for missing the Parthenon. As we passed
I launched a silent message out across the water to the god of the sea:
Thanks for everything.

The world remained hazy and Greece slipped by, Gaidaro Island,
Makronisos.

1540 *Sonnet* broad reaching at over six knots under a cloudy
Greek sky, a very pleasant sail, but there's something else going
on, with Steve being here. Inexplicable water in the bilge (might
be the drip in the packing gland but I doubt it), inexplicable
crack in the Plexiglas of the forward hatch, and I'm ready for this
era to be over, the movement of this boat from one place to the
next toward the distant distant goal of northern Greece. (And
then, as that hits me again, as I remember how far away the Med
seemed from the North Atlantic, how far away Greece seemed
from Spain, the pride swells in me.) Not tired of it, exactly, but
excited about a world in which there's more than that, ready to
hear the news, ready to learn something of the changing face of
Bulgarian politics, ready to do pottering-type jobs on *Sonnet*, not
the jobs crucial to getting her back out to sea.

1700 Steve naps, I read *Coasting*, and it all blends together. I'm
happy out here with my boat and my book and my journal, with

overcast skies and a coolish breeze. Mainsail looks a bit rattier than it did at the start of this voyage, inspected the top of the rig by binocular this morning and noticed all the scars on my re- cently painted mast but that's fine. Wondering if I've sailed more miles in just over three months than Tony did the entire time he owned her; even if no (my guess yes), *Sonnet* is becoming mine, becoming ours.

The wind picked up in the early evening, out of the southwest, sending us nicely into the channel between Evvoia and Andros. Short days, well past the equinox, dark by six o'clock.

I launched into dinner preparations, nothing more elaborate than a salad and some packaged pasta, but the spirit was right.

The wind was behind us—Andros to starboard and Evvoia to port—as I stirred the pasta Parmigiana into the boiling water. The boat was slewing around a bit with the Monitor steering, so I suggested that Steve hand steer, if it sounded like fun.

He steered. I stirred pasta. The wind was building. I realized that Steve had never steered this boat downwind, and this might not be the best time to get a feel for it. Damn, though, two meals in a row would have been some kind of record.

I took over the helm, and he took over the galley. I didn't really want to appear concerned about the wind, and I was really hoping I wouldn't have to reef. I kept telling myself this was a funneling phenomenon, the wind was likely to let up at any moment.

The wind kept building.

I steered, trying to keep the boat balanced, to keep things nicely controlled. The apparent wind was stabilizing around twenty; I figured as long as it stayed around twenty this was no big deal. A few gusts to twenty-three, twenty-four, no big deal. Then stabilizing up where the gusts had been; shit.

Steve stuck his head up to ask how much longer the pasta should take. I wrestled the wheel. Oh, four or five minutes maybe. He disappeared back into the galley.

Boat slewing, rushing, hitting nine knots. I told myself I'd have to reef if it stayed steady like this at twenty-five. Hopefully it'd drop back down again.

Well, maybe steady like this at twenty-seven.

Hmm. It seems to be over thirty.

No way out of it; I had to reef. I called Steve back up, said maybe before we eat we should reef, and he said fine, do you want me to steer since I don't know how the reef lines work. I said no, you might have trouble steering in this wind since you don't know the boat, why don't you just handle the mainsheet and we'll let the wind vane steer. He settled himself by the mainsheet, I waited for what seemed like a lull, activated the Monitor, hooked my tether to the windward jack line, and hurled myself forward.

It was the most desperate I'd ever felt, reefing. I was actually shaking, fumbling, terrified that something would go wrong. All I wanted was for this to go quickly, smoothly. All I could visualize was an accidental gybe or a blown-out sail. All I could think about was how this must look from the cockpit, me at the mast, wrestling with halyard and Dacron, fumbling with winches, the sail whipping, the wind howling, imagining Steve imagining me doing this alone, a thousand miles from land.

I put in all three reefs; what the hell.

We ate our pasta.

30 Oct

0400   Interesting little sail. It's lighter again, *Sonnet* sailing politely at over five knots, 15–17 knots of apparent wind, the reefing fiasco is already receding slightly.

I think, in my pleasure to have him on board, I was focusing on the vacation-home part of it, pleased to have surfaces wiped down, *Sonnet* looking beautiful. Harder with all this sailing stuff; he doesn't really *like* it. Which we both knew, which is why he has zero interest in passage-making.

He said, earlier, that it was very different to *own* the boat, stressful. Different from sailing on other people's boats. The responsibility. Some of what I was feeling the first leg, I think. I've become more accustomed to the reality of boat ownership.

Another realm: I'm aware of his size, on this vessel that's only known women. Amazed by the size of his shoes. Needing to squeeze down the binoculars after he's used them. Aware of the sound of him, his weight in the cockpit when I'm below.

We took turns on watch, two hours on, two hours off. The wind died completely around 0600. When I rolled off the engine cover— heeding Skyli's admonition always to check the oil—I found the top of the Westerbeke frosted with salt; yesterday's bilge water obviously had come from somewhere high enough to spatter the engine and dry there.

I asked Steve to turn on the engine just long enough for me to see what the problem was, and discovered the raw-water hose leaking at the hose clamp near the pump, spewing out a fine steady spray.

We turned off the engine and I pulled out tools. Steve hand steered in the slop while I made repairs. He was exhausted from an odd-sleep night he wasn't used to. He was ready to be on land. Skyros was off our starboard bow, rugged and utterly inaccessible.

He was not having fun.

Engine back on at seven, overheating at 1400 rpm's. Off when we got a bit of breeze. On again at eight, temperature okay at 1200 rpm's. Approaching Linaria.

0830   Here's the reality: He *hates* this. He'd much rather be in Sofia, working on his Gypsy cable. At first it all was slightly amusing; now (after a long night) it's mostly wearing and sad. It makes me question my own love for sailing, makes me see it in his eyes—the exhaustion, the constant complications—and ask myself what there is to love.

Also, I feel guilty, I feel the weight of him not enjoying him- self. Why exactly did I choose Skyros? The myth stuff intrigued me; this is where Achilles, disguised as a woman, was hidden by his mother to keep him from going to Troy, until Odysseus tricked him into showing his true colors and he sailed off to meet his destiny. But there's nothing *here*. Chose it partly because we could go alongside, don't have to wrestle the Bruce out of the forepeak.

At 0915 we slipped alongside the quay in Linaria, between a brightly painted fishing boat and a gray-drab military cruiser. Just across the road was a pleasant *taverna*, cane furniture on a terrace, and Steve migrated that way while I did a thorough freshwater rinse of the engine, got himself a coffee, asked about the little hotel at the end of the harbor, asked about buses to the main town of Skyros, asked about fuel.

He lined up a room in the hotel—for an afternoon nap and a shower; if the beds were uncomfortable we could still sleep on the boat—and then lined up a cab to take us around to Skyros.

We made the ten-mile trip across the rocky island. The cab dropped us at the main square of Skyros, and we wandered through narrow streets until we found a tiny four-table restaurant. The cook motioned us into her kitchen, lifted lids of pots. The chicken stew looked wonderful; two bowls. And a salad, bright tomatoes, crisp cucumbers, good Greek olives, and feta cheese.

Cold beers, going straight to the head. Sure, he wasn't wild about the sailing part, but look where it had delivered us.

We talked about Bulgaria. He told me about the ironclad prejudice toward Gypsies, parliamentary votes of no-confidence, the hardheaded female staff of the female vice president. It was fascinating stuff, and I was glad for his grasp of it; I felt ready to plunge back into the periphery.

After lunch we made our way up through the maze of narrow streets. White houses, flat roofs, cone-shaped roofs on churches, cats, narrow red-tile stairways leading up to narrow wooden doors, painted wooden handrails, painted window frames, painted doors, vivid blue, teal green, pale enamel gray, the walls always flat white, the light and the shadows, bougainvillea and geraniums and grape vines. In the courtyard of a little church Steve stretched on a bench and napped, and I sat with a cat on my lap, absorbing her purring.

We walked on up to the ruined castle, up to a view down to the northern shore, aqua water, a snaking road along a snaking coastline, brown hills and stone.

Back to the town and our taxi date.

Evening light. Steve is in the taverna, I update my engine log, then look over and realize I feel something akin to affection for this misbehaving Westerbeke of mine. A degree of knowledge. Ready to learn more.

Tired of the entire business earlier today, sick of it, seven months now of virtually nothing but this boat. And now the comfort and affection, source of pride and repose, a part of the whole not the whole.

At dinner in the cane-chaired taverna, maybe from the fatigue, Steve's mood deteriorated. He said he was stressed by the existence of this huge object in his life, this yacht. He said he just felt low, felt *what now*, felt *what matters*. He said he wasn't designed to be alone so much, these long periods separated.

He said he couldn't quite imagine how much time he would want to spend on the boat. I knew he liked space, bright lights, hot showers, room for all his clothes, had known it for years, knew it when we went to Nikiti and stayed in the comfortable Porfi Hotel, but I felt a flush of anger, needing from him at least *some* recognition of how tough what he was saying might be on me. I said if you really don't want to spend time on the boat maybe I should keep it in Thessaloniki rather than Carras, lashing out a little, knowing how much he liked the Halkidiki.

31 Oct

1000   When was it, last night, this morning, just wanting all
this to be all right, praying to Aeolus for two days' pleasant sail.
And today it seems that Steve is trying, he's interested in the
chart, navigates us through the narrow Valaxa Island Pass,
around the rocks off the next point, sets a course for Skopelos,
goes forward to raise the mainsail. And then what strikes me is
this: He's not *trying* for my sake, the way I'd be trying for his.
He's looking into his own past, his own knowledge of sailing,
and seeking out the things he likes, making the best of this for
himself. And these are the things I value in him. He's not trying
to bend himself to my needs like Monica, not going silent like
Eileen. We're never going to sail oceans together and that's fine;
I'd much rather sail oceans with Skyli.

Goes deeper and more complex than all this. Hints in myself
at the restaurant last night of the old demons, wondering if I'm
not who he needs, if he needs someone who'll always be there,
do his shopping do his laundry have his children. But then,
walking back to the hotel, we stopped and he just held me tight,
standing there on the quay, in a kind of nowhere land between
Sonnet and the taverna and the hotel. Held me close, these two
bodies, two people so closely joined who haven't been in touching distance hardly at all in the past seven months.

He's restless because he's productive, not the kind of lazy that

I can be. Restless when his creative powers aren't working, when he's not working on his book.

Thinking this morning of how he's tried so many things, more than I have. Which doesn't make him flighty, simply brings into focus the things that work for him: writing, walking. He gets excited about sailing for a while but in fact he would much rather be in the Sierra; he buys himself a ten-speed in California and a mountain bike in D.C., and in the end he walks to language school every day, even the days I drive. Black Lycra biking shorts with an electric-blue stripe, blue backpack, doing his Bulgarian flash cards through the Glover Park woods, across the campus of Georgetown, across Key Bridge and into Rosslyn. Happy. Happy as no one I know to get up at 8 a.m., make himself a cup of coffee, and sit down in front of the computer to write. Even before he had any idea if what he wrote would sell, morning after morning month after month in front of that screen in Costa Mesa. Even in Paris, working at the typewriter in our tiny *chambre de bonne*. Carving time into his life as a diplomat to write, the discipline of that, the focus. Love him for all this.

1415 What could be more pleasant? Engine runs at 1100 rpm's, enough to do some good without driving me nuts or overheating itself or the interior. Steve reads *Jurassic Park* on the starboard bunk. I read a dated *New Yorker* at the chart table. My watch goes off (set for every 8 minutes) and I go on deck: 305°M, just right, mainsail pushing us along with the engine, speed above five knots, engine temp below 180°, islands in the distance all around us, not a ship in sight. Dip back below, cool breeze coming down through the hatches.

It was a longish day under way but easy, forty miles north-northwest to the scattering of islands that form the northern Sporades. For most of the day we motor-sailed; at the very end, after entering the channel between Alonnisos and Skopelos, then powering through a narrow passage between two tiny islands three or four miles from the harbor entrance, the wind filled in from the south. We rolled out the jib, shut off the engine, trimmed the sails, and *Sonnet*—in that merciful silence—

gathered way across the flat water, heeling, white foam forming behind her on the blue. There's nothing in the world like the way a boat feels when she takes the wind in her teeth and sails; Steve loved that moment off the coast of Skopelos as much as I did, loved it with utter clarity.

My guidebook told me we'd have to drop a stern anchor and go bow-to-the-quay, but the harbor was virtually deserted this late in the season, no other cruising boats, and there was plenty of space for *Sonnet* to go alongside the southeastern jetty. To port we looked across the open bay to a hillside dotted with olive trees. To starboard was the town—spilling its whitewashed way down to the harbor—and the green piney slopes above it.

Nearly sunset. We walked for forty-five minutes through the narrow cobbled streets of Skopelos, wending our way without bearings as the light faded, then found ourselves back at the waterfront and headed left around the harbor, surveying the three open restaurants before making our choice. We ate outside on a red-checked tablecloth as the smell of cooking fish wafted to us from the open kitchen.

Fifty miles to cover tomorrow to Carras; I wanted to allow twelve hours, the way the engine was overheating, best to leave before dawn. As we walked back to the boat I told Steve I'd take *Sonnet* off the dock in the morning myself, so he could sleep.

I slept peacefully that night, the boat moving lightly on the water.

I got up at five in the darkness, dressed quietly, moved quietly around on deck, stepping on and off the quay as I got things ready. I removed the spring line completely, coiled it and stowed it, looped the bow and stern lines around bollards on the quay and led them back on deck. I turned on the engine, let it warm up at low rpm's, moved forward to remove the bow line, moved aft again, throttled back, shifted into forward, throttled forward, released the stern line, taking *Sonnet* alone off the final dock before her final destination.

1 Nov

0600 Faint hint of sunrise behind the dark outline of Alonnisos. Stars. The lights of Skopelos at my stern, the north star at my headstay. Stars, no moon. Blinking lights off the tip of Alonnisos and the tip of the smaller of the islets we gated through yesterday evening. Sky, sea, islands, stars.

Powered between them yesterday, then the breeze came up and we turned off the engine and sailed. Steve said, "This is heaven."

0710 The sun has just risen over Alonnisos. Steve is still sleeping. I stand on the engine box to warm my feet, elbows on companionway, logbook in cockpit. This is all pretty amazing; an end of something and a beginning.

A definite release; the push is over. A good sense of focus and perspective. Work on the boat when I'm on the boat. Create a space in Sofia where we can live comfortably. Study Bulgarian, seek out my sailing contacts so I can integrate the boat with Bulgaria.

No shortage of boat projects, but it doesn't overwhelm or upset me, she's sailed thousands of miles, she could do it again. See this and use it for what it has the miracle of being: Something to do. Something to feel a connection to. Something to ward off the demons of depression.

Steve woke up around eight, made himself a cup of coffee and a bowl of cereal and breakfasted in the cockpit. The wind a bit earlier had been from the north-northeast and now was nonexistent.

He settled below to finish *Jurassic Park*, which Monica had left on board; the number of pages in his left hand increased steadily as those in his right hand decreased. I knew he'd rather be home, working on his own novel, grappling with Bulgarian political dilemmas, but he was doing okay, a bit like a lion accepting his cage, knowing he won't be in it for long. Found a nice gazelle bone to gnaw on, would rather have zebra but hasn't had gazelle for a while, so might as well enjoy it.

I'd always envied him, how fast he could read.

The engine was overheating at anything over 1200 rpm's, so we kept it below that, powering along at just under five knots. Amazing how many hours of the past three days I'd spent under power, without crawling the walls. Maybe lower rpm's bothered me less than higher. Or maybe it was because I was sailing with Steve, wanting him to like the boat, keeping my grouchiness at bay.

We read, we talked, we made ourselves lunch and ate it in the cockpit under a hazy Aegean sky.

1245 "I'm not a passagemaker," Steve says. "I'm a day sailor." Talking about our cross-country drive, California to D.C., that he basically hated it, hates protracted voyages. Then thinks again. "No, that's not true. If I'm on my own two feet I'll go any-where."

Those, for what it's worth, were the final written words of the voyage, the final words in the journal with the farm on the front. No pages left; the book lasted exactly as long as the voyage did, forty-five thousand words or so scribbled between its covers.

We never did get wind, that final day sailing to Carras. We never even raised the mainsail. We had hoped to see the Halkidiki peninsulas as we approached—Kassandra, Sithonia, maybe even Akti to the east, a glimpse of the sacred Mount Athos—but it was way too hazy and we closed the distance by GPS and chart. By early afternoon the haze was alternating with bona-fide fog, and we sighted Paliouri—the southern tip of Kassandra—only on the radar screen.

At 1415 the point was abeam. *Sonnet* entered the bay of Kassandra in zero visibility, still powering north.

An hour later the fog began to lift. Slowly, slowly the lovely coastline of Sithonia materialized on our starboard side, pines and olive trees coming right down to the water, vineyards and citrus groves in the laps of hills, tiny aqua-watered coves. Four miles ahead was the silhouette of a turtle-shaped island; to its east were the two white hotels at the en-trance to Porto Carras.

So there it was, the final destination. Close to an hour still to go.

I went below to make a log entry, feeling both elation and a strange detachment, sat at the chart table and took the log from its space above the radar. Steve and I were using the simple blue book I'd bought in Malta for the passage to Greece; there'd been plenty of pages left in the alphabet-tabbed log Skyli I had used from Fuengirola, and in the printed log I'd used alone and then with Monica, but both had felt completed, so I'd bought a third.

I made the entry, slid the log back where it belonged, then shifted on the seat so that my back was pillowed against the hull, my legs stretched out on the engine cover. Rested a moment, looked around the interior of the boat, the familiar shapes and surfaces I'd first seen on a freezing day in Maine, *Sonnet* inside a shed in Southwest Harbor, her mast outside on sawhorses in the snow.

I opened the top of the chart table, dug around at the back, and pulled out the log from the first two legs of the voyage, spiral-bound, a gaff-rigged schooner on its sturdy plastic cover. I flipped through the pages, running my eyes down the comments columns ("Out of the Chesapeake/ sailing sweet and slow" . . . "another low forecast—back to 3rd reef "), line after line filled with my handwriting, then alternating with Monica's, position after position, always farther east.

I set the book aside, lifted the chart table again, and found Skyli's and my log, warped and water-stained from the into-Malta storm. Pages with log entries. Pages with poetry attempts. Well past the end of the log entries, on Page L—presumably for Lydia—I found the following:

Ha!

15 or so Oct, and we're in Malta and I won't soon forget how brave I've been, not the sailing stuff which was way too easy and not the ditching Lisa, Liebchen, Antelope Medicine thing, which wasn't brave, if anything it was typical, if not cowardly, Ha! It was the head on the chopping block of chance thing, and handing you, a stranger (even worse a strange woman), the axe. But I liked the looks of this stranger; and luckily she didn't chop off my head. Phew.

18 Oct: I-Lean says you may grow sad this Bulgarian winter, propinquity of Sonnet notwithstanding. She thinks it would be a good idea for me to send you things to help buoy your spirits, which will be heavy with Communist-era architecture. So, whadya want besides cat food?

24 Oct: To wit—the nicest thing you ever said to me, and the thang that will carry me further than Antelope Medicine, even, was that around me you felt smart. Notice, please, how I refrain from the usual glib butthole remark that "anyone would feel smart around me because of my double digit I.Q." Naw, mon, I was very touched. We're strange little cosmic mirrors of each other with, I think, un-

canny similarities and antagonisms. Let's use this. "The best kind of friend is like iron sharpening iron." (SHRIEKBACK.) I'm happy you're a sailor—if you came to life at cockfights instead, I would love you no less but it would be kinda boring. Waaaa?

Sweet my Lydia, take care of yourself, your Steve, your Butch and your black sloop, in that order.

Don't forget me, eh?

Skyli